IF

a Memoir

RICHARD WEST

Cover design by Casey Gerber Creative

Illustration by Jamie Noble Frier

Disclaimer: This book shares both a literal and metaphorical journey. Memoir is always a re-creation, a re-imagination of events – it can't be otherwise. Nonetheless this writer tells his story with an integrity of intention and emotional truth. The author aimed to open a window onto the fragility of sobriety and in so doing compressed real characters and events into a readable narrative. While the names of some people have been changed to protect their privacy, the names of others have not.

For Dominic
Maureen, Gabby and Jamie

ABOUT THE AUTHOR

 Richard West is a recovering alcoholic who accepts his hard-won sobriety can all too easily be lost. His son and ex-wife were killed in a car crash. Grief and guilt followed. Richard spent 25 years working for an American bank with ten years in overseas positions that fuelled his passion for adventure - and hard drinking. Richard died several times. By fate - and his own hand. Born in London, Richard lived in Italy, Saudi Arabia, Greece, Kuwait and Papua New Guinea. Teaching English in China for a year spurred him to study journalism at the University of the Sunshine Coast. But Richard needed more: he needed to challenge his demons. At 62 he bought a motorcycle and rode 16,000 solo kilometres around his adopted Australia – and discovered himself. A master's in creative writing followed. Now Richard lives in the present moment, helping himself, and others, through his writing, and as a speaker for Beyond Blue. Read more www.richardwest.com.au

CONTENTS

THE END

I sat in my office on a tired Brisbane Tuesday morning. Dark clouds greyed my window to a city just beginning its day. Staff shuffled past in a haze of steaming coffees and *good mornings*. A normal day. Another day. But a baseless fear settled in my gut like a gathering storm scares a dog. The air stilled. Drizzle turned to rain. I felt alone in a building thick with people. And began to tremble.

My mobile rang.

'Dad!' Jamie screamed. 'Dad …' He struggled to continue. 'Mum and Dom …'

The call came from England. In the witching hour. Jamie wailed. I gripped the phone. Dominic, his younger brother, was twenty; Gabriella, his sister, still a child. They lived with Heather, my first wife. We'd divorced ten months earlier.

'Dad,' he sobbed, 'there's been a car crash …'

'Tell me.'

Jamie couldn't answer.

'Tell me!'

'They're dead! Mum and Dom are dead.'

'Gabby?'

'She's unhurt,' he said. 'Gabby's okay.'

My daughter survived. Dominic and Heather had not.

'I'm coming, Jamie. I'm coming home.'

England - 1954

The man who would lose a son was born in London. It was the best of times; it was the worst of times. Winston Churchill led Britain; Menzies Australia. An auspicious yet uncertain time to be born. Mao and Khrushchev threatened from the East. NATO's nuclear muscle pushed from the west. France retreated from Indochina giving birth to Cambodia, Laos, and two warring Vietnamese twins. A king ruled Iraq, and a Shah reigned in Iran. Perón shed tears for Argentina, and Tito's iron fist gripped Yugoslavia. Doris Day sung 'Secret Love', Rocky Marciano held the world heavyweight boxing title and Marlon Brando won an Oscar for his role as a washed-up fighter. The man grew up believing he was capable of many things. But never murder.

Australia - 1 July 2016

I thought about IF as I mounted my motorcycle and touched my tattoo. The bald eagle spread from the top of my shoulder to the bottom of my bicep – a father's act of rebellion: when Dominic had dared the dare. When my son was alive.

1770

Australia - 1 July 2016

'You're crazy,' said Maureen. My wife repeated what she'd said every day since our wedding twelve years ago. But today she meant it. Really meant it.

'Agreed,' I said, mounting my motorcycle, head bobbing to underline the obvious.

Maureen waited. And watched my every move.

A mid-winter Queensland day had become a magical Christmas morning and a twenty-first birthday wrapped into one. Except I was sixty-two years old. Ageing was tough, growing old mandatory, but I held to the theory that growing *up* was not. Like Jack, I sprinkled water on my dreams and prayed my beanstalks would take me to the giant. I needed to kill him.

Today I would begin a solo circumnavigation of Australia on a motorcycle bought ten days earlier with money I couldn't afford, excitement I couldn't control, and goals I couldn't explain.

I confirmed Maureen's fears: 'You left out old,' I said. 'I'm *old* and crazy.'

Humour belied my fear.

'I'm gonna do it.' But my bravado sounded hollow.

The man behind the mask pleaded for another chance. A chance to write the final chapters of his yellowed, dog-eared history – drunk with dreams and footnoted with failures.

'I know,' Maureen said, blonde hair flying every which way in the breeze.

She had faith. And trust. I had neither.

In times of doubt, my mother's dirty tale would push its way to the surface. Often, it proved to be an apt parable of self-fulfilling prophecy: I saw my three-year-old self sitting on a potty in the kitchen of a South London council house. A pair of steel knitting needles, common in those days, found their way in my little hands. This bad boy thieved these miniature javelins while straining to deliver a pile of poo – a packet he knew would be paid with praise: *what a good boy.* But as the steel conductors plunged into the A/C power outlet, the accolades escaped in the explosion. Shit, piss and the baby boy tsunami'd across the kitchen floor. I think this was where it all started.

My Yamaha 1300cc motorcycle stood waiting. I'd christened her Yammie. Candy-red paintwork and chrome jewellery dazzled under the bright, morning light of Coolum Beach – a quiet Queensland seaside town – and my home of fifteen years. Leather panniers hung on each flank; a rear parcel rack held a luggage carrier crammed with gear I would need and gear I didn't. Lashed to the pillion seat was a large black swag with a tent and camping equipment that had never been used. Despite being overloaded, Yammie still oozed elegance and power – a thoroughbred, unlike the mongrel who rode her.

The distant surf crashed and boomed; a salt-rich breeze whispered fragrance of ocean. Dry and mild. Perfect conditions. A good omen.

'You're crazy,' Maureen said again as she threw me an anxious smile. 'Be good ... be careful.'

A nod was the best I could do. I turned the ignition.

We kissed.

I pulled on my helmet.

Maureen's eyes watered as she silently mouthed, *I love you.* She picked up Tess, our dog, and placed her in my arms. Sad eyes peeped from under a bundle of white and apricot curls.

I tussled the silky hair, felt her warmth and held her close. My helmet hid the sting of tears. Steel knitting needles. Time to go.

My fingers opened the throttle and pressed the starter. The bike's twin pistons exploded and Yammie snorted a cloud of exhaust and petrol fumes. She throbbed with an urgency that pulsed through my hands, my legs, my backside. Yammie's rhythm was my rhythm: rock-and-roll. Yammie was ready and so was I.

My helmet and the noise of the bike made it difficult to speak. I nodded a farewell. Maureen said nothing more. Her silence said everything.

My left boot pressed down on the gearshift. A solid clunk. I eased out the clutch and my bike edged onto the road, a powerful mare under rein. I twisted the throttle and felt the intoxicating power as I lifted my left foot on the gearshift and worked her speed upward through the gears. Clunk, second. Clunk, third … Don Quixote and Rocinante hit the trail.

I raised my left hand, 'Love you,' I said, unheard into my helmet.

At the bend at the bottom of the road, I turned my head. Maureen stood like a lighthouse. She didn't wave again. I imagined she stood for a long time listening to the sound of my bike as it faded into the sea breeze. I imagined her fear.

Five hundred metres ahead, red traffic lights stopped me before I could start. My heart pounded. I waited at the lights. Yammie idled next to a large truck. I felt the future. I could touch it. The lights stayed red. A young man's arm leaned across the sill of the truck's open window. A handsome twenty-year-old's face beamed at me with kind, sleepy eyes. Dominic. Traffic sounds dissolved. Light faded. The truck driver's window cast a frame around his face, like a funeral painting, edged in black. But the driver smiled a familiar smile, a cheeky grin, a ten-year-old, a twenty-year-old. Time ground to a stop like a locomotive with a final chug and lurch. No sound, no movement could invade the illusion. My heart no longer pounded a nervous beat but heaved with an ocean of grief. A car horn screamed its impatience. The traffic lights had turned green. I opened the throttle and Yammie sped forward from the pack; a glance in my wing mirror showed the truck's windscreen bursting with light from the reflection of the sun. I was on my way. And the image of my son dissolved.

Yammie was on fire. We headed to the iconic town of 1770 – 406 kilometres north. A big first day's ride for both of us. My motorcycle riding experience dated back to teenage years. This was the first time I had ever ridden over one hundred kilometres in a single ride. Yammie had been a 'second bride' and I had not yet become fully acquainted with her idiosyncrasies. We had only known each other for ten days, but now we would ride 15,000 kilometres, anti-clockwise, around Australia's perimeter in a sixty-two-day pilgrimage. I hoped we were a good match.

———

Months before I had been restless. Fearful. Guilty. Frustrated. Salt and pepper receded into white as sad memories sharpened the past. The present lacked meaning. I needed – *something*. Like a final drink for the road. Maureen knew it too. My heart bled to believe that what was done *was* done. I needed to prove it, but I was terrified of what I might discover and terrified of what I might not.

My *something* started with *Wild,* Cheryl Strayed's memoir. A spunky story of a young woman, a heroin addict, searching to expunge her demons. She walked the Pacific Crest Trail, an 11,000-mile solo hike through the states of California, Oregon and Washington. It was an impulsive decision. She had no hiking experience and faced snow and desert heat, bears and rattlesnakes, pain and dangerous men. She made it. Strayed's addiction and self-destructive behaviour mirrored mine. But the movie was the spark that blew my fuses. In a moment of mind-boggling bad luck, Strayed, played by Reese Witherspoon, lost her boot when it tumbled off a cliff edge into an abyss of forest below. The sound of one hand clapping echoed across the ravine as she pitched her other boot to follow the first. Now she was barefoot. Witherspoon's expletives of courage and calamity exploded in the same instant I jumped from the sofa and punched the air.

'That's it,' I said.

'That's what?' said Maureen.

'I'm gonna do the same thing.'

'You're crazy.'

I didn't sleep that night. Thoughts raced. Ideas came and went. By dawn I had the answer. I would walk, run, or cycle around Australia. I told my wife the next morning.

'Insane.'

My research started with intense training and long periods of deep thought. I poured months of concentrated sweat into distance cycling, gym workouts and twice-daily hikes up Mount Coolum. Then a serendipitous encounter offered a simpler, saner solution.

I had just delivered a much-needed coffee to Maureen, a registered nurse, who was working late shift at an aged-care facility. On the drive home, I saw a biker bloke wheel a large red motorcycle onto his drive and park it against a hand-scrawled sign: FOR SALE. I cruised past … but turned my head like a corkscrew.

Don't even think about it, said my sensible self. Two minutes later, I pulled into the drive alongside the bike. The owner appeared.

'Hey,' I said. 'Just looking.'

'No worries.'

A minute of silence passed.

'Why are you selling?'

The man pointed into his garage where a huge Indian motorcycle sat gleaming like the chunk of gold she cost. Blazing mustard yellow, tinselled chrome and leather tasselled saddlebags. Spanking new.

I grinned.

The biker's orphaned motorcycle crooked a finger and invited me to take a closer inspection. Stunning looks: wild and elegant – a lady with punch who didn't show her age, despite her 2007 birth certificate: A Yamaha 1300.

'Here,' said the man handing me a spare helmet. 'Take her out. Follow me. See what you think.'

My circumnavigation of Australia began ten days later, my pockets $7,000 lighter.

. . .

I planned to ride solo around Australia's 15,000-kilometre perimeter: North towards Townsville, a left turn to Darwin, onwards to Perth, south to Augusta and then east, across the Nullarbor Desert towards Adelaide, Melbourne, Canberra, Sydney and home. The choice of route would not turn back the clock, but it would offer a greater probability of tail winds. A shove up the backside was more than a metaphor. Sixty-two days was not a random choice. I would take one day for every sixty-two years of my life. It would be a spiritual journey: a time for solitude and a time to think. Maureen had given her blessing.

To leverage my trip, I decided to raise funds for a good cause. I chose Beyond Blue: a charity that provides support to those suffering from anxiety and depression, and aids in the prevention of suicide. I felt a close connection. Within a day, they created a page for me on their EveryDayHero website called 'A Ride Around the Block'. Beyond Blue provided a window for my project and simplified the administration, but now I also had an added layer of pressure. I *had* to succeed.

Everyone believed the ol' Pommy boy was tilting at windmills, pushing barriers, exorcising a mid-life crisis. Maureen knew otherwise.

———

An exhilarating ride. A beautiful day. Yammie cruised with a subdued roar as the road raced beneath my boots. Wood smoke, mown grass, grazing stock. The smell of bush and motorbike smouldered in an intoxicating mix. Wayward bugs splattered Yammie's windshield and hit my legs like gunk-filled rubber bullets. I passed through cattle pasture, forests of pine and seas of sugar cane. The tall fibrous stalks over four-metres high covered millions of acres: an ocean of cane topped with fine flowers glittering silver-pink under the warm afternoon light. The cane swayed in a gentle motion orchestrated by the wind. Small-town sugar refineries belched sweet, rich smells of processed cane. I sped on my way towards the small town of 1770, across regional Australia's rum industry. The day was warm and dry.

Push bike training had made me fit and lean. A new dawn and a new dusk; I was feelin' good. But my conviction needed proof.

The town of Agnes Waters touches shoulders with 1770. The liquor store deserved its label: CELLARBRATIONS. I stopped Yammie outside, pulled off my helmet and cradled it on my tank as I sat and thought. Five minutes. Ten. Fifteen. I strode into the store and found the whisky like a wolf catching the scent of a chicken, except in this case the chicken was me.

I didn't need to think. I didn't need to choose. One litre of Johnny Walker Red Label nested in my hand as I strode to the counter and paid.

'Will that be all?' said the checkout woman with an expression forecasting ugly weather.

'That's all.'

I bound that bottle in a black bag and buried it in the bowel of my saddlebag – banished from thought, exiled into darkness.

Fuck you! Johnnie screamed in defiance.

'You already have,' I said.

Ten minutes later, Yammie cruised into 1770, the site of Captain James Cook's second Australian landing. My first victory. The small town gave me a sense of significance, and dread; one foot on the edge of a new frontier, the other on the edge of a dark and dangerous abyss.

I pulled into the first camping site, secured a patch of dirt, and pitched my tent under the testing gaze of seasoned campers, wallabies, kookaburras and scavenging ibis.

Erecting my canvas home for the first time, I did exactly what the directions said to do. No embarrassing mistakes. Day One. Four hundred and six kilometres.

The cortisone injection dumped into my shoulder before leaving had held up. An old tendon tear in my right shoulder had morphed during my push-bike training into a major concern. An ultrasound showed that it was chronic – a full-thickness tear of the supraspinatus tendon. The steroid, like magic snake oil, had done the job. At least for the time being. No pain at all.

Maureen's beef sandwich helped me celebrate the moment before I crawled exhausted into my sleeping bag. A big ride. A big day. I did it. 14,600 kilometres to go. I drifted into a restless sleep of dreams, scattered thoughts and fears.

Be good, I heard Maureen whisper. *Be careful*.

BUTTERFLIES

I slept well, packed my tent, stored my stuff and loaded Yammie. 'Get your engine humming,' I sang with garbled lyrics as Yammie roared north. 'Born to be wild…' *Easy Rider* triggered old memories.

Day Two, and I had been blessed with another bright day: fresh, dry and fanned with a light breeze. Perfect riding conditions. We headed for Marlborough and a 350-kilometre ride. My attention wandered. Abstract thoughts and faded images. The road raced under my bike: straight, strong, immutable. Each day gave me time to think. I had sixty left.

———

At thirteen years of age I knew I wanted to fly. The Air Cadets offered opportunity and adventure. I joined. Wings grew from a butterfly effect I didn't yet understand, and my flight took a different path …

Whaaaaack! The leathered glove smashed into my gum-shield and ripped my lip. A hard punch. Blood ran in my mouth, down my throat, rich and copper sour. It rocked me. My opponent, a sixteen-year-old reform-school inmate, signalled his surprise. He expected me to go down, back up or at least register the strength of his punch. I didn't. I went in hard. Right jab, right jab. Bang, bang. Left cross. I led with my right, a southpaw. Right-handed too. That was unusual. My right lead packed a powerful punch.

Ding Ding Ding. The bell rang. End of round one.

My trainer wiped blood from my mouth and held the sponge to stem the flow. He kept it there and waited for the bell.

I was sixteen years old too, an air cadet sergeant fighting in the British boxing finals for my Mitcham squadron. I had been fighting since I was thirteen. I was good. He was good. Two more rounds – it would be a hard fight.

After months of eliminating bouts, I had made the finals. My opponent was several inches taller. A street fighter, a gang kid. His reach had the range to pick me off from a distance: damaging punches that would score valuable points *before* I could hit him. My plan was to step in close, take the punishment and pack punches hard into his body: short right-left combinations.

Ding Ding Ding.

Round two. The sponge oozed blood as my trainer took it from my mouth. I stood and rushed into the centre of the ring. The second-round tactics were a replica of the first. We hurt each other in different places. My mouth exploded in a mess of blood; his ribs and guts were sore and bruised. We both scored painful points.

Ding Ding Ding.

I flopped on the stool. The trainer pushed the sponge onto my bloodied mouth. Cool water mixed with blood. I spat out the rusty cocktail. One round to go. The gang kid was tiring. So was I.

Ding Ding Ding.

Strong strides to the centre of the ring masked my shaky condition. We touched gloves in a silent salute. A short-lived courtesy. *Whaaaaack!*

Three rounds, three minutes each – not a long time. A fucking eternity!

By the middle of the third, our exhaustion was clear, and still my right hook remained unused. In the last minute he caught me again, hard on the jaw. My legs wobbled but stood their ground. I attacked. Another surprise. I feinted with my right and caught him in the gut with my left. A good punch. He did what I expected. He lowered his arms in response to the pain in his belly. My right hook hit him hard on the jaw. Short and sweet with all the strength of my shoulders behind it. He sank to his knees, gloves on the canvas. His confused look said it all: *Where the hell am I?* Animal instinct lifted him to his feet. The referee looked into his eyes, wiped his gloves, and signalled for us to get to it. 'Box,' he said.

I hit him again. Hard.

Ding Ding Ding. The bell saved both of us. The fight was over.

A tough final. My mouth looked like a mess of sloppy lipstick; my eyes bruised with an overindulgence of purple eyeshadow. His face: red, swollen and sore. The referee held my right glove, my opponent's left. Stained with blood, snot and sweat, our gloves told our story. We waited for the judges.

'A unanimous decision and in the blue corner …' the referee raised my hand.

I punched the air. The gang kid looked at the canvas. His ego hurt more than his body.

My jubilation soared for days and the fight delivered a valuable lesson. But not from the ring. After the fight, I sat hunched in the dressing room, euphoric and exhausted. A squadron leader appeared beaming over me. He had influence in deciding which cadets won coveted glider-pilot training courses at RAF Kenley.

'Well done, lad. Good show.'

'Thank you, sir.'

'Would you like glider wings?'

'Yes, sir.'

'It's done. You'll get notified soon.'

'Thank you, sir,' I said to his retreating back.

The officer did what he said he would do. Six weeks later, a letter confirmed my place. The win gave pride to my squadron; it gave me opportunity. The RAF trained me to fly open cockpit gliders from a winch launch: an air cadet's dream. Every Sunday for seven weeks I flew tandem. Me in the front, instructor in the rear. Then, on one cold winter morning, I flew solo. Like an eagle, proud and free, my three solo flights became a profound memory as real as the fight. Boxing had given me wings.

At seventeen, I completed an intensive two-day RAF aircrew selection assessment at Biggin Hill, England's famous Second World War fighter station. But the medical delivered a knockout blow. I was deaf. And blind. An exaggeration, but my eyes and ears did not meet the high standards required. In reality I didn't cut it. Not good enough.

Butterflies flapped ferocious wings.

At eighteen, confused about my life and where I should head, I used my meagre savings to tour the United States, Mexico and Canada by bus. I travelled alone from New York to San Francisco, Juarez to Toronto. Easy Rider on six wheels. I slept on the Greyhounds at night and checked out the cities during the day. YMCAs offered longer stays. Shoestrings, pizza, Coke and a lot of luck got me back to London. Now I needed work – a career – but what? My eyesight and hearing shot down all dreams of becoming a pilot. Instead, I looked for a job where 'travel' sat at the top of the perks list. Of course, I wanted to get paid for the privilege too. Naivety came easy for this eighteen year old. All I needed was a blue-chip international corporation that wanted a kid and would pay him to travel. *Easy.* But which one?

First National City Bank travellers' checks supported my USA adventure. *So why not? They were* American, global, prestigious, and had an office in London. I wrote to them.

A tsunami of butterfly wings followed.

Citibank, as we now know them, gave me a job. At eighteen, I began my banking career as a junior clerk. My career spanned a quarter of a century. I departed as a Vice President and my travel dreams came true. It's a long story – old age overtook the boy – alcoholism overtook the athlete. But the young, sober man was never far behind. He was always trying to catch up. One day, maybe he would.

A career developed and a life evolved, but not before alcoholic fuck-ups became a regular feature. I often wished for an *Etch a Sketch* to turn today's canvas upside down and shake yesterday's clean.

Alcohol became my confidence builder and pressure relief valve. It never worked. My screw-ups could never be rescripted; my failures never redacted, but it took a half-century to realise *Ground Hog Day* perfection was just a movie; *Etch a Sketch* a toy. Life was real. There were no rehearsals.

————

Yammie growled like a tiger waiting to pounce. She spat Ks with a speed that demanded unwanted attention. A speeding ticket could be our downfall. I eased the throttle. A warm breeze caressed the day. Mid-winter and a glorious twenty-five degrees Celsius. I smiled. My adrenalin simmered, and the land passed: sugar cane, lush pasture, low hills, braying cattle, gentle valleys. Freedom and anonymity wrapped an invisible cloak around my addiction.

The day continued to be kind. Late afternoon. Marlborough was close.

A 'hotel' beckoned one kilometre from the highway. The colonial structure sat decaying across the road from the railway line. It flashed its services like a red light marooned in Las Vegas. *Meals, pokies and accommodation.* I needed two of the three. My boots carried me up the wooden steps into the old, wood-walled, corrugated-iron-roofed pub. Scuffed pool tables and dining benches still damp with beer lined up in mess-hall orderliness under a large, cathedral-ceilinged gallery. Travellers from antique lands had filled the walls with nomadic scribblings. Gratuitous graffiti, brilliant marketing – a distraction from the deteriorating decor. A haze of musty air, French fries and stale beer added to the hotel's welcoming, addictive atmosphere.

A drinker sat at the bar, hands wrapped around his glass as though someone might snatch it at any moment. The barman saw me, raised an eyebrow, and telegraphed his question faster than words.

'Any camp sites?' I asked.

'Five bucks.' He jabbed his thumb toward the rear.

I pulled a note and handed it to him.

'That includes the shower,' he said.

Tired, I tramped back to my bike and rode to the rear of the hotel. Three caravans and one tent occupied polite patches of dirt, discreetly selected to maximise personal privacy. I chose my spot.

Nestled beside the backyard of the hotel was the ablutions block. I showered longer than the three minutes mandated by the washroom rules. The water was hot; the heat reached deep into my aching muscles. 'Clap along if you feel like a shower without a roof...' I sang, as my naked body gyrated, bounced and bopped, while steam circled around me like theatrical stage smoke. Adrenalin had kept my hunger at bay; now my body commanded me to eat. Anything would do, as long as it was hot and greasy.

Refreshed, I sauntered back to the pub.

The barman returned. He raised the same eyebrow.

'I'll take the sausages, mash and peas,' I said.

'Drink?'

I hesitated. 'Soda water.'

He looked at me for a second. He knew.

'Sure,' he said. 'No worries. Seventeen dollars fifty.'

This was a Saturday night and a soda water warmed in my hand as weekend regulars got stuck into what looked like a long night. Pool balls cracked as they ricocheted across worn felt, eighties music blared, pokies chimed, rugby raged on TV, blokes chugged beers and girlfriends smiled. The whole kit and caboodle happy as clichéd pigs in a surfeit of shit. And why wouldn't they be?

As I ate my sausages, the waitress asked, 'Another drink, love?'

'Yeah, thanks. Soda water.'

'No worries.'

But it was. My addiction blazed on my forehead as obvious as a night labourer's fluorescent jacket with flashing lights and a police escort. *Hi, I'm Richard and I'm... an alcoholic.* Present tense.

'Second thoughts ... forget the soda. I'm done. The sausages were great.'

'No worries,' she said. But the waitress knew too.

'Night,' I offered over my shoulder as I walked out into the dark field and my canvas home. My tent loomed from the night; Yammie stood shotgun.

'Screw the present tense,' I said stooping low to draw the tent zipper that sealed me into my tiny world, my blackness. 'Screw it,' said my soul refusing to go gentle into that good night, my dreams, my fears.

A road train swept its headlights through my tent exposing the old fraud like a delicate darkroom image. A dog barked as the lone truck rumbled south along the railway road. Darkness descended again.

My sleeping bag smothered my exhaustion.

I slept. Johnnie stayed in the saddlebag.

CRUSADERS AND DESERTS

A cold Sunday morning. I woke early and crawled from my tent, joints and muscles groaning in displeasure. Dawn signalled a spectacular start to the day. Spray-painted cirrus clouds of reds, oranges and gold drifted over the blue-black canvas of first light. A magical beginning. I grabbed my camera. This old man and his motorcycle wanted more than Santiago's fish carcass to prove he did it. My Canon would provide evidence, but images could never capture what I felt.

Grey pairs of nomads emerged from three identical white caravans. Early risers, busy with rituals, ablutions, loading, packing, checking, hitching, departing. We exchanged nods as I ambled across the paddock's wet grass to find the breakfast room hidden inside the pub. A door opened to a dim corridor leading into the depths of the pub's back rooms. A sign declared the kitchen for the use of *In-House Pub Boarders Only* – not dirt-patch, $5-a-night bikers. All quiet – 6.55 am – an empty kitchen. I committed a crime. And trespassed. Despite warnings not to use the kitchen, my need to charge batteries and equipment trumped the embarrassment of discovery. I boiled water in the kettle and remained undetected despite its steaming rattles stoking my sin. I brewed coffee from my supply of instant powder. Stealing electricity didn't register as a crime in my book. Coffee did.

My third day, and this city boy discovered camping had its challenges. Food and water and petrol were essential; but my technology with its parasitic batteries craved AC: iPhone, laptop, cameras, iPad, GoPro. I disconnected one of two 1970s toasters and attached my hungry digital babies to the teat. Cables snaked like untidy spaghetti across the wooden table laid for the breakfast of the pub's 'house guests'. I sipped my coffee. And waited.

A goods train creaked and groaned past the pub, hauling coal-dusted boxcars clunk-clanking south, trailing behind their locomotive mother.

The kitchen door opened and startled my thoughts. A young couple, late twenties, walked into the scene of my crime.

'Sorry,' I said. 'Morning! ... I've taken over the power outlet for the toaster.'

They looked at the mess on the table, then turned their gaze to me.

'It's fine. We're just having tea and cereal,' said the guy in an English accent.

'Thanks. Where you from?'

'Marlborough,' they said in unison.

'That's Marlborough in England,' said the woman.

'Bloody hell. What a coincidence,' I said. 'Where you heading?'

The man replied, 'We've got relatives in Australia. Spent a week with them in Sydney but planned a six-week tour up the east coast before flying home. You?'

'I'm traveling around the coastline of Australia ...' I blushed. 'On a motorcycle.'

'Wow!' said the woman. 'How long will it take?'

'Sixty-two days. At least that's the plan.'

'Goodness!' the guy said. 'How far have you covered?'

'Just started.' My blush became an inflamed sunrise. 'This is my third day.'

'Good luck,' they both said reaching for the cornflakes.

'You too. Enjoy Australia.'

I'm travelling the coastline of Australia, blah blah, on a motorcycle, blah blah, this is my third day, blah blah. I hadn't even been on the road for forty-eight hours. *Fraud.*

I gathered my equipment, eager to get started when another traveller, a man, mid-forties, walked into the kitchen.

'G'day,' he said, cheerful and confident.

We all returned the greeting.

'Anyone heard the election result?'

The man's question rocked me to my boots. Just two days on the road my adventure had wiped Australia's general election from my thoughts. A blank disk. The nation voted yesterday. My wife and I had ticked our horses on the ballot paper just two days before in an early pre-election vote. Politics and current affairs were another addiction. Forty-eight hours on the road had weaned me. No cold turkey. Election blackout.

We shook our heads and looked to him for further news.

'It's a close thing. Neck and neck. I'm guessing it's gonna take a while to announce the winner. Turnbull must be shitting himself.'

The English couple looked confused.

Political pundits considered the Prime Minister's double dissolution a reckless gamble.

'Interesting. Gotta go. Have a good one,' I said stuffing spools of untidy cables into my backpack.

After a shower, a shave, and more coffee, I packed the tent and loaded my gear onto Yammie. Sunday morning. Great weather: cool but with higher temperatures forecast for later.

Yammie fired up instantly despite the cold night. The roar of her pipes hit me with satisfying comfort. Today I had a potential date with biker blokes from *The Cooktown Crusaders*, biker blokes I hadn't met – real biker blokes. They had camped at Midge Point, 335 kilometres north. The fraud didn't think he was ready.

Unbroken fields of sugar cane blurred like a blaze of swaying sentries *with* spears held to attention. 'Sugar, sugar everywhere,' the

ancient biker mumbled, 'and every drop available to brew and drink.'
The rich smell of sugar refineries was strong and pungent. Warming,
comforting, sweet. Bundaberg country. I couldn't smell the rum, but
imagination trumped reality as my mouth watered and nostrils
twitched. A true dog of Pavlov, my reaction was a condition: a trigger
pulled by memories, dust and need ...

————

Where did it start? Hard to say. Alcoholism is never more obvious than
when you try to stop. The best time is before you start. The second-best
time is today. The third-best time is when you live in Saudi Arabia.
And I did live in Saudi Arabia. But I didn't stop.

Twenty-five-years ago and the memory was still sensual.
Intoxicating smells, sweet and rich like the Bundaberg refineries once
percolated my Saudi Arabian villa. The aroma was as sharp today as it
was a quarter of a century earlier. Riyadh, 1990. I lived and worked in
this Desert Storm Kingdom in the Gulf War nineties. Ironic that a
drinker would live in a dry country – a country where alcohol was
illegal, forbidden by Sharia law, and where public beheadings were
executed every Friday after midday prayer. If the Saudi police caught
me with alcohol, it would mean instant imprisonment, a possible
lashing, deportation and an abrupt end to a career. *A good deterrent*, I
hear you say. 'Alas, 'twas but a minor impediment.' Ironic, too, that
my chosen profession was that of financial policeman. Saudi American
Bank used me as their deterrent and enforcer of policy and procedure
and internal rules and external regulation: the man who identified risk
and made sure it was mitigated. A responsible role for a responsible
person. The holder needed to be a firm believer in financial religion
and the culture of the interest rate, despite *usury*, despite *Riba*. I was a
banker. My coat label read *Boss*. My business card read *Chief Auditor*.
My football-playing pub mates said 'Wanker'. A chameleon of shifting
social sands. Riyadh became my home: an island of Islamic extremism
surrounded by dry and sober deserts.

I still had intimate feelings for the two twenty-litre plastic containers that filled a corner of my bathroom: stout and sturdy, bubbling Buddhas, bursting with hope, promise and fulfilment. Home brewing was an illegal pastime for many but a physical necessity for some. I wed grape juice from the supermarket with several litres of sugar, a handful of raisins, a mug of honey, 15 tea bags and a touch of stardust, the mystical powder called yeast. Surgical gloves provided a touch of theatre: a single rubber 'hand' functioned as my brew's 'airlock', secured by elastic bands around the 'wrist' in a stranglehold around Buddha's neck. I pricked the 'middle finger' to give the brew's breath a licence to exhale and refuse entry to airborne contaminants that might infect the infant potion. *Voila*, said the magician as he showed the witch his improvised insulating and pressure-release valve. I tied the other 'fingers' down for aesthetic reasons. As the brew hubbled and bubbled with toil and trouble, that beautiful 'middle-finger' would rise and proclaim its proud erection as my personal gesture of rebellion. The containers simmered with growth – an orgasmic creation. Triumphant progress permeated the bathroom with gentle, sweet, beautiful whispers of promised potency.

The brew gave birth thirty days later. Prematurely, if need dictated. In tandem with every creation, a regenerative batch began, an evergreen cycle. Red or white? An irrelevance, but a continuous supply was essential. I drank my brew after work and on the Saudi holy day: Friday, the big day of prayer. It delivered my needed fix, often with a palatable taste and flavour. And when it didn't? Well, it was still strong stuff.

Hi, I'm Richard. I am an alcoholic.

Alcoholism attacked me with horror and guilt. Terrible tales and true stories. But the narrative was not the script of others. I penned the true-life articles – creator, writer, editor, publisher – I was the gatekeeper to my addiction.

But the bloody present-tense affirmation was tough to swallow. '*I am*' wedged itself between yesterday and tomorrow and refused to budge. The present tense seared *Alcoholic* onto my forehead with the intensity of a branding iron.

I had lost my sense of refinement forever. *Alcohol and elegance didn't belong on the same song sheet*, my inner-bogan booze buddy would say. Aficionados cloaked wine in a veil of mystical language. Masonic wink-winks, knowing nods, pursed lips. Wine-tasting rituals were a ruse, a Mickey Finn, slipped in by the host to advance social standing. Many believers would go to great lengths to speak the cryptic language without understanding a word. Instead, they mimicked a script and squawked like parrots to audiences eager to listen. Social status became as addictive as the alcohol.

Aficionados sniffed the brew, twirled the glass, waxed lyrical with spluttered clichés about symphonies and structures, bodies and bouquet. Titillating and sexy. Their stories stressed an imagined status. Perhaps today's wine was an exemplar of a fondly remembered vineyard, an ego opportunity for the connoisseur to reveal how the wine's unbridled barnyard brilliance would marry beautifully with the veal bum and bull's bollocks. As a refined alcoholic, I knew, without a note of floral hesitation, that wine was not a question of taste. Everybody knew taste was secondary. Alcohol was the real deal. The only question – how strong?

———

Before leaving Coolum, I had considered catching-up with The *Cooktown Crusaders*. These blokes made an annual twelve-day return ride to Cape Tribulation. I had their itinerary. The Crusaders started from the Sunshine Coast on the day after my departure but were already a day's ride ahead of me. They were raising money for autism. The leader's young son was autistic. The owner of the motorcycle shop where I bought Yammie's accessories told me the *Crusaders* had invited me to join them. He worried about me. I spoke like a newbie, had owned a big bike for just ten days, didn't know diddly shit and told him I'd ride my bike around Australia, alone. No wonder he worried. He suggested I start my ride with these guys. 'Get to know the ropes,' he said. I declined. Not that I didn't need help. I did. But I didn't need someone to tell me I was stupid. I knew that already. Now I reconsidered. Should this fake rookie rider catch up with real-deal bikers?

Roadkill left an ugly trail along the Bruce Highway as I rode north. A twenty-five-kilometre section of isolated road was an open mortuary. Fourteen dead kangaroos and wallabies. Eight in a three-kilometre stretch. Travellers had warned me not to ride in the early morning or at dusk. A close encounter of the third kind with a full-grown kangaroo at 110 kilometres an hour would be fatal. A wallaby just as dangerous. These animals would bounce off a truck or cause significant damage to a car but for bikers: steel knitting needles.

I pulled into Midge Point late afternoon. Fraud or not, I would meet up with the *Cooktown Crusaders*.

Boom gates barred my entry to the camping site. I parked Yammie and poked a hesitant head into the visitors' hut. A middle-aged woman beamed a big welcome.

'Friends of the *Crusaders* stay for free. '

'Thanks,' I said. *Fraud,* I thought.

The woman gave me directions.

Yammie on tick-over took me at walking pace towards the bikers camped in a small clearing behind the trees. I saw the motorcycles first. Eight or more. All loaded with gear but not as top heavy as mine. The riders lounged in folding camp seats swigging beer from iced bottles. I brought Yammie to a stop in front of them. My bike cooled; the metal tink-tinked as the heat left her engine. The Fraud, the Bad and the Ugly whistled menacingly between us as we eyeballed each other. One second. Two. The fraud with no name backed down and introduced himself:

'Hi, I'm Richard and I'm … I'm looking for Heckle.'

'Hey, Richie,' said a guy with a bandanna and a long goatee beard.

'Hey, I thought I'd say hi … catch up…'

'Great,' Heckle said. 'Put your bike behind ours.' He waved with a bottle in his hand to the bikes mustered behind them. Their motorcycles gleamed with passion and pride.

All eyes inspected the intruder. I removed my helmet and jacket and strode over, hand extended.

Heckle, a medium-sized guy, gave me a shake like I was a long-lost dog who responded to *Paw!* 'Glad you came,' he said as he took me by the arm and introduced me to the gang. Tension over.

The youngest appeared to be of Samoan descent: a huge, powerful-looking man. The oldest had shoulder-length hair crowned with a bald pate like a mediaeval monk.

Heckle – that was the leader's surname – and another rider, his cousin, had the *Cooktown Crusaders'* colours tattooed on their biceps. Early forties, I guessed. Still feeling like an impersonator, I sensed these were nice blokes. A gang of rough, respectable guys – veteran bikers, riding for a cause. The *Crusaders* said they had organised a sausage-sizzle fundraiser for later in the evening. They said raffle tickets and *Crusader*-tattooed stubbie holders would be on sale. I took this as an order, not a discretionary purchase recommendation.

I erected my tent as fast as a magician flashes his rabbit. A show for the *Crusaders.* The ablution block was nearby. I showered and prepared myself like Cinderella for the ball in reverse: dusty clothes, stained jeans, frayed shirt, scuffed boots.

The evening was full of camaraderie and blokey humour. Camp guests and grey nomads gathered around a campfire. Sausages and onions sizzled nearby. The Crusaders had rigged a stereo with a TV monitor; a karaoke session began.

Heckle took the 'stage.' In his best gravel voice, he sang, 'There is … a house … in New Orleans…' An awful rendition delivered with a heart of gold.

Sausages, onions, bread rolls. Five-star cuisine.

Heckle thrust a beer into my hand as I sucked a stray onion into my mouth.

'Here you go, brother,' he said.

'Uh … I have a drink.' I waved my bottle of water.

'Nah, have a beer.'

'I don't drink.'

He knew.

'No worries,' Heckle said with a sober look.

But it was. Present tense.

We spent the evening listening to war stories that only bikers could tell. Rich and meaty, dished with plenty of juice. Crashes and near misses. Broken bodies. Smashed bikes. Drunken feats. Seized engines. Reckless runs. Stupid stunts. Travels and adventures remembered with a tear and a swipe of the sleeve. *Crusaders* liked beer and beer liked *Crusaders.* As the night drew late and the fire burned low, the stories grew bigger and faster than Pinocchio's nose. The tales of horror did not faze me. Except one. Heckle recounted a time he'd started off at dawn after a camp out. Within minutes, a monstrous huntsman spider crawled from *inside* his helmet onto the visor, a centimetre from his nose. I shivered.

The gang was interested to hear about my adventure. I told them, thankful for the flickering shadows that shielded me from the redness burning my face.

'Sixty-two days?' the older, long-haired biker with the bald pate asked.

'That's the plan.'

'You'll never do it. Two hundred and fifty K a day. One day off, you gotta do five hundred K the next. Two days off and you gotta do seven hundred and fifty to catch up. Tough gig,' said the old guy. 'Bad weather, bike problems, fatigue. Maybe you will, maybe you won't.'

Beery-eyed, he looked towards a dark horizon somewhere behind my eyes and said, 'I done it.' Then sighed and added, 'Took five months.'

'Well, I'm gonna give it a go,' I said, not convincing them or me.

'And,' he said looking over at my bike, 'you'll need a jerry.'

'A jerry?'

'Yeah, a ten-litre jerry. Outback and distance between fuel stops will blow your mind. Northern Queensland is a bitch. They run out too!'

'Run out?'

'Yeah, the servos run out of petrol. 'Specially the little ones. So here you are, bike sucking air, pulling in to grab your fuel, then you see the sign: *No Petrol.*'

'Shit,' I said. 'I never thought a service station would run out.'

'Get a jerry,' he said.

With thoughts of huntsmen, the outback and a dry tank, I crawled into my tent and slept. I didn't want to fail. I didn't want to look stupid. I needed to be strong and sober. Not weak and wasted.

Fifty-nine nights before the finish line.

SUPERSONIC

F ourth of July. No fireworks. I woke at 5.00 am in my small tent. The Crusaders slept in swags under the stars while their motorcycles guarded the perimeter like sentries. Sleep was a symphony of snuffles and snores punctuated with grunts and groans and beer-induced mutterings dragged from dreams. Discarded bottles lay scattered among the slumbering riders. A naked arm stretched from a swag, motionless amid the empties. The camp was still and dark. I needed to take a leak and shuffled toward the toilet block, narrowly missing a clothesline strung like a hunter's snare across the path. A dim yellow light illuminated a small wash house scented with soap and tainted with urine. Cloud cover added a layer of protection against the open coldness of the night sky.

I retraced my path back to my tent. With no chance of sleeping, I grabbed my torch. A sandy path led through wallum onto a beach where a cool breeze spiced with brine stirred the dawn. No surf. The tide ebbed gently, lapping at the shore. Ripples of cold water snaked around my naked feet; sand swirled between my toes. A sea bird squealed its presence across the dark and empty shoreline. Alone – Crusoe on Midge Point. My fourth day. Difficult to believe. The adventure had become a reality: three days riding, 1,000 kilometres. Standing in the shallow water, I breathed the rich sea air and listened to the sounds of a breaking day. I could do this.

Heckle boiled water back at the campsite while the big Samoan devoured the remains of a cold sausage from the previous evening's sizzle. The others still slept.

'Grab a coffee,' said Heckle.

'Thanks,' I said, spooning several heaped teaspoons of powdered coffee into a large, chipped mug.

'Great night,' I said. 'Thanks for the invite.'

'Thanks for coming. You wanna ride with us up to Cape Tribulation?'

The diversion would add nearly 1000 kilometres to my trip. Cape Tribulation was 500 kilometres north of Townsville, the town from where I would head west into central Queensland.

'I'm already worried I won't make the trip in sixty-two days, so I'm gonna say "no". But thanks anyway.'

'No worries. You have my mobile. Call me if you have any problems.'

I drank coffee and watched the riders wake. They stayed silent as they ate, packed and loaded their bikes. A smattering of grey nomads came to watch their departure. After bear hugs and high fives, with helmets secured, the Crusaders fired up their machines; the morning came alive with throaty roars, throbbing bikes and pumping exhaust.

'Wagons, ho!' Heckle said as the Crusaders raised hands in farewell.

The morning emerged, dull and stark. Swags and bikes disappeared, leaving giant footprints in the grass; the roar of engines now a soft purr as the Crusaders headed north.

At the campsite kitchen, I finished my coffee and found a cold sausage: the sole survivor from the night before.

. . .

Yammie carried me north towards Townsville: 305 kilometres. Grim clouds promised squalls. Riding in the rain would not be fun. Four days and it felt like forever.

The Crusaders didn't discuss Australia's general election. Neither did I. Each day, I weaned myself from addictions. *The ride* was everything: my only present tense.

The power and throb of my bike was seductive. My hand wrapped around the throttle, and like a child, I wound her up. Yammie jumped forward, a wild horse racing into the wind. The speed soared and the cowboy grinned. I eased off after ten minutes. My driver's licence had sucked up too many demerit points over the last three years; another offence and I would lose it. Deep shit. Adventure over. But impulse made me do it again. The thrill was addictive. Power and speed. My bike, the alchemist, turned back the clock; the ol' boy felt like a young man. A crazy young man …

―――――

April 1989

Heathrow's first-class lounge had faded like an old photo, but speed restored the memory as solidly as the road ahead. Thirty-four-year-old me waited to board Concorde for his supersonic flight to New York.

A strong gin and tonic sat in my hand, heavily iced, topped with a smiley-faced lemon. 10 am. My third.

Concorde's arrogant eagle eyes stared at its wealthy passengers. The supersonic jet sat alongside the lounge's floor-to-ceiling windows. The lord of the skies offered only first-class tickets. Concorde's precious people didn't have to walk kilometres of corridors to board. The aircraft's doors were fifty paces from the lounge; its seats waiting to honour wealthy bums.

Relaxed, I placed another spoonful of finely diced onion onto an unsalted cracker loaded with caviar. The eggs popped delicately in my mouth, smooth and nutty, with a breeze of ocean. I tried hard to radiate nonchalance. I couldn't. Velocity and alcohol were an exciting combination. My gin and tonic vanished in a final gulp. Already fuzzy, I stood to make a refill when a tray of fully loaded champagne flutes appeared at my side. I took one look and nodded to the waiter. 'Thanks,' I said, noting other passengers didn't offer such common courtesies.

My champagne was empty before I reached the bar. Exquisite backlit bottles of wines and spirits glowed with the soft ambers of sapphires, rubies, quartz and emeralds. The world's finest liquors. Self-serve. I did; I filled my glass with ice, selected a bottle of Tanqueray, poured a generous slug, and added a touch of tonic. I returned to my seat with a full glass. Whispers of juniper, fresh and sharp, a hint of citrus. The gin hit my stomach with explosive satisfaction.

The Tannoy announced the departure. The elite-of-the-elite sauntered towards the sleek bullet that would propel its fat-cat cargo to New York at twice the speed of sound. I picked up my briefcase and followed. Unsteadily.

Concorde – more like a *missile* – had a narrow, cramped cabin with two-by-two seats of twenty-six rows. Row thirteen didn't exist. An aisle seat waited for me in row fourteen.

I nodded to the aristocratic gent who would rub elbows with me for the next three hours. I was rewarded with a sour look. As my backside moulded to the contours of the fighter-plane seat, an attendant thrust a tray of champagne and orange juice toward me. I chose champagne.

'Thank you so much,' I said with slow words and a smile too big for my face.

Concorde's engines thrust its rich, beautiful people into an adrenaline-fuelled take-off, donkey-kicking thrusters forcing bodies deep into leather seats. The afterburners shut down after a few minutes. The sudden removal of warp speed slowed all sensation. I felt like I was floating in honey.

'What can I get you, sir?' said the pretty flight attendant reappearing by my seat.

'Gin and tonic,' I said. A request I would repeat many times over the next several hours.

Champagne, canapes, and G&Ts slid down as fast as Concorde's

Mach 2. Drunk, speeding at 2,150 kph at over 60,000 feet above the Atlantic, I could see the curvature of the earth. I nudged the guy next to me, gave him a sloppy smile and nodded toward the window. He didn't look. He shook his *Financial Times*, frowned, and gave me the aristocratic equivalent of the middle finger. *Up yours* too, I thought, and pressed the attendant button for a refill.

Three and a half hours later, I arrived at John F. Kennedy, ninety minutes before I took off, but the cabin crew could not wake me. It took forty minutes to bring me back to life. My legs carried me in a stagger from the supersonic rocket to the snail-paced luggage carousel. My Concorde ticket included a helicopter flight to Manhattan's East River. I missed it. Instead, I stumbled through the 'green' channel where I offered immigration officials a crooked smile and a passport. A long queue waited in the rain for yellow cabs to whisk them to their futures. Mine took me to my minibar.

A long and lonely New York night separated today from tomorrow.

———

Yammie's engines roared; Townsville lay two hours further north. Foul weather was imminent. The sugar cane bent in anticipation; cattle laid grimly expectant, and the sky blackened. I stopped and pulled on my waterproof leggings. Thirty minutes later, torrential rainfall descended on the road. Headlights swept through the downpour, red and orange, refractions and reflections, spray and shit. It was difficult to see; rain hit my eyes like needles. I pulled down my visor; my helmet was now a cocoon against the cracking bullets of the storm. I eased back the throttle, bent my body low behind the windshield and rode sixty-five calamitous kilometres into Townsville. Lit by neon confusion, I reached the outskirts of the town and followed the road looking for shelter. The weather stunk. No tent tonight. I stopped at a caravan park, took a cabin, and unloaded Yammie under dim light and a torrent of rain. I shuffled to the communal toilet block thirty minutes later: wet, cold, exhausted, anxious and desperate for a hot shower. On my first day of bad weather, my sanity questioned my strength; my despondency demanded a drink.

'You've earned it,' said Johnnie, the oily-tongued salesman that sat on my shoulder. 'Just one.'

I saw his leery grin.

'You'll be fine,' he said. 'Trust me.'

DESERT STORM

I slept well. The sun shone through a humid, subtropical Queensland morning. A new beginning. Clear skies had eclipsed the darkness of the previous night. Today I would take a left turn and head west into Australia's outback but first a ride to Castle Hill.

The pink granite monolith towered 286 metres above Townsville. Yammie followed the winding narrow road that led to the summit as we zigzagged through walkers, runners, cyclists, dogs and careless cars. The stunning views added icing to my improving mood. Magnetic Island sparkled like a jewel beyond Cleveland Bay and into the Coral Sea.

A wooden promontory jutted from the easterly tip of the monolith where tourists gathered to ogle and snap. Mid-winter and it was hot. A handsome twenty-year-old man smiled at me from the crowd. A memory. When I reached the lookout, he had gone.

I grabbed my camera. Packs of Asian tourists wandered into my composition to snap group selfies. They tilted heads and pointed tongues, posed under V-shaped fingers and punctuated their giggles and squeals with an alien language. Suddenly, like cicadas, the buzz stopped. The group lost interest and wandered elsewhere with solemn faces, heads low, fingers flicking mobiles. My turn. I took some shots of the bay then strode back to Yammie. Time to go. I had a big day ahead.

The Flinders Highway would carry me to Hughenden: 384 kilometres west. An empty road that cut through plains of tough grass and little else heralded my entry into outback nothingness.

Petrol had not been an issue until now. I had ridden 160 kilometres since quenching Yammie's thirsty tank. Torrens Creek was close. My map showed a service station. Twenty minutes later it was clear I had unwittingly passed the town. I stopped at a railway crossing where the train track ran parallel with the tarmac road to Hughenden. The railway lines ran hard, straight, unbending until they merged into pinpricks, east and west. A rutted dirt track crossed the train tracks and the road to Hughenden. A wooden signpost pointed to places not listed on my map: a rough trail, yet the furthest location was Aramac, 270 kilometres south. And Torrens Creek had passed without a trace. The town couldn't be far. I'd just have to turn around and go find it.

How had I missed Torrens Creek? I rode east, back from where I'd come. Five minutes later, I found an old pub with a single bowser. It seemed Torrens Creek and its population of twenty had escaped my attention.

I pulled up next to the bowser. An ol' boy with a weathered bush-hat held a beer bottle to his lips. Slumped in a wicker chair, he rocked back on its rear legs. Like a scarecrow he sat silent and unmoving. The bottle stayed glued to his mouth; wrinkled eyes followed my movements like an owl stalking a mouse. Sand, rust and grime covered the single bowser. I turned off my engine, removed the ignition key, unlocked the petrol tank, took off my gloves, unstrapped my helmet, pushed out the kickstand and slung my left leg high to swing out from the seat. The mechanical parts of my replacement right hip made this manoeuvre look like the old man I was. I hung my helmet on the handlebars, stretched my back to ease the tension in my arms and shoulders and reached for the bowser. The old man's eyes missed nothing; the beer remained frozen in time.

'No petrol 'ere mate,' the ol' boy suddenly said, eyelids drooping as if he'd fall asleep before he finished his sentence. 'We run out.'

My shock sparked his two-word solution. 'Ninety kilometres,' the scarecrow said pointing west with a bony, liver-spotted hand still wrapped in a stranglehold around his bottle.

Ninety kilometres later I crawled into Hughenden with only fifteen kilometres remaining in the tank. Close. Too close. But by a stroke of luck, a small service station at the edge of town was just closing.

'Anywhere I can sling a tent?' I asked.

'Out back,' said the woman behind the counter motioning behind her with her jaw. 'Ten bucks.'

'Done.'

Yammie could wait until morning, but without a mobile connection I couldn't call Maureen. She would worry.

Tucked beside the service station, a small patch of sparse grass in a billabong of dirt offered an intimate space for two caravans and a tent.

The day's heat quickly dissipated. The setting sun threw gold and amber onto my scrap of scrub as the balmy day bled into a bitterly cold night. The service station closed, as did any opportunity for decent food. My excuse of a camping stove brewed a mug of cook-in-the-cup noodles. It had been a long day.

Hughenden ticketed itself as dinosaur country: volcanic basalt mountains and sweeping black soil plains were scattered with fossils, including 'Hughie' – a seven-metre-tall Muttaburrasaurus. Sleep came easily despite the icy temperature. A heavy sweater and a snug sleeping bag kept the cold out and the hot noodles in. Excavations, fossils, bones and relics. Past into present or present into past?

———

Saudi Arabia 1990

Iraq invaded Kuwait during the white-hot Saudi summer of August 1990. My office overlooked the military airstrip in Riyadh. During the five months that followed Saddam's attack, coalition forces built their muscle: planes, soldiers, weapons, munitions and supplies. Operation

Desert Shield. The logistics were a modern-day marvel. Huge Lockheed transport planes stacked three or four high – all day, all night, every day, every night – hung like fixtures in an unchanging sky. This gargantuan military operation defied imagination. Cargo planes landed, discharged, refuelled, took off. Within minutes another plane would repeat the same manoeuvre. Next.

The Desert Shield build-up was the biggest and most expensive in aviation history. The huge Berlin airlift of the Cold War paled in comparison. The immensity of the operation unveiled itself from my office window. Air-raid sirens wailed random alarms, but still Saddam's scud missiles remained on their mobile truck launchers. Saudi Arabia was safe. For now.

The anxious inhabitants of Riyadh waited. The city expected coalition forces to attack within weeks. Speculation bleated from tongues of every language. Today, tomorrow, next week. A month passed. No-one knew what horrors Saddam Hussein might unleash in response to an allied assault. The city's tension spread like a disease. Impasse created fear through uncertainty. Citizens needed decisive solutions. 'The sooner the better,' we said.

Essential staff remained at the bank where I worked. Citibank evacuated non-essential staff and their families to the 'safe' city of Jeddah or transported them to secure locations outside Saudi Arabia.

Iraq's response to a coalition attack was the subject of great debate: like a sports event, everyone discussed each side's strengths and weaknesses in extensive and unnecessary detail. The date of the showdown was still unknown. No-one knew whether Saddam possessed the capability to load chemical weapons onto his scud missiles. No-one was sure whether the missiles could reach Riyadh. No-one was sure whether the missiles could find Riyadh. No-one was sure of anything. Except fear. Western embassies issued their lucky citizens with gas masks. Most bank staff – Saudis, Indians, Pakistanis and Filipinos – had no protection. It felt dishonourable to have gas masks while non-Western workers had nothing. I gave mine to my maid. Off-duty US marines wore T-shirts that screamed their frustration: ***Send us in to kick some* or *send us home to get some!***

On the 17 January 1991 at 2.20 am, the air above Riyadh exploded like a volcano. Operation Desert Storm began. After six months of build-up and preparation, the coalition forces released waves of allied fighter planes to 'kick some'. The marines would not be going home to 'get some'. At least, not anytime soon.

Strike aircraft screamed low across the city, shaking the dusty red buildings for heart-pounding hours. Air-raid sirens like heavy-metal banshees wailed eerie screams across the cowed night sky as American and British fighters roared north towards Kuwait and Iraq. The real war had started. Now Riyadh waited.

The first Iraqi Scud missiles reached Riyadh in the days and weeks that followed. Saddam's retaliation was not unexpected, but the outcome was. Military experts compared the likelihood of Saddam hitting Riyadh to a child throwing a cricket ball into a bucket at the far end of a football pitch. Saddam had never played cricket, but his missiles found the bucket. The American Patriot Defence system brought down most Scuds. But during the initial missile attacks, civilian naivety caused most of us to believe the Scuds scored direct hits. The population hid in buildings and bedrooms, and shuddered from what they thought were the shock waves of missile strikes. The inhabitants of Riyadh were wrong. The shock waves came from successful Patriot intercepts. The American missile defence 'worked' eighty per cent of the time. Occasionally our patriotic shepherds just nudged the Scuds or hit their tail, leaving the warhead to fall and explode on the unfortunates directly beneath. Irrespective of the outcome, an aerial Patriot-Scud marriage sent shock waves that shook walls and windows like an earthquake.

The Scuds had no chemical warheads and the Patriots revived morale. We began to feel safe.

Soon the city peeped out from its dusty tension; wary inhabitants sniffed the air, pushed the fear into their pockets and returned to businesses and their lives. Riyadh went about its daily affairs despite the air-raid warnings. The wail of sirens often competed with the wail of a million mosques. A discordant duet followed.

Statistics suggested that the odds of death by missile were unlikely, like shark attacks: horrifying but improbable. Except on the roads. If you were unlucky enough to be driving along a busy city street as the air-raid sirens began their wail, you lowered the probability of survival. Not from incoming missiles, but from dipshit Riyadh crazies. These citizens sped like lunatics to a place of sanctuary that didn't exist. The sane solution? Pull over. And let the road carnage play its course. Stop. Wait. Survive.

During one air attack, I pulled onto the hard shoulder and stepped outside into a desert Grand Prix of car horns, revved engines and tyre smoke. I scanned the sky to see if I could see the Scud. The kid received his reward. A Patriot traced across the sky hunting its quarry until its kill was confirmed by anyone who dared to watch. Flash, sparkle, BANG! The 'bang' caught up seconds later, but the Riyadh Grand Prix continued – chequered flags would not be waved until the sirens stopped.

One night an American colleague invited Hans and me for 'drinks' at his villa. Hans was Dutch. We all lived in a compound called Mirabella. The American's wife had stayed and was one of the few Western women remaining in Riyadh. We abandoned formalities. And hit the only topic open to discussion when the wail of air-raid sirens split the air like a parting sea. The American and his wife quickly and politely excused themselves to the 'safety' of an unused bedroom where they had rigged a spare mattress under an oak dining table. Here they would huddle until the 'all-clear'. Hans looked at me, and I at him. Then we looked at the illicit whisky bottle on the table. We eyed the forbidden fruit and shrugged our shoulders. The two of us sealed the deal. Hans said nothing, picked up the bottle, and poured the amber liquid to the rim of our tumblers.

'Proost!' he said.

I grinned and we chinked glasses. We spent the next hour boozing while the air-raid sirens screamed, and the Americans hid under their mattress.

No conversation was possible. None necessary.

The night closed with a stumbled stagger to my villa under a black cloud of memory fog.

After some months, when commercial flights resumed, my Dutch drinking partner moved back to Europe, back to his wife, back to his family, back to normality. Before his departure Hans bequeathed me a special leaving gift: his invaluable portfolio of red, muddy, smelly, beautiful homemade wine. Fifteen felicitous bottles of Riyadh's finest.

Hans died of cancer a few years later.

Proost.

KROK-KA-DEELS

After a cold night, the roadhouse exploded with morning. I crawled from my sleeping bag, stiff and cramped, into the backyard of my overnight home. Galahs perched on a telephone line, heads tilted downwards, all eyes on the stranger below. Their feathers rippled in the breeze; pink chests and silver-grey plumage glinted like armour in the first rays of sun. Curiosity flickered across their crests while the crazy guy beneath stretched a little life into his brittle body.

Hughenden stirred from its bitter winter night. A truck had pulled up at the bowser. Eggs, bacon, sausages and all things fried floated in a gentle whisper to taunt my hunger. I had eaten little the previous night; my belly rumbled in ravenous anticipation. Breakfast.

But first things first. My ten-dollar exchange the previous night rewarded me with a toilet key. I pulled the key from my jeans and opened the male ablution block. A shabby-looking construction: one toilet, one sink, one shower, no urinal. The green badge on the single stall declared it 'VACANT.' I opened the door. A huge truck driver sat regally on his throne with a newspaper spread over hairy legs dusted in cement.

'I just sat down, mate.'

'No worries,' I said as I turned on my heel and shut the door to the crinkled rustle of his newspaper.

A constipated volcano erupted as I reached the toilet block door; vile vapours followed the explosion. I decided to use the next roadhouse for my own ablutions, so I headed for the diner.

As I entered a stout, no-nonsense bush woman – the owner of the establishment – held a phone to her ear. She looked at me and her furrowed frown cemented my status as 'city-boy nuisance' lost in the outback.

'You Richard?'

'Yes!' I said excitedly. *My God*, I thought, *this social media stuff really works*. I was raising funds for Beyond Blue and my pre-trip blitz with the local press seemed to work. I naively expected the caller to be a journalist or charity donor.

'It's your wife,' she said as she passed me the phone. She left me in shock while she busied herself with frying pans sizzling with bacon, eggs and sausages.

I didn't have a mobile connection, so a call to my wife the night before had been impossible. Maureen had no idea where I might hang my hat. Or even if I would hang it at all.

'Where have you been? I've been worried sick,' Maureen said. She had called every roadhouse, hotel, pub and patch of dirt that lined yesterday's ride. Including those with populations that barely exceeded plurality. She even spoke to my 'no petrol 'ere, mate' friend at the Torrens Creek pub. I knew Maureen would worry. I intended to call her as soon as I had a mobile connection. She beat me to it. Maureen said everyone recalled the ol' white-haired boy on the red motorbike looking for fuel. Well, well, the immensity of the outback suddenly shrank to a small-town. Internet eat your heart out: meet the Bush Telegraph – an Australian phenomenon.

'I'm sorry,' I said.

'Are you okay?'

'All good.'

'Call me later.'

And that was that. Maureen was at work. I would call when I could.

Breakfast never tasted so good. I had everything and washed it down with a mug of tea. A slice of toast and marmalade added a touch of English luxury to an awesome spread. I picked up a discarded newspaper:

The North West STAR

A family of four were rescued on Monday, July 4, after being stranded in the bush between Mount Isa and East Leichhardt Dam. The family had abandoned their vehicle with two flat tyre. They were found ten kilometres south of Mount Isa on the Duchess Road. The family had no injuries. A private helicopter and a police vehicle started the search at 2.30 pm and located the family at 4 pm.

I had an emergency tyre-repair kit. Anyway, this stuff happens to others. *Right?* With my stomach full, Yammie refuelled, and my flask filled with coffee, I rode out of Hughenden and continued west on the Flinders Highway. The first Europeans passed through Hughenden in 1861: Frederick Walker's expedition. Walker was searching for the famous explorers, Burke and Wills. He never found them. I believe it. No helicopters to help them.

The sheer beauty of the emptiness was breathtaking: black volcanic soil, rich with the bones of fossilised dinosaurs spread to my left, to my right, and as far ahead as I could see. The first kink in the road interrupted the geography about seventy kilometres from Hughenden. My entry into outback Queensland had convinced me 500 Australian kilometres were longer than that of any other country. Travels across China and the Tibetan plateau (on a train) and the American Midwest prairies (on a Greyhound bus) felt like nothing compared to the

Australian outback on my Yamaha. Sheep and cattle speckled the openness like dust on an empty canvas. Farms or cattle stations must surely be out there. Somewhere. I just couldn't see them.

The mild weather continued at least while the sun shone. By late afternoon the cold would begin to strengthen. Frequent coffee from my flask kept me alert; fatigue could be fatal.

The bush surrounded me with the fish-eye perspective of an ant struggling to grapple with the immensity of a million galaxies. *Surrounded?* The wrong word. Nothing surrounded me. Just *girt* by emptiness. Clumps of yellowed grass covered a rich, rusty earth that stretched across a shimmering 360-degree horizon. Lone trees dotted the otherwise empty plains. The outback did not register my presence. I was less than nothing. I received no judgement. No personal history. I breathed. *Freedom.*

Richmond was ahead. The ubiquitous railway line ran parallel with the road. Another red dirt road crossed the Flinders Highway. A small tin shed had been slung alongside the railway tracks. A waiting room for one and a half passengers. Perhaps shelter for anyone waiting for the biannual 14.39 to Townsville. Unlikely but perfect for a coffee stop.

One hundred and twenty kilometres had passed under my boots as I approached Richmond. Across the railway tracks, several hundred white corellas fossicked on a narrow side road. I grabbed my camera and approached like a butterfly collector in the Amazon. The birds rose in an angelic cloud reaching for the sky as a single soul. The fluttering of their wings disturbed the tranquillity for a stitch of time before peace settled and all was still. I missed the shot.

Replica dinosaurs for tourists lined the road 500 metres further ahead opposite the roadhouse. A sign warned this stop offered the only fuel until the next roadhouse 146 kilometres west. I filled my tank. The scenery continued with breathtaking emptiness for exactly 146 kilometres to Julia Creek.

The outback amazes. It's unique, Australian and bizarre. If its roadhouse was any indication, Julia Creek's population of 368 souls possessed a strong and unconventional sense of humour. I filled Yammie's tank and wandered into the roadhouse to pay.

A truckie stood in the queue in front of me. While I waited I read the messages peppering a large noticeboard next to the cashier. One advertised brightly coloured knitted garments tailor-made for penises. *Willy Warmers*. I piss you not. Beautiful full-colour photographs illustrated the product for which the models, 'Nathan and Me', received full credit. Measurement appointments were essential. Another proclaimed the vagina to be 'the best engine in the world'.

In 1912, the world-famous Austrian gynaecologist, Dr Herman Otto Kloepnecker, M.D. PH. D. published the following:

The best engine in the world is the vagina. It can be started with one finger. It is self-lubricating. It takes any size piston. And it changes its own oil every four weeks. It is only a pity the management system is so fu**ing temperamental.

This is a truck stop. No other patrons gave the noticeboard any thought. Friends are like undies said another:

Friends

Friends are like undies...
Some crawl up your arse...
Some snap under pressure...
Some don't have the strength to hold you up...
Some get a little twisted...
Some are holey...
Some are cheap and nasty...
And some actually do cover
Your arse when u need them to

My face broke into an embarrassed grin as I took a photo.

'So you like my notice board?' a voice said from over my shoulder.

I looked behind me to see a thirtyish-year-old woman point a finger at another note: a poster of the Great Wall of China. This was the backdrop image to a certificate awarded to Wendy Horne by the National Breast Cancer Foundation for the 'Great Wall Trek 2016'.

'Wow,' I said. 'That you?'

'Yep, just came back.'

I had pegged Julia Creek like Chester's Mill: a fictional American rural town cocooned in Stephen King's novel *Under the Dome*. Residents from Julia Creek in China? The Great Wall? It just seemed odd, is all I'm saying.

'Congratulations,' I said. 'Good on you … interesting noticeboard.'

'Glad you like it,' said Wendy, the roadhouse manager.

I paid for my fuel and left smiling, impressed that brave people do what they do.

Curious, a quick Google search told me that forty-four people did that trek. Wendy was one of them. They raised $290,000 for cancer research.

Good on you, I thought as I mounted Yammie. *Way to go.*

I said a silent goodbye to Julia Creek's Adventurers, Willy Warmers, Female Engines and Underwear Friends.

I reached Cloncurry fatigued. A long 405-kilometre ride. A caravan park was conveniently shouldered against the road.

A hot shower invigorated my tired body, but the thought of noodles brewed on my camping stove soured with the discovery of a sign that read *All-You-Can-Eat Buffet – $25 – Camp Canteen*. My discretionary budget spend went south.

I decided on the roast: beef, baked potatoes, broccoli, peas, all drowned under a carpet of thick gravy. I had eaten a big breakfast but had no lunch apart from a packet of peanuts and an apple. Now I was on a roll. A help-yourself ice cream counter looked irresistible. I squeezed chocolate, vanilla and strawberry into a dish that physics said was too small. My addiction to sweetness pulled me back for a second go. *Please sir, can I have some more* … But nobody lifted a cane to whack my backside as I ladled childish mountains of ice-cream into my empty bowl.

The Discovery Park gave a home to more FIFO workers than travellers. Fly-In-Fly-Out had become an Australian phenomenon. But tonight, curiosity created an even stranger cat. A Chinese man, mid-thirties, approached my table as my last spoonful of ice cream disappeared into my mouth.

'Can I ask question?' he said.

'Sure.'

'Have you ever travel to China?'

'Why do you ask?' I said, failing to hide my surprise.

He gestured over his shoulder to a table on the other side of the canteen. Seven Chinese men sat staring at me expectantly.

'We take bets you visit China.'

'What did you bet on?' I asked.

'That sometime, you go China.'

'You're right. I did. I lived there for a year.'

My answer pleased him. His question amazed me. A bizarre encounter where the ol' boy became the subject of a strange bet. Stranger still: the gamblers were Chinese workers living in the Aussie outback. We talked for a while. The man had worked in Australia as an engineer for several years, a professional, but as he said, 'English, need improvement.'

I ambled back to my tent. It looked like I had company. A one-man tent had been pitched alongside a yellow Volkswagen Beetle convertible twenty metres from my humble canvas home. It was almost phosphorescent. A dim light exposed the shadow of the tent's single occupant: a woman. She was humming.

I shrugged off my curiosity, unzipped my tent and burrowed into the comfort and warmth of my down-filled cocoon. Six days into my adventure, and self-doubt questioned when bad luck would hit. Negative thinking. Cold air cloaked Cloncurry in an icy blanket. Despite the temperature, and without willy warmers, I fell asleep dreaming of China in the outback.

Kunshan, Nr Shanghai, China 2009

Temporary backpacker accommodation in Coolum took on a more permanent outlook. Alcohol abuse had forced Maureen to abandon me. With good reason. When I had sobered up, she might take me back, but for now, I had no other options.

'Dry' did not come easy. The Queensland heat squeezed my sobriety like a python. I shook my newspaper and the communal kitchen coughed dust and regret. Employment was as elusive as my abstinence. *English Teachers* said the ad. *Jobs guaranteed in China.* I looked closer. *No prior experience. We teach you everything. Just $1,499.* My resume lay in the darkness of a desk drawer, a cemetery of dead applications and rotting rejection letters.

I made my decision.

On a hot, humid Monday, six hard, studious weeks later, and $1,499 poorer, an envelope arrived. The certificate inside said I had completed a TESOL Diploma. I officially became a *Teacher of English to Speakers of Other Languages.* Respect inched closer *and* sobriety stumbled stubbornly alongside.

My flight arrived in Shanghai five days later. And on a cold, wet Friday night, another newly minted English teacher joined the expat job queue. An airport bus ferried me to the city centre; a taxi did the rest. I never imagined Shanghai would look like Manhattan. Wide roads weaved through deep valleys of glass and concrete lit by molten trails of car lights. Blazing ads the size of football pitches segued from Coke to cigarettes, SUVs to smartphones. Rain refracted the brilliance of the night onto an Asian humanity pulsing like a heaving sea as Shanghai moved closer to the Chinese New Year. Rat to Ox. A city alive.

My driver honked as he criss-crossed the city and edged into another world. Gone were the gaudy lights. Instead, narrow, steam-filled backstreets whispered another story: hard lives hidden in shadows.

The taxi arrived with a screech of tires and guttural words. *We're here*, I guess the driver must have said.

My budget boarding house turned out to be very … budget. The *HUNG RU HOTEL* lived in a dark and dirty lane. Its neon 'N' and 'G' no longer worked: '*HU RU*' flickered in dull yellow lights offering a weary welcome to stray guests, but I didn't care. I had done it. 'HU RU' worked for me.

But my initial euphoria faded with every day that passed. I shivered through twelve days of Chinese rain and Artic cold. My room, a small monk-like cell with no heating, became a prison. A mobile phone and the use of an old computer in the dingy foyer gave me freedom to search for employment. *Jobs guaranteed,* the ad had said.

Twelve days of endless googling; twelve days of online, real-time rejections. Each teaching position demanded a copy of my passport and a current photo. My fifty-five years creased my face in hard lines like barbed wire after an explosion. And despite being lean and fit, the photo that glared at prospective employers did not show youth or energy. Just despair. Old and beaten with eyes that screamed.

'No,' said the emails with digital words colder than the weather. Polite Chinese platitudes loaded with poor English filled the refusals. *Xie Xie*, they wrote. Translated, it meant, *don't call us, we'll call you.* I was broke. And every failure fuelled my fear.

Reject. Reject. Reject.

A drink would help. A drink would help a lot.

The old fighter bobbed and weaved, backed onto the ropes and soaked up the humiliation. Until a surprise win: I was asked to attend an interview at *Cri-Kee International* in the nearby town of Kunshan.

The head teacher, Harry, sent me an email. *Let's catch up*, he wrote, *eyeball to eyeball.*

Shanghai's super-fast bullet train shot me fifty kilometres to Kunshan in eighteen minutes. Harry and I had arranged to meet in a fast-food coffee house next to the train station at 8.30 am sharp.

Harry was American, young, mountainous, overweight. Long hair escaped from beneath a Snoopy baseball hat turned backwards while a shirt three sizes too large hung past his knees and billowed in his wake.

'Hey,' Harry said.

I was easy to find. The coffee house exploded with harsh voices padded like sheep against the cold, shrouded in steam breath and cigarette smoke.

We looked an odd couple.

'Pleased to meet you,' I said, my surprise hidden in the nicotine haze.

Harry wasted no time. 'Man,' he said, 'we need a teacher. Yesterday. Pronto. What experience you got?'

'None. But I have a TESOL diploma. And I've given workshops to banking employees about products and procedures.' My voice had the sound of one hand clapping, the sound of the long-term unemployed.

'Man,' he said again. 'No English-teaching experience. Shit. An Australian!'

'English, actually.'

He waved his hand dismissively. 'You speak any Mandarin?'

'No.'

'Jesus! But you *do* have the diploma. But hey, you look … experienced. The school's owners, Latisha and Leo, want to meet you for lunch.'

'Really?' I said, and started to sabotage my opportunity, protesting against my skills, doubting the efficacy of my application. Fear and doubt. I could hear my weakness.

Harry looked surprised. 'You want the job or not?'

'Yes.'

'Good. Rock up to this address.' Harry handed me a slip of paper. 'Noon! Twelve on the button,' he said. 'Just talk crap – confident crap. You'll be fine.' Harry had scrawled a map on the back. He heaved his bulk out of the chair and pushed his way to the exit. The Chinese parted like a biblical sea as Harry waded his mammoth frame through clouds of cigarette smoke.

'Tzai Jien,' he shouted in Mandarin over his shoulder.

I wandered the streets of Kunshan, a small village of two million people. Modern tower blocks and glitzy, cheap shops and even cheaper products lined the main roads near the station. People crammed into this town tighter than the Melbourne Cricket Ground on World Cup Final day. Aggressive gestures accompanied loud conversations. Staccato words rose and fell with an intensity that alarmed rather than welcomed. I understood nothing. People pushed. People shoved. People stared. I had seen no other Westerners other than Harry. Without warning, two teenage girls hugged onto my shoulders as they squealed with laughter. One on the left, the other on the right. Long tongues lunged towards my ears as their fingers, with black-painted nails, pushed a *V* towards the third girl who snapped a photo. I was the star attraction. They melted into the crowd before I could open my mouth. The girls flitted into the flock, laughing at the white-haired Western man staring at them from their cell phone.

Small lanes like a network of capillaries pulsed behind the facade of the main street: cigarette vendors and hawkers, cats and dogs, washing and children, garbage and food. Always food: dumplings, boiling soups, skewers of meat, vats of rice, steam and sizzle. Addictive smells of a hard life. Firecrackers exploded nearby. I jumped. The locals served firecrackers as entrees before weddings and family celebrations.

Three hours later, I found the school in a drab office tower hidden in a backstreet. A dirty elevator took me to the eighth floor where Cri-Kee International exploded in colour. Bright cartoon characters painted on every wall: Bambi, Mickey Mouse, Cinderella, Donald Duck, Dumbo, Pinocchio. Young adults filled every glass-walled classroom: an even mix of girls and boys, mostly late teens and early twenties. A shy receptionist dressed in a purple Snow White dress with yellow bodice ushered me into a spacious back room. Walt Disney in the teaching area; Confucius in the owner's private offices. A carved table peaked out from beneath a mountain of Chinese food. A fish head stared at me from a bowl of murky soup as four faces peered at me through a salty haze of cigarette smoke laced with sweet and sour.

Two Chinese men slouched by the table: Leo, the owner's husband, short and stocky, and a young Chinese teacher named Lucifer. A Chinese woman, early forties, black hair past her backside, sat at the table and smiled. 'Please,' she said sweeping her hand theatrically over an empty seat. 'I am called Latisha.' She was Leo's wife and the school was her baby.

Harry mushroomed over a seat at the far end on the table, backside hanging over the edges, baseball cap still in reverse. Leo held out a limp hand and shook mine like he was pumping water from an empty creek. I caricatured the action until personal embarrassment and Western etiquette dictated withdrawal to be the best strategy.

'Welcome, welcome, welcome,' Leo said. He pushed a can of Tsingtao into my hand, while my terror hid behind my need for the job.

'Thanks,' I said, hoping my confident smile covered my fear.

'Drink!' commanded Latisha. I watched them gorge: noisy, sloppy, heads down, bowls lifted to mouths. They chatted and spat in speckled English and Mandarin. Leo piled food onto my plate and pushed beers into my hand. A 'no, thank you' would have translated into a Western middle finger. They did not take prisoners. I talked. I ate. And I drank.

Leo smiled, said nothing. Smoke drifted from the cigarette poised in his left hand while his right clicked chopsticks at the speed of light. He stopped only to guzzle Tsingtao … and to press more beers into my reluctant hand with a nod that needed no interpretation: *Drink up!*

Latisha directed questions at me in reasonable English: 'You have krok-ka-deels in Australia,' she said solemnly.

'Yes …' I said with the gravitas. Harry's advice nudged my narrative: *Talk crap with confidence.* 'Dangerous crocodiles.' And I told tales of life in Australia shoulder-to-shoulder with koalas, possums, wallabies and kangaroos. I scored a win with kangaroos.

'Aaah kaang-gaaaah-roooos,' she said stretching the syllables far enough to snap. 'Mmmm, very, very eeeenteressing.'

'Yes,' I repeated, 'very interesting.'

Leo drunkenly impersonated a bounding kangaroo, hands poised in prayer in front of his nose, body undulating in sexual rhythm, nose twitching like a mouse. Leo beamed, ecstatic he had picked up the conversation's thread.

'Kang-gaaah-rooo,' he said Tsing-Tao-loud, bouncing up and down in his seat.

I was drunk, exhausted and surprised when Latisha offered me the job. I could start in the morning.

Interview over. I stood, unsteady and confused.

'G'day,' said Leo as he pushed two more beers into my hand. 'Takeaway. You take,' he said as he spat ash and food into my face, his cigarette still clinging to his lips.

'Hey, man,' Harry said, 'Congratulations.'

'Yeah, man,' Lucifer said, his first and only words.

'Yeah, man,' Leo mimicked.

I stumbled to the elevator, past Snow White, crystal classrooms and a million Chinese eyes. They stared at the ageing, alcoholic addition to the school's teaching staff. I returned a crooked smile, leaned against the wall beneath Pinocchio, and waited for the elevator.

'Holy shit,' I said as the lift sucked me down to the ground floor. I staggered out of the building and stood, swaying, thinking. I pulled the ring from one can. Foam oozed over my fingers. I pulled the ring off the other and put it to my mouth, ready to gulp. I froze, then raised my arm over my head and hurled the beer into the garbage on the other side of the lane. The remaining can stuck to my hand like a limpet. Shell shock. My arms fought the addiction until I raised the second can and held it high like a grenade. With the scream of a marine sergeant, I threw the frothing, explosive beer at my demons lurking in the dirty gutters across the cobbled street.

'You bastard,' I yelled to no-one, everyone and myself.

Tomorrow I would fight again.

YELLOW BEETLE

First light edged onto the campsite. Two cold nights in a row. My sleeping bag begged me to stay. My joints and muscles were stiff and my shoulder throbbed. The steroid had begun to wear off. Perth might be the right place and time for another injection. A long way still to go. The sun had yet to rise but already muted torch beams flickered across my tent followed by the mutterings of early risers. The clack-clack of camping mugs eager for coffee motivated me more than an alarm clock. Rise and shine.

The yellow Beetle and the humming woman had already packed. The naked imprint in the grass betrayed her earlier presence. I hadn't heard a sound.

Motorcycle camaraderie had already proven its power. Bikers understood. Whenever we passed on the road, riders raised a hand or threw a 'G'day' nod. But another group was stronger: antique travellers with white hair. *Grey nomads*. Their gravitational pull was inescapable: addictive personalities, conversation polarised to attract, outback explorers on a mission to discover Australia. And themselves.

The campsite kitchen bustled like a village square for elders, a Roman forum, a place to share, an opportunity to meet and greet. Old men, avatars of an ageing Oz, shared welcomes that assured us all we were from the same tribe and spoke the same language. Cloncurry was no Pandora, but the urge to look these fellow travellers in the eye and say, 'I see you,' was a difficult compulsion to overcome. But as Burke and Wills needed water, nomads needed conversation. Each morning started with meetings almost as momentous as Stanley discovering Doctor Livingstone. A handshake, a smile, and then actors from the edge of the stage would take their cue and move with a discreet but amiable amble towards the meeting. The outback's social media took a more analogue form: firm handshakes and weathered faces.

The first rays of sunlight had just licked the camp as I took my first sip of coffee and an outstretched hand reached for mine.

'G'day, I'm Pudd. Where you headed?'

'Pudd?' I said with a smile that smothered my urge to say, *Dr Livingstone, I presume?*

'Yep, I was an eighteen-pound delivery. Dad nicknamed me Pudd,' he said.

'Right,' I said, without a nod to the aptness of his name fifty years later.

'I'm Richard and I'm … pushing west. Shooting for Camooweal today.'

'Me too,' Pudd said.

We soon got down to detail. Where we had been, how long on the road, the price of fuel, the length of our journey, the cost of camp sites, Mr Turnbull's long-term economic policies. And arthritis.

Then David joined us. He didn't say, 'I see you,' but Pudd and I understood – we wore the same feathers – white hair. We were mates. Nomads from the same tribe.

David told us his ancestors originated from Tipperary – Irish immigrants escaping the famine. His great-great-grandfather stole a loaf of bread while starving in London, that's why he lives in Australia, he said. David told us his unmarried mother had given birth on the beach behind a rocky outlet somewhere in South Australia, but she later married a wife-beating alcoholic. He had just escaped from prison and was still on the run. David owned a Harley. 'And it's not stolen,' he said. But never rides it now. David was now a retired corporate lawyer. Agnes, his wife, had arthritis too.

Then Francis joined us. Another convict. He had no immediate family in prison although his uncle was an MP. Then Simon. His forebearers included wealthy sheep farmers. They made fortunes and went into pharmaceuticals.

The five of us talked like brothers-in-arms at an annual reunion. The 2019 Cloncurry Nomad Reunion. We spoke of everything and anything. But we knew the meeting had reached a denouement of sorts once we had agreed on our plans to put right in the world everything that was wrong. Job done. Meeting over. Well, nearly over.

'Capsaicin,' Simon suddenly said. We all looked at him. 'It's an active component of chilli peppers,' he added. Our confusion continued until he added the magic words: 'For Arthritis.'

'Right,' we said. 'Right.'

Meeting over.

Firm handshakes, a grip on the forearm and a hearty, 'Good luck,' 'Take care,' 'Safe travels,' 'Catch you later.' My heart glowed to be part of the tribe. It was nice, and only 8 am.

The ride to Camooweal revealed rugged rocky outcrops, hills, bends, escarpments – wild scenery. Cowboy movies from my childhood filled my imagination: *Red River*, *Stagecoach* and *True Grit*. John Wayne appearing from behind the next outcrop of rock would not have raised an eyebrow. *What's your business, mister?* But with local landmarks like Dingo Creek, Possum Bend, Kangaroo Crossing and such, the possibility seemed remote.

Termite mounds like alien colonies populated hundreds of acres of bush: a fantasy world of blindness, workers, soldiers, reproductives, kings and queens. Red-earth structures like mediaeval castles, over a metre high, with turrets and tunnels, chimneys and dungeons. The mounds spread either side of the road like military forts protecting the trail.

Today my usual superlatives seemed weak. After stopping Yammie somewhere on the road between Mars and Uranus, I poured coffee from my flask and looked over the land. Not a soul. Just me. The mute power of outback nothingness threw out an invisible strength and wrapped me in its comforting glove. Time to go. I pulled myself from its hold and pushed west.

Mount Isa shattered the outback like an industrial sore. Smokestacks leeched pewter vapour across open mines cratered like the aftermath of an artillery barrage. And buried under the forgotten blood of the Kalkadoon on Battle Mountain lay copper, lead and zinc. I refuelled, deferred coffee and continued towards Camooweal.

Three kilometres west of Mount Isa, a road sign warned of kangaroos for the next 190 kilometres. Soon I saw, and smelt, a decomposing roo; its rotting flesh rich still warm and wet. Another roadkill lay ahead. A big one. A bloated apparition took form at the side of the road: grotesque, all four legs pointed skyward – a white cow – now a cartoon caricature, swollen with gas, ready to explode or perhaps float upwards and drift in the heat across the outback.

A yellow convertible Volkswagen Beetle rattled ahead with its hood down.

Yammie roared past. But not before the blonde, mid-fifties driver looked up and threw a cheerful smile. The VeeDub suggested attitude; a quirky dashboard daisy confirmed it. Her hair blew every which way around oversized sunglasses. *Thelma and Louise*, I thought. Except she was alone. I glanced in my wing mirror to see a tanned hand wave a salute. *G'day*. I lifted my hand and returned the greeting. *G'day*. The Beetle stayed in my wing mirrors until it became a bug. Two more dead cattle rotted by the roadside over the next twenty-five kilometres. The bush became a blur. I didn't see more roadkill, but the sporadic smell of rotting flesh said others had died close by. Riding at night, dawn or dusk was a risk too far

I pushed on.

The Post Office Hotel greeted me at Camooweal. I decided to stay. It had been a long day. The alternative was a three-hour ride further west. It wasn't an option. I took a room. No internet. No mobile connection.

I needed to get a prescription filled at a pharmacy, so I asked in the 'bar'. It was Friday, late-afternoon busy, and half the town's tradies had already settled for the night.

'Tennant Creek, mate – 450 kilometres that way,' said one of the grizzled patrons, as he pointed a dirty finger to the west.

My surprise was clear.

'Or you can always go back to Mount Isa – it's only 188 kilometres.' He laughed at his own joke as he hooked his thumb towards the east.

'Right,' I said. 'I'll take a rain check.'

'A rain what?'

'No worries. Thanks.'

I turned back to the barmaid. She looked at me with a question, then offered an answer: 'Beer!' she said, expecting her exclamation mark to be beyond debate.

'Soda water,' I said. 'Thanks.'

The barmaid opened her mouth, then decided she had heard correctly the first time and scampered away to chuck a lonely ice cube into a glass, fill it with soda, decorate it with a straw, and crown it with a look of disgust.

I placed five bucks on the counter. 'Thanks,' I said with as much enthusiasm as I could muster.

She knew.

A dim hallway, stale and sweet, laden with the silky mustiness of floor polish and disinfectant, led me fifty paces along a worn, cracked linoleum floor to my room. Two bunks and a single bed offered a choice of mattress. I guessed I had the room to myself but still shifted my gear against the door. I'm not at my best when disturbed by late-night surprises.

A *No Smoking* sign hung on the wall above a small plastic table furrowed with dark, ugly cigarette burns. Dust drifted on the warm air fanned by the late afternoon sun. A faulty smoke detector bleated from somewhere down the hall. My room nested in between the bleat from the smoke alarm and the *baa baa* from the pub. *Bleat – baa baa – bleat–baa baa*. Friday evening and all was well.

I didn't bother to unpack. A service station blazed its lights at the edge of town, 500 metres west of the Post Office. The Post Office bar looked compelling, but the BP servo was safer.

The roast pork made a good choice. The waitress handed me a plate with what looked like a whole pig floating in a shipload of gravy; its escape contained by a perimeter wall of veggies and potatoes. A meal for two hungry adults. The cold evening overtook the warm day. I sat in my motorcycle jacket shovelling dinner into my face when a mid-fifties blonde woman with windblown hair walked into the diner. I don't know why, but my fork froze mid-air. She smiled.

'Hi,' she said in my direction as she walked over to the meal counter.

I watched her choose her food, my fork stayed where it was until she turned and looked for somewhere to sit.

'Can I join you?' she said.

I put my overloaded fork back on my plate. 'Sure.'

'You passed me on the highway several hours ago.'

'Yellow Beetle?'

'Yes, cute isn't it?'

'Nice daisy.'

'You're observant,' she said, blue eyes holding my gaze as I turned to look at my fork.

My words spilled across the table loaded with fake confidence. 'I'm touring Australia,' I said too quickly. 'This is my seventh day.'

'Me too,' she said with a collaborative smile. 'My twelfth.'

We sat silent for a minute.

'Melanie,' she said, with an outstretched hand.

'Richard.'

Simultaneously, we asked the same question. I won.

'Where did you start?' I asked.

'Newcastle,' she said. 'You?'

'Coolum Beach.'

She began to eat. I off-loaded food from my fork and began again, more mannered.

The conversation bobbed along, comfortable and at ease. Two travellers dancing to the same song sheet.

She had just divorced. Three adult kids. A third marriage gone wrong. Her adventure was an escape. A three-month hiatus before she 'started over' again. Ninety days for her. Sixty-two days for me. My conversation paralleled hers. Except I wasn't divorced. And my escape had a different purpose. He sat in my saddlebag. But perhaps our goals were the same.

'You must have a wonderful wife,' she said.

'I do,' I said.

We finished our food. My belly politely swollen.

We were both staying at the Post Office.

'Would you mind walking me back?' she asked.

'Sure.'

The night was dark and cold, the street empty. She had camped out back. The tough biker had taken the easy route and paid for a room. We walked the 500 metres in silence. The pub was rocking, full swing. We needed to walk through it. The exit to the campsite was out back; my room was at the end of the corridor.

We stepped inside.

'I guess you'll be having a beer,' she said.

I hesitated, 'I don't drink.'

'Alcoholic,' she said, without raising an eyebrow. Kind and gentle. Not an accusation. Not a question. She understood.

'Yes,' I said with shame and regret.

'Me too,' she said, 'I stopped ten years ago. Sleep well.' And without another word she walked towards the rear door that led to her tent nestled alongside a yellow Beetle.

'Night,' I said to the shadow of the Beetle lady sashaying into the night.

I hesitated at my door. The bar's scent followed me like a mate demanding company. My best friend. My worst enemy. Alcohol's oxygen was at once both life-giving and poisonous. Mates, beer, conviviality and man talk. Words amplified by beer that flowed, drunk by men who plunder. An exhaustion settled over me that I knew well. Too tired to sleep. A drink might help me relax, ease the ache in my body, prepare me for tomorrow. I walked back into the bar. A young barmaid looked up, caught my attention, an eyebrow asked and answered her question. She reached for the beer pump. My big, fat, muted lip-synch gave her my reply: *No thanks!*

She didn't believe me. I didn't believe me.

'What time is breakfast?' I said, thinking of escape and distraction.

She looked confused, then raised two hands and six fingers.

I thanked her with a balled fist and a thumb pointed to heaven.

She knew.

I needed to sleep. Tomorrow would be a long ride – 460 kilometres to Three Ways – with just a single roadhouse in between: Barkly Homesteads, 267 kilometres west. Maybe I could squeeze 250 kilometres out of a single tank, maybe more with a tailwind. But the slightest headwind would leave me dry. *Get a jerry,* said the old bikie from Midge Point. I would. In the morning.

I tried to sleep. The smoke alarm bleated, and the barroom laughter rose and fell. *Bleat–baa, bleat–baa, bleat-baa…*

Ten years, the woman had said. *Did you hear that, Johnnie?*

Hazy memories, fluttering here, settling there. Men at Work surfaced through the ether, taunting me with their lyrics. 'Are you trying to tempt me… I come from the land of plenty?' The words passed into my dreams and danced around my glass brimmed with whisky quivering in shaky hands. My right hand tried to raise the glass to my mouth. It couldn't. I put the glass on the table and clamped it with my left. Now with both hands, I raised the glass in slow motion, slow enough not to shake, and for my mouth to kiss and greet the whisky in a successful embrace. My lips locked onto the glass and anchored its contents while I chugged: needy as a dying desert drunk at a water hole. The alcohol slid in a fiery cascade into my empty, ravenous stomach. I began to calm. I felt assured – a full bottle was close, my glass half-full. I waited a few seconds, the urge to vomit subsided, and the glass moved towards my mouth. I finished the dregs, reached for the bottle and filled her up. My mouth squeezed tight until good manners edged the corners upwards into a wicked, grateful grin.

MAN FLU

My Saturday morning began with a dark, cold dawn. The Northern Territory border straddled the highway twelve kilometres west – Three Ways a further 450 kilometres. Barkly Homesteads hid somewhere in between, as did my petrol.

A lead cloak of exhaustion shrouded my body. Today would suck energy I didn't have. I sat on the bed and let my hands massage my face, attempting to work life into a mind and body that needed more sleep. A grimy window framed the gravel carpark where outback winds ruffled Yammie's black cover. On the far side, I could see caravan and tents huddled in a sprawl – a yellow Beetle and a single tent stood out from the herd.

Too lethargic to head for the breakfast room, I made coffee in my room. Power cords strewn across the room sucked AC to revive my caboodle of digital equipment. They burst with energy I could only wish for. A hot shower helped. Ten minutes later I shouldered my gear and crunched my way across loose gravel to Yammie. I stowed my stuff and fired her up. The pub and Camooweal township knew I was awake. My hand wrapped around the throttle and I revved Yammie's engines to share the beauty of her throaty roar with last night's noisy revellers.

I had overloaded Yammie from the start. She was bum-heavy too. But that's the way it was. The loose, shifting gravel of the Post Office car park made me splay my feet like a duck and 'paddle' cautiously towards the tarmac road. My foot slipped and the bike keeled over. As I heaved it up, pain tore across my left forearm. 'Shit, shit, shit.' My left arm felt buggered. I shook with pain and frustration. Torn shoulder tendons had been a problem from my first day. Steroid injections the day before my departure had helped, but now this. I sat astride Yammie, breathing hard. Movement of my forearm was painful. But to stay another night in the Post Office felt too dangerous. My arm would improve, but not for a few days. Manoeuvring at slow speeds was a strain, normal riding fine; but I'd need to protect the muscle from further stress. I made my decision and carefully paddled Yammie onto the road.

Petrol first. Down the deserted street, the BP logo pulsed yellow and green.

A customer information board outside listed distances. The sign confirmed my fears: the first fuel stop would be Barkly Homesteads – 267 kilometres west. As I filled Yammie's tank, I knew I wouldn't make it without a jerry. I paid for my fuel but discovered the servo only sold ten-litre jerries. Too big, even if I didn't fill it up.

'Where are you headed?' said the woman behind the cash register. I told her. She smiled and wished me good luck. 'There's a mechanic down the road. He works Saturday mornings. I'm sure he'll have a five-litre jerry.'

Buried in the outskirts of the Camooweal metropolis, the mechanic had an early start. I found him in a workshop, his head buried under the bonnet of a weathered ute. The mechanic had three old five-litre jerries and was prepared to part with one of them. He would take twenty dollars to cover the cost of a replacement.

'I don't know whether I'm doing you over …' he said, before I cut him short.

'Twenty dollars for peace of mind? Done deal.'

I rode back to the BP service station to fill my can. Five litres translated into roughly an extra seventy-five kilometres. I filled her up, lashed the jerry to my already overloaded bike and started Yammie's engines. On tick-over, we paddled slowly towards the main road. My left forearm still throbbed and distracted my attention. I didn't notice the commotion that had erupted behind me. The cash register woman had rushed outside and was waving a hearty goodbye. It was a robust wave, a hearty wave, an emotional wave. I waved back. But she didn't look amused. She looked pissed off!

I stopped. 'What's up?' I shouted from across the road.

'You didn't pay, mate!'

'Shit.'

My anxiety about dry tanks had turned me into a criminal. Fill and flee. I'd forgotten to pay for the five litres of petrol now sloshing around my jerry. My attempted theft had amused the other customers. Red-faced, I handed over my cash, then sped like a criminal to the Northern Territory border and the safety of the state line.

After a five-minute getaway, I reached the border: Welcome to the Northern Territory, the iconic sign said. A Landcruiser had already stopped beneath it. I pulled up next to the driver.

'Can you take a shot of us?' said the driver as he handed me his phone.

'Sure.'

A boy and a girl pushed smiling faces out the back window, while his wife leaned close to her husband.

'Cheese!'

'What about you?' said the man.

'Great.' I handed him my phone.

Don Quixote and Rocinante stared back, or was it Butch Cassidy and the Sundance Kid?

Then we sped deep into the Territory and left my crime behind.

Hallelujah! The Northern Territory had jacked-up Queensland's speed limit from 110 kph to 130 kph. And the road trains were longer too. In Queensland, road signs warned of road trains fifty metres long. As I travelled farther west and came closer to the border, the signs became more alarming: fifty-three metres. But now the Northern Territory warned of road trains fifty-three-and-a-half metres long.

Maybe NT truckies wanted to boast about the extra half-metre they held over their Queensland competitors? The rivalry must have been so great, the NT government needed to spell it out. *Their* truckies were half-a-metre longer. It was official: size mattered. Western Australia might prove insightful.

The outback generates a sense of lawlessness. Riding a motorcycle in the outback is like being in the Wild West. NT's 130 kph speed limit had been generous. Get an inch, and take a mile … After an hour Yammie roared west at 145 kph, but now I needed a leak. I checked my phone. *Say what*? After thirty minutes, I had travelled 120 kilometres. I knew I was speeding, but 120 kilometres in 30 minutes? The bowser at Camooweal must have dispensed rocket fuel. It took a few seconds to work it out: NT time is thirty minutes behind Queensland, and my phone had set the new time zone automatically.

But maintaining 130 kph hour after hour wasn't easy. I pushed Yammie to 150 kph to relieve the boredom. It helped a little. Until I hit two small, undulating bumps I hadn't seen. My body catapulted from the seat, while my hands stayed on the handlebars. I took five seconds to stabilise Yammie, fifteen minutes for me to stop shaking. Concentration. I needed it as much as fuel.

The scenery, always immense, offered subtle changes every day. This morning was no different. Yellowed bush carpeted the emptiness, while a couple of isolated trees broke the monotony. The sky was empty too: not a whisper of cloud. A universe of outback … difficult to comprehend.

A sign stabbed the vastness of nothing: *Soudan Station*. A caveat deterred unwelcome visitors: *Sorry, No Petrol*. Perhaps thirsty stragglers had pissed off the station and arrived, unannounced, hoping for thimbles of fuel.

I passed two separate cyclists battling towards Barkly Homesteads. Two! About 80 kilometres apart. The distance between lattes was 267 kilometres. Brave adventurers. Intimidating road trains were, well, intimidating, even on my heavy Yamaha. On occasions, when I roared past these steel monsters, the wind draft had been so great, I had to lean the bike way over to keep going in a straight line. Scary for cyclists. I hoped tomorrow's roadkill list didn't add push-bike riders to the rollcall of cows, roos, wallabies, and other unidentifiable carcasses.

Road-train truckies had a sense of humour. Often, I overtook the same road trains three or four times in a day. I'd scream past, exhaust pipes yelling both *hello* and *goodbye*. Twenty minutes later I'd stop – click a few photos, grab a handful of peanuts, wash them down with a swig of coffee, then back to the road. *Waaaaaah, waaaaaaah*, screamed the same road train's air horns bellowing yet another *G'day*. The drivers waved a farewell *hooroo* with trumpet encore: *Waaaaaah, waaaaaah*.

A road sign passed in a blur*: We Like Our Lizards Frilled Not Grilled*. I assumed this was a fire-danger warning, not a Northern Territory delicacy. Another series of signs warned of quarantine dangers: *Prickly Acacia* and *Mesquite,* and *No Bananas Past This Point*.

Yammie cruised along the highway and passed a bizarre stretch of road where the ubiquitous termite mounds lined either side. But travellers had dressed them! In singlets, T-shirts, shorts, skirts, sacks, baseball caps, blouses, dresses, scarves, jeans, construction hats, and even a sequined wedding dress. A 'fashion' creation flashed by every thirty metres. Despite my propensity to share the midday sun with mad dogs and Englishmen, these termite mounds stretched my sense of sanity. Surprise morphed into Freudian analysis. Australian rural art? An expression of outback loneliness?

I passed at speed but some demanded a second look. Was that a kid lost in the bush? A little girl left to fend for herself in the outback? A height-challenged construction worker capped with a yellow hard hat? Too many miles in surreal isolation. One had a huge, nine-inch length of wood between what one might imagine being a pair of legs. A yellow hard hat crowned his head. Was this Northern Territory's answer to the Milan catwalk? An outback fashion parade with a sense of humour. Versace? Gucci? Draped in a blue duffle coat, red fisherman's hat and matching Wellies, one termite home doubled as Paddington Bear – perhaps on an outback walkabout in the NT. The pudgy bear waved at me. I checked my mirrors – no-one behind (surprise) – and I waved back.

Barkly Homesteads loomed out of nowhere, and I still had eighteen kilometres to spare in my tank; the jerry hadn't been necessary. Tailwinds had given me a gentle push. I strode into the roadhouse, shoulders rolling forward like John Wayne ploughing through a saloon full of gunslingers. Large groups of truckies stood chatting, gulping coffee, munching sandwiches, talking shop. Imagination and exhaustion slowed my brain. The saloon broke into a hush as all eyes landed on the bad bikie. A real John Wayne would have broken the silence with manly words about 'injuns' or 'bears' or 'wolves', or maybe the Big Man would say ... 'A hundred Apaches were on my tail...' as he let the gravitas of the moment settle. 'Whisky,' he would demand as the bartender slammed a shot glass on the bar while the subdued saloon waited to hear the cowboy tell his tale. And me? Yeah, I was the alpha bikie man, the Yamaha rider. I stared at the truckies and spat my hard-arsed cowboy words out like bullets from a six gun: *Hey, any of you guys see Paddington Bear back there?* A sliver of sanity kept my mouth shut. Instead, I managed a smile and a 'G'day' as I ambled to order food and coffee with a manly extra shot. The truckies, no doubt, needed space to brag about their extra half-metres.

Another 190 kilometres farther west, and after a ride of 460 kilometres, I pulled into Three Ways where I paid $12 for a patch of dirt. I crashed for the night, but not before a shower and a mixed grill of truckie proportions. Tomorrow would see a change in compass bearing as I headed north towards Darwin. My body lay inert in my tent. Exhausted. Shoulders and upper-body muscles tense and tight. The rips and tears in my shoulder and forearm throbbed. I tried to relax, to forget the pain. I needed to sleep, on a mattress thin as a gym mat and hard as a stretcher ...

———

Coolum Beach July 2005

Memories of Maureen rose sharp and clear. My wife worked her laptop on a cold winter's day in our home office where we ran our mortgage-broking business. I pecked at the keys on my computer too, but sullen, and unable to concentrate. An antiquated heater laboured to push a little warmth around. Running a business on a hard diet of net profit and pressure created a tough working atmosphere. Mostly we dealt with it.

I had never been prone to sickness or ailments like colds, flu or stomach bugs. If ever contagion broadcast its impending arrival, I'd go for a run. A good sweat made me sweet. Not that day. Bad throat. Every swallow tore my oesophagus like spinifex forced by desert winds down a dry riverbed. Hyperbole? No, this was beginning to feel like man-flu.

Maureen, a registered nurse by trade, took my temperature. In her firm matron voice, she gave her diagnosis without compassion: 'You have a sore throat.'

'Yeah but …' I protested.

'Take a lozenge.'

'Okaaay,' I said, sounding like a disbelieving, insolent child.

Later I floated, peaceful and calm. Not sick. Just high. A feather drifting across the office, rising out of myself, conversation a pleasant mumble like bees on a sleepy afternoon. If I didn't swallow, there was no pain. I tried not to swallow. A fever had made me light, dozy and dreamy … four-gin-and-tonics dreamy. It was late afternoon and winter hovered beyond the office heater as perspiration drained my energy and sapped my soul.

'I don't feel right,' I said, vainly attempting to assert the severity of my condition.

'Take another lozenge.'

I did.

Early evening: I made a manly management decision. 'I have to go to bed.'

'Good idea,' Maureen said, 'Take two Panadol and I'll put the lozenges next to your bed … in case you need them.'

I undressed, didn't shower, collapsed into bed. The room rocked like a drifting ship, rising and plunging on huge swells. I began to fall asleep and swallow. 'Shit.' I gasped, as the mother of all sore throats began to choke me.

My gin-and-tonic dreams rolled me across deserts and storms, cattle carcasses, ships and thunder, lightning and bouldered riverbeds.

Three am. I sat up. I couldn't breathe. Nothing. I sucked for air. Nothing. My body heaved to draw oxygen. *Nothing.* Maureen slept. *Water,* I thought ... *Drink!* I staggered towards the kitchen, bouncing off walls. I got to the sink, ran water, drank. Consciousness began to fade. I couldn't swallow. Nothing. Couldn't breathe. Nothing. I was dying.

Like a wounded elephant, my body shuddered in one last attempt to draw breath; a huge heave. Nothing. I died.

My glass smashed on the floor at the same time as my head. The commotion woke Maureen. At least, that's what she told me. She screamed for Gabby, my thirteen-year-old daughter, to call for an ambulance. My wife gave mouth-to-mouth.

Gabby made contact. 'Is there a pulse?' she shouted, repeating the emergency operator's question.

'Just,' said Maureen as she continued to blow, 'how long?'

'How long?' repeated Gabby to the emergency operator. 'Four minutes.'

Maureen didn't show her fear. She told me later that mouth-to-mouth had made my gut swell like a balloon. Air was not reaching my lungs. My skin was the colour of ash from a fire that died long ago.

The first ambulance arrived. Blocked airway. Pandemonium. Time stopped. The lead paramedic, mouth tight like a clam, shook his head, 'No pulse.'

A second ambulance arrived. Maureen dropped to my side, pumped my chest. No result. Maureen pumped again. This time a heavy wheeze punctuated the silence like a tyre slashed with a knife. The second crew took over. Oxygen was fixed to my face. A little made it to my lungs. Still unconscious, oxygen levels dangerously depleted, my body rasped in its struggle to suck air.

I remembered nothing after my collapse on the kitchen floor. I saw no dark tunnel. I saw no bright light. When I struggled to the surface, I was in intensive care in Nambour Hospital. I felt as though I had drunk a whole bottle of gin. I floated like a butterfly, soft and dreamy, under the balmy lights of an ICU.

A nurse dressed in angel white said, 'Don't pull the tube. Leave it be.'

I pulled again at something in my arm. A mask covered my face. I heard machines, *beep ... beep ... beep.* Lights and monitors. I breathed as though under water with a scuba regulator. The nurse from heaven took my hand from my arm, held it at my side while a twenty-year-old male orderly hovered in the background of my vision. He looked familiar. The handsome young man smiled encouragingly while giving a nod like a blessing. His image faded as I fell back into a morphine-induced, dream-laden sleep. The nurse chased me into my sleep: 'You're going to be okay,' she said.

The morning after felt like I had awoken from an untimely resurrection after a big night. Like I should feel hungover but was still drunk.

'How are you feeling?' said the nurse from heaven.

'F i n e ...' I said, realising I was not wearing the regulator and not swimming.

'W h a t h a p p e n e d?'

'Epiglottitis,' said the nurse.

'Epi ...?'

'Epiglottitis,' she explained. 'A potentially fatal medical condition that occurs when the flap of tissue that covers the windpipe during swallowing becomes infected and, in your case, shuts off the windpipe. You're lucky to be alive.'

'Sheeeet,' I said.

'Pardon...'

'Schokay, feeling a bit boozy ... woozy...'

She smiled.

The hospital discharged me after five days, fit and fresh and cool as a winter morning.

But the episode had been, well, unsettling.

Two weeks later I met with a specialist to pose the question that no-one else would answer. 'Could this happen again?'

His answer spurted truth like a burst artery. 'Does lightning strike twice?'

'Steel knitting needles.' I said, not needing to know more.

George Washington died of epiglottis in 1799. It's rare. When Maureen pushed my chest, the resultant pressure forced the flap covering my windpipe (the epiglottis) to lift, just a little, giving the medics their opportunity. Maureen's act, her persistence, saved my life.

Thank you, Maureen. Perhaps we'll just forget about the lozenges.

But this would not be the last time Maureen saved my life …

PINK PANTHERS

It was a cold night. A thick jumper and a sleeping bag created a marsupial pouch that kept this joey snug. It was tough to haul my body out, but I had a big, big ride ahead.

Petrol first. It was a ritual, like cleaning my teeth. Mostly, I did my teeth first. Nine days of riding, four in the outback. Now I would head north towards Darwin – Katherine first.

I pulled into the Three Ways roadhouse to refuel. The bowsers presumed guilt before innocence: *NO I.D. NO PETROL. NO EXCEPTIONS*. I stepped into the service station smoothing down my lightning-frizzled hair. My purpled and peeling nose added a further notch to the fear factor. The yellow star that burnt my face all day, every day, had blitzed my face. Scouring winds finished the job. My helmet shaded the outer circles of my eyes while the exposed tops of my cheeks had blistered into burnt stripes of natural war paint. I queued to reach the girl behind the till. She had a thick German accent. My turn. I held out a sun-burnt hand and offered my driver's licence. My photo looked nothing like me.

The girl stared at the radioactive racoon before her. Three embarrassing seconds later, she returned to her efficient and disciplined self.

'No need for ID,' she said without blinking.

'But ...' I began to argue.

'Not necessary,' she said dismissing me before turning to the next in line.

Sympathy or fright? Maybe both. News of escape from my border-town fuel theft had obviously not made it to Three Ways.

'Thank you,' I said, humbled by the trust bestowed.

I filled Yammie's tank and returned to pay.

The German girl dealt with the long line that waited for service. She was blonde, tanned, attractive. Her co-worker too. A roadhouse 'manned' by fraulines.

Back to the point. On first glance, I didn't notice, well, maybe I did. By the second visit, I recognised the sales and marketing technique the service station used to full effect. One of the German girls had a shapely figure which she kindly presented through a low-cut blouse. Three Ways received the gong for the busiest roadhouse and the politest and most patient truckies. The long queue snaked out the door, but the road-train drivers stayed studiously focused. They waited to pay their bills and retrieve their IDs. But in this roadhouse, in the middle of the Northern Territory, the lads displayed rare chivalry. I heard a courteous, *'After you'*, followed by a *'No, I insist, after you'*. All to remain in the queue a few more minutes.

Today, fuel didn't look like a problem. My map showed service stations every 150 kilometres, hopefully not empty.

A Brit served me at Jenner Springs. He came from Brighton. At Dunmarra, a girl from Brittany in France. At Three Ways, two German girls from the Bavarian Alps. Foreign nationals at every roadhouse: a cosmopolitan surprise in the Aussie outback.

After Dunmarra, I throttled back to the official speed limit of 130 kph. Long distances and high speeds lulled my senses and blurred the bush. I leant into a long, gentle bend before a horrifying discovery: a small cluster of Brahman cattle stood in the middle of the highway. I tensed; the cows relaxed. Shock, more than danger slowed my response, but I still hit the brakes in good time. The cattle clomped to the other side. I opened the throttle before they waddled back. In

England, drivers would consider the Stuart Highway a B road: narrow single lane on both sides. Kangaroos and livestock exponentially upped the risk. Driving at night would be like Russian roulette, and I had no intention of playing.

In Cammoweal the previous night, a pub patron in the Post Office had told me the nearest pharmacy was in Tennant Creek, 450 kilometres away. Now Tennant Creek was just a short twenty-five kilometres ride south. But the town had shut for Show Day. The German girls at the Three Ways roadhouse told me I wouldn't find another pharmacy until Katherine, 650 kilometres north. This Pommy couldn't compute that distance and size. It couldn't be correct. What if my prescription was for chronic diarrhoea? I would be in deep shit.

It was late morning and the temperature hit a dry thirty-three degrees Celsius. Northern Territory mid-winter. The fleece lining in my riding jacket needed to be removed. There was no room anywhere, but I squashed it into a pannier. Johnnie Walker's belligerence had not improved. *Fuck you*, he said. My jailed tormentor never slept.

A calm day, hot, no hint of bad weather and not a whisper of a breeze. Tranquillity at 130 kph. Peace.

Whuummmpp!

A tempest torpedoed Yammie with the shock of an explosion amidships. It hit me like dysentery at a black-tie dinner. Unseen and unexpected. Yammie staggered – all composure lost – and we quivered, but I kept her upright. We stabilised in three seconds that spanned a lifetime.

Later that night, a local explained the torpedo had been a *willy-willy* – that's Aboriginal for whirlwind. A mini-whirlwind had hit us. *Shake, rattle and roll* took on a new meaning; riding with one hand, a new level of risk. My imagination scripted tomorrow's newspaper headlines: *Willy-Willy Kills Pom*.

I needed to rest. The ubiquitous railway line that paralleled the road offered an opportunity and a coffee break. I climbed down the embankment, serenaded by a million cicadas that electrified the silence. The railway line, a land ladder to nowhere, climbed to the northern horizon. The top rung a speck on the horizon of my journey, the bottom rung solid in the present. I stood like a Wild West gunslinger waiting for a train to rob. A regular Jessie James. I listened: cicadas. Outback. No train. I rolled the moment in my mind, and enjoyed the serenity like a prayer, wanting to accept the things I could not change, the courage to change the things I knew I should, and the wisdom to know the difference. The conductor snapped his baton. The cicadas stopped. I swigged the last of my coffee. Silence. Time to go.

The AA prayer never failed to give a boost. I had survived a *willy-willy*.

I scrambled back to Yammie, where she waited on the hot tarmac, engine tink-tinking as she continued to cool. 'Short break, baby,' I said, as I fired her up. We continued north and left *willy-willy* nightmares behind us.

I arrived at Larrimah and looked for the service station. I didn't see one, but I saw a huge sign for the Pink Panther Pub. Larrimah *is* the Pink Panther Pub. I followed the arrow. A surreal fantasy appeared from the outback 500 metres later. Two four-metre pink panthers greeted me, escapees from an unsound mind. One sat in an armchair drinking a beer; the other slouched in the pilot seat of a miniature steel helicopter. Both panthers guarded a giant bottle of NT Draught. All 2,250 gallons of it. Welcome to the Big Stubby. The owner had painted the pub's smaller outbuildings pink, including a menagerie of exotic birds, wallabies, emus, lizards, snakes and a crocodile: a three-and-a-half metre salty called Sam. Willy-willys, Pink Panthers, frauleins, bottles from Brobdingnag. Mad Max country? No, just Larrimah in outback Northern Territory.

The pub had character – beat-up character five decades past opening time. Larrimah boasted ten local inhabitants. Two of them huddled at a table on the far side of the bar: old Aussies, Akubras, singlets, bullwhips coiled neatly under their stools. Both held serious beers to serious lips. If this were a movie, now would be the time for the croc to escape, the Pink Panthers come to life, all hell break loose, and Max Rockatansky to burst through the doors blasting a sawn-off shotgun while Crocodile Dundee brandished his outsize knife.

It had been a long ride. I walked over to the bar.

'What you having?' said the Aussie bartender with a shaved head, drooping moustache and mandatory singlet.

'Soda water,' I said with a big smile. 'Thanks'

He threw me a disdainful look and pointed to the far corner of the pub. I wasn't sure whether the barman had ordered me to stand in the corner because I had asked for a soda water or whether he meant that I should search for my poison elsewhere. I decided on the latter. I followed the direction of his finger and found a freezer with soft drinks. I grabbed my soda and made history. A bloke had not stepped inside this venerable public house and asked for something other than beer since its opening in the summer of 1952. I went back to the counter to pay. The two Aussies looked up from their beer to examine the alien Pommy. A snarling, pink rubber pig with bloodied fangs and a policeman's hat sat next to the cash register staring menacingly at me and my soda.

I paid. 'Any petrol?' I asked.

'No, mate.'

'Okay, but my map says there's petrol here.'

'I don't care what your map says there ain't no petrol 'ere.'

I nodded, pausing uncertainly before raising the confidence to ask my next stupid question: 'Where's the nearest fuel?'

'Mataranka … Seventy kilometres up the road.'

Shit. Touch and go. I sipped my soda and checked the map again. The petrol icon stamped next to Larrimah was irrefutable. I moved with purpose back to the bar, ready to tap a firm finger on the section of map that proved my petulant point. Maybe not. As I left, I saw him glance at the two ancient Aussies patrons. 'Another soda, mate?' he shouted at my back

I knew he knew.

'All good,' I said, as I walked out the door. But it wasn't.

A year later a local resident went missing. His dog too. Police suspected foul play. And in a small community plagued by deep enmities, the disappearance echoed the death of a British backpacker sixteen years earlier. Dozens of others have gone missing. Camping

here didn't seem a smart option. Particularly for those that drank soda water in the Pink Panther.

Onwards. Seventy kilometres to Mataranka.

I made it, but the service station had closed. 'Shit, shit and shit!'

'What's wrong?' said a young woman walking past.

'I need petrol. Can't believe this is shut.'

'There's another one three hundred metres down the road.'

'Three hundred kilometres?' I said in desperation.

'No – three hundred metres!'

My neck craned out into the road. Neon lights blinked from farther up the road. In Mataranka the servo sparkled like a Christmas tree in an outback desert night. Two petrol stations. One was open. I offered a silent prayer to anyone, everyone, and the young woman walking down the street.

One hundred kilometres later, I pulled into Katherine. Near the outskirts of town, a decaying two-seater plane had crash landed on the edge of a paddock a decade or two ago. Although fatigued, I stopped to take a photo. Images of a dead pilot, engine failure, bad weather filled my imagination. *Pilot error*? Too tired to think, too tired to erect a tent, I found a motel. *Crossroads*. It was perfect. Anything would be perfect. My longest ride yet: 649 kilometres. I needed a shower. To eat. To sleep. Darwin was 305 kilometres to the north. I would dream on it. As I drifted into sleep, I thought of the pilot of the two-seater plane. Maybe his map showed fuel at Larrimah too, maybe a beer too many at the Pink Panther, maybe steel knitting needles. Maybe…

———

Papua New Guinea 2007

Saved. A random application for an overseas job materialised into a consultancy position in Papua New Guinea: a huge career opportunity and a well-paid, one-year contract. The position offered an escape from mortgage broking and a job I detested.

I worked in Port Moresby. A dangerous place.

My role required the delivery of internal audit training to national and regional government staff. In an earlier life, I had been a corporate auditor, risk mitigator, compliance manager. Opportunities existed to leverage my experience. Opportunities existed for me to feel valued. Opportunities to prove myself. Opportunities.

All employees had to adhere to strict personal security procedures. Safety policies even required that all staff carry Walkie Talkies. My employer insisted on gated and guarded accommodation, had endless lists of where you could and couldn't go, and procedures for most foreseeable 'mishaps.' I should not, for example, change a flat tyre. Instead, I should lock all car doors, call security on my Walkie Talkie and wait for their arrival. On no account should I get out and change the tyre. The procedure had no interest in preventing back strain but rather to lessen opportunities for local hoodlums, lovingly called *rascals*, to attack and rob you, maybe worse. Good risk mitigation.

Maureen did not join me for six weeks. Loneliness was a risk; nightmares were often my only companion. I found somewhere to live, set up an apartment and worked. Papua New Guineans were nice people: simple, polite, uncomplicated, happy.

In the evenings most expats did two things: drink or work out. The statistics tilted heavily in favour of the former, though in one place you could achieve both – The Yacht Club – and the official 'home' of expats in Moresby.

I lived alone and went to the Yacht Club often. I drank coffee. I drank soda. And I knew everybody knew.

The decision chose me and we shook hands: the gym. I opted to work out and surprised myself. My once athletic body responded, and long-term fat began to firm and dormant muscles tightened. I ran, skipped, pounded the heavy sweat-stained punch bag, hefted weights, and whispered mantras and affirmations. I visualised a successful end to my 'tour'. While the drinkers huddled upstairs at the Yacht Club bar, I worked out in the ageing gym on the ground floor. Workouts became my alcohol. I grunted and groaned, serenaded from above by tinkling glasses, drinking and loud laughter. The social breeze floated through the gym's large windows: a cocktail of alcohol, salt, seaweed, cigarettes and petrol. Yachts sat moored in military lines and, like obedient white horses, bobbed gently to the chink of chains, halyards, ropes and rigging.

I grunted as each gloved fist slammed into the punching bag. It looked as worn and lined as me. A right lead, bang … and again … bang, and again … bang… and a one-two … bang, bang. Sweat stained my singlet; pain and concentration contorted my face. Grunt, bang. Grunt, bang. The bag swung; I danced. Ballet interrupted with fury.

Workouts and soda water made me fit and strong. I lost weight. Working out became a routine, a lifestyle, a habit – an addiction. I was doing fine.

Maureen and Gabby joined me just before Christmas. We had enrolled Gabby in the international school in January but soon decided against it. Boarding-school kids visiting their parents for the holidays convinced Gabby that the 'uncool' Port Moresby International School didn't cut it. Before the semester started, Gabby pleaded to attend boarding school in Brisbane. I hesitated. Fate decided.

Gabby was fourteen. To prepare for our time in PNG, she completed a PADI open-water scuba-diving certificate. Her bravery made me proud. Enthusiasts labelled Papua New Guinea as one of the world's best dive locations. Soon we would dive together. We had goals. Before any plans to dive, I needed to return briefly to Australia to finish some personal affairs. We would all fly home to Brisbane on Friday afternoon. A ten-day break and we would return to PNG. Then my job would start again in earnest.

I rose at 5.30 am on the day of our departure and hit the gym. Not the Yacht Club gym. That morning I used the small, claustrophobic gym in the basement of our apartment block. On the few occasions I'd used this gym, it had been empty, and that morning proved no exception. Ancient equipment crammed the dusty gym. Relics of rusted steel spread across its floor like steel skeletons on an archaeological dig.

I attacked my routine. Thirty minutes later, a set of bench presses on a Smith's machine would conclude my workout. I loaded it with sixty kilos. Ten repetitions completed three times. A two-minute breather sandwiched each session. The weights slid up fixed bars, so the weights moved either up or down. When completed, with arms fully extended above my head, a slight twist of the wrists would secure the bar on its anchoring hooks.

On my last session, I pushed. Grunt ... one, grunt … five, grunt … nine, *huge moan*, grunt … ten. My outstretched arms held the weight. I twisted my wrists to lock the bar and its sixty-kilo load. *Yeah*! I edged my hands slowly away. All good. I began to shimmy my body from under the weight. But … Jesus … no … it couldn't, but it did … The bar shuddered. The weights fell. A crashing train loaded with sixty kilos cannonballed towards my head. I couldn't move. The steel mass bludgeoned my throat like a sledgehammer smashing soft carcass. Time stopped. The air stilled. Dust motes froze. Silence.

Then I screamed, except I couldn't scream. 'Fuck,' I shouted, except I couldn't shout. Sixty kilos pinned my throat to the bench. Three seconds of shock before my hands gripped the bar and heaved. Survival fuelled a herculean effort and my arms rose a few inches to free my head from under the bar. I jerked upright. Sat still. No pain. None. But I couldn't breathe. My lungs struggled to suck air down a crushed windpipe. A blunt dagger had slit the inside of my throat. I was drowning in blood I couldn't see. My hand searched my throat. No lacerations. No open wounds. I gurgled. The stale gym air vibrated with monstrous, ugly, guttural wheezes. The sound of one man dying.

I rose and staggered to the door. Leaden legs dragged my body up two flights of stairs to a security door that led to the elevator. My security swipe card was in the gym. *OMG*. To go back was impossible. False religious alliances formed in a lightning second. And that door, that door that always, always returned to its locked position, had not fully engaged. It had remained open. I pulled the door, reached the elevator, pressed the button, and waited. Fifteen seconds later it delivered me to the sixth floor and our apartment. Maureen was asleep. I smashed the door with my fists, my body, my feet. Maureen opened the door. My contorted face and butchered efforts to breathe struck her like a wicked slap from a nightmare.

'My God,' she screamed. 'What's wrong?'

No response. I was dying. Maureen didn't understand. I ran shaking fingers like a slashing knife across my throat.

'Heart attack?'

'No, no,' I wanted to scream. *No Air* said my panicked face as I began to drown in muted silence. Desperation took over. I stumbled across the hallway to the other apartment on the floor. I slammed my body against my neighbour's door and kicked and pounded.

'What's wrong?' Maureen screamed again.

Michael, our neighbour appeared, shock cleared his bleary eyes. He looked at me, then Maureen. 'Jesus, what happened?'

Maureen was frantic. 'I don't know, I don't know.'

I sank to the floor wheezing for air.

'Let's get him to my car. Quick. Take his arms.'

They stumbled with my weight; my legs did little to help.

'Shit look at his throat,' Michael said.

'My God … Oh my god.'

My neck had swelled like a beer-bloated bladder about to burst. My throat had merged with my shoulders. I groaned and wheezed as Michael bundled me into his car. I couldn't breathe. No air. None. I felt sad. So sad.

'Faster,' I heard Maureen scream.

I brushed my lips against Maureen's. A kiss. Words worthless. *Goodbye.* Maureen understood.

No tunnel. No bright light. No angels.

Maureen gave mouth-to-mouth. Michael raced for the hospital. The car careened through Port Moresby.

'Michael, he's gone. Richard's gone.' Maureen's voice became a shrill command: 'Faster.'

We reached the hospital. In an instant, Maureen told me later, that nurses, doctors and paramedics had assembled around my lifeless body like a rugby scrum.

RED-SEA SOUL MATE

My eyelids stirred to the chirp of birds. A sweep of the blackout blinds uncovered a beautiful morning. Sunlight filled my room. Katherine: *Crossroads of the Outback.*

If the Christian God were metric, he might have commanded the tenth day be a day of rest. Coolum to Katherine: nine days on the road and 3,600 kilometres behind me, but on this Sunday morning – Day Ten – I decided Darwin would have to wait. Today would be my sabbath. *Crossroads* was prim and pleasant. Across the carpark the inn's restaurant offered breakfast. A yellow Beetle was parked in the far corner.

The previous evening, Ben, the proprietor, checked me in. He was a motorcycle enthusiast too. I told him of my goals, not my tactics. A week before my journey, I thought about charitable leverage. I hoped my trip might raise money for others. I chose *Beyond Blue*. Ben and his wife donated one hundred dollars on the spot. Today I had collected over $4,000. The biggest gift had come from Jetts gym. They donated a dollar a day for every day I had been a member: a whopping $1,100. Ben lent me tools to fix a wing mirror that had worked its way loose. Yesterday it twisted and turned at high speeds, reflecting the sun's rays in a dazzling display of visual Morse code. But breakfast first, wing mirror afterwards.

A few minutes with Ben's spanners, and my wing mirror was locked tight.

'Problems, Richard?' said a mid-fifties blonde.

I looked up. Surprised.

'Hey, Melanie. All fixed,' I said with a bright and breezy confidence I didn't own. 'We've got to stop meeting like this.'

Beetle lady laughed and extended her hand. 'Hey.'

'Hey,' I said as we shook hands. 'Not camping?'

'I needed a rest.'

'Yeah, me too. Headed to Darwin tomorrow. I need to layover for another night. I'm doing Katherine Gorge today. '

'Ditto,' she said. 'But breakfast first. Maybe I'll see you on the trail.'

'Maybe. Try the omelette.'

'I will.'

Melanie, the yellow Beetle woman, turned and walked towards the restaurant.

I returned Ben's tools but found his wife instead. 'Thanks for the spanners,' I said. 'And your donation.'

'No problem. We both wish you good luck. Ben dreams I'll let him do the same thing one day,' she said smiling. 'Not a chance.'

I smiled, then hesitated. 'Do you ride?'

'Yes.'

'Do you have a helmet I could borrow?'

Katherine Gorge was a short twenty-minute, thirty-kilometre ride away. Mid-winter had not cooled the temperature. Thirty degrees. Shorts and singlet weather. My motorcycle jacket stayed in my room with my panniers and luggage.

Katherine Gorge offered trails that climbed high into escarpments promising serene sunsets over the river and vistas of the ancient land of the Jawoyn people. *Nitmiluk* they called it: *Cicada Dreaming.*

Melanie walked out of the restaurant with a smile.

'You still here?' she said.

'Just about to leave ... You want a ride?'

She smiled again. 'I've never been on a motorcycle before.'

'You'll love it,' I said. 'It's addictive.'

'I don't have a helmet,' she said.

'I know somebody that does.'

Our friendship began before we arrived.

'Breathtaking,' Melanie said after twenty minutes riding pillion. 'Wow.'

The gorge had a mystical tranquillity. Jawoyn ancestors walked these trails 45,000 years ago. The immensity of this knowledge settled on our shoulders, at once both heavy and light.

The Rainbow Serpent, the Jawoyn said, slept under the ground until she stirred. Then she pushed and pushed until she surfaced. The Rainbow Serpent voyaged across the land, resting when tired, but every time she continued her journey, she left behind deep trails that mirrored the imprint of her gargantuan slumbering body. When she had traversed the land, she returned and summoned the frogs. Their bellies were full of water and made them slow. The Rainbow Serpent tickled their tummies. The frogs laughed to free the water from their mouths to fill the furrows and hollows to spawn the rivers and lakes and billabongs to wake the animals and plants to follow the Rainbow Serpent across the land.

Thirteen gorges meandered under the Nitmiluk umbrella. Deep ravines over seventy-metres high shadowed the Katherine River as it carved a twelve-kilometre deep-water channel through ancient limestone cliffs and sacred Aboriginal sites rich with Indigenous culture and history. Crocodiles, rapids and plunging waterfalls. Peaceful, calm, restorative.

The serenity of our setting and the simple intimacy of a shared hike led to easy talk. Small talk led to big talk. Past, present and future. In Camooweal Melanie had fearlessly told me she was an alcoholic. We formed a bond – one we understood well.

'Are you closer to what you're looking for?' she said.

'One day at a time,' I replied, 'but I'm getting there.'

Melanie flicked her blonde hair from her face and looked for understanding. 'Getting there?'

'Yes, just to be here. The outback is' – I wanted my thoughts to be clear – 'life changing. The outback has underlined the insignificance of me. And my problems. What about you?'

'I've found freedom,' she said. 'Peace too. But the future is too far to figure.'

The trail began to rise; our breathing deepened. The gentle, sloping track, like our conversation, headed uphill. The sandy path changed to rocky outcrops. We were alone in the outback's beauty and its blessing.

'Agreed,' I said. 'Out here,' I continued spreading my hand, 'I'm addicted to the vastness of it all. The anonymity. 'To be frank, *today* is more important than *tomorrow*. And yesterday's memories fade with what I'm doing in this moment. I'm happy knowing that I've arrived today. That I'm here.' I paused. 'Tomorrow I want to believe that I can look at today in the same present moment that I'm doing now. Maybe *that's* what I'm looking for.' Melanie didn't answer. We climbed steeper. The escarpments lined the horizon. 'And with each day I love my wife even more. Few wives would give their blessing. For such a crazy stunt … to a crazy old man.'

'She must be special.'

'She is.'

'What's her name?'

'Maureen.'

'And you're not old,' she said. 'Crazy? ... maybe.'

The warmth of the day gloved us in comfortable silence. We hiked higher and higher; circling eagles observed our progress while a colony of fruit bats hung unconcerned in a cluster of trees.

'Where did you meet?' Melanie asked.

'Twenty metres under the Red Sea.'

Amusement and doubt flickered over her face. 'You're kidding?'

'I used to live in Saudi Arabia …'

Saudi Arabia 1999

The Red Sea shimmered as the small boat crammed with wannabe divers pottered out of the Saudi port of Jeddah. Early morning and already the heat pressed down on its excited passengers. The men wore Western swimming togs; the women abayas: long, black flowing cloaks that hid their bodies. Sharia law demanded it. And we would obey, but only until the boat escaped the jurisdiction of the Saudi coastguards. When safe, the women would discard their raven robes, and reveal … swimsuits and bikinis. Welcome to Saudi Arabia.

The twenty student divers on this trip had been training for their PADI open-water diver certifications. All of us were green but eager to learn. The men included oil workers, engineers and a banker. Me. The women were nurses. A mixed bunch, our passports labelled us as American, English, Dutch, Canadian, French, Australian. And one young Saudi woman, an inspiring rebel for us all. We were all single. Or separated.

The instructors gave details and instructions for the day. We would make our inaugural open-water dive on Horseshoe Reef: mid-depth, around twenty metres. Most important, they told us, was to 'buddy-up'. The divemaster would assign buddies. In the previous weeks our swimming-pool training had instilled in us the mantra of a marine: *Look after your buddy.*

'Okay, people, listen up,' said the instructor as he looked at the huddled group of divers waiting like wilting wallflowers for a partner.

'Pete hook up with Helen, Carol with Debbie, Dave take Michelle,' and so it went. Until … 'Maureen and Rich.' We smiled at each other and nodded. 'Follow the anchor rope to the bottom,' said the instructor, 'and wait there.'

Maureen was a nurse, about my age, late-forties, a little nervous but full of energy and enthusiasm. Her apprehension didn't sit right with her avid desire to leap over the side. Maureen looked like she was both ready to fight and flee at the same time. I flattered myself with the thought the instructor had tagged me as capable and calm – a good match.

'Rich, you go first,' said the dive master. 'Maureen, you follow.'

We kitted up, readied ourselves on the edge of the boat and

prepared to execute our first backwards tumble into the water. I placed my hand over my mask, wrapped my arms over the hoses and attachments, and fell arse over pec into a calm sea. Disorientation met me in a cloud of bubbles and metallic hisses. My body spun as the sky revolved around the darkness below. Echoed breathing followed. I surfaced a few seconds later, equilibrium restored, and telegraphed the diver's signal to confirm successful entry: a touch of the hand to the top of the head with an elbow extended sideways.

Maureen stood on the deck, her breath shallow and rapid. Hesitating. Thinking.

'Away you go,' said the instructor.

Maureen's chest rose and fell, just a whisper short of hyperventilation, until she tumbled over the side.

Oh my god, I imagined her saying.

She surfaced next to me; the fear gone. She smiled. I did the same and added a thumbs up: *Well done.* The other divers followed in varying stages of anxiety and ungainly splashes.

We swam across the placid water to the anchor rope. Here we released air from our buoyancy control devices to start our descent. I gave Maureen the thumbs down signal, *Going Down.* Me first. Maureen on top. I looked up at my buddy. She dithered. I signalled with my thumb and forefinger joined to form a circle: *OK?* Maureen looked at me and answered my question: *OK!* Down we went, slow and sure, bubbles bursting around us like squalls of inverted rain. I looked up often.

OK?

OK!

Take care of your buddy.

We landed on sand, circled by a horseshoe of coral. Yellow angels and blue butterflies darted and drifted across the reef – a few fish we could name among a universe we could not. We gawked like children at the skeletal coral glowing in pink and green, orange and purple. Silent, save for the hiss of our breathing, we marvelled at our new world.

The dive boat bobbed twenty-two metres above us in the sticky

Arabian heat. But on the seabed, the cool water chilled us while we waited for the other divers who were slowly descending. Two by two. Metre by metre. Maureen began to shake. My buddy was cold.

Then a strange thing happened. In my teenage years, alcohol meant courage, and a pint meant inconceivable words became conceivable: *Wanna dance?* Maturity hadn't changed a thing, except under the Red Sea a barman was as scarce as a mermaid. And Saudi law forbids both. But, in that moment, in that instant of insanity, my hand reached out to my buddy. I clasped Maureen's fingers in mine. Electricity. I didn't know the diver's signal for: *Did you feel that?* But despite being hugely embarrassed – and not a little smitten – I hoped it was mutual. I didn't raise the underwater phenomenon during the post-dive debrief. Neither did Maureen.

We married five years later, but not until horrific floods had crashed under a rickety bridge.

―――――

'Amazing,' Melanie said. 'Truly amazing.'

'It was.'

'So, this was your first marriage?'

'No, my first ended in divorce.'

'Oh,' she said with understanding and sadness. 'I married three times.' Her face tightened. 'The last one started to beat me in under a week.'

'Shit.'

'It lasted six months. One hundred and eighty-eight days to be precise.'

'Alcohol?'

'Yes,' she said. 'I was sober; he wasn't.'

We both knew we suffered from the same illness, but my present tense was more present than Melanie's. I didn't tell her that Johnnie Walker slept in my saddlebag.

'I'm sorry,' I said.

She shrugged.

We hiked in silence. The warmth cloaked our hike in a heavy peace. The Katherine River snaked far beneath us where a boat chugged westwards like a silent comet ahead of its tail of sparkling water. The path became rougher and steeper, leading to a tableland high above the bush.

'We made it,' I said, breaking the silence. 'Coffee?'

Melanie smiled. A pair of white cockatoos circled above us. A huge boulder, metres high, begged us to climb. I held out my hand – King of the Castle – and hauled Melanie to the top. We stood dumbfounded on the boulder staring across the gorge that cut across an infinite horizon of nothing. Then Melanie suddenly spun on her toes, her arms stretched theatrically upwards to the sky. A blonde ballerina in boots and baggy pants. A curtsy concluded the show.

'Bravo,' I said, as I handed over the coffee flask as though it were a flute of champagne.

'Thank you, kind sir.' She held up her hand for a high-five.

Melanie took a sip of my black coffee and handed it back. I took a swig too. We sat on the ledge, legs dangling over the side, sharing the flask, backwards and forwards.

Katherine stunned us with her beauty. Conversation flowed as easily as the river that rolled through the gorge. The day's warmth began to cool.

'We should get going,' Melanie said.

I held out my hand and pulled her to her feet.

'We should.'

The sun had dipped below the horizon by the time we reached Yammie. It would be a cold evening.

Yammie fired into life. We did not speak on the ride back. Melanie's hands held my waist. Twenty minutes passed in seconds. My senses discarded the cool night, the wind and the rich evening scent.

The motel car park arrived none too soon. Melanie dismounted, took off her helmet and studied her boots. A minute passed. Silence.

Melanie broke it. 'Hey,' she said, 'great day!'

Another silence. Seconds ticked by in long sweeps of muted unease.

Melanie broke it again. 'Call me,' she said. 'You might get a flat tyre.' She laughed, took a pen and notebook from her backpack and scribbled her phone number. She ripped out the page and handed it to me. She waited. Said nothing.

I stood still. 'Of course,' I said, like a student snapped from a daydream by his tutor. 'Sorry.' I scribbled my phone number and handed back her notebook.

'Thank you,' she said. 'For so much.' She turned and walked back to her room.

I waited until Melanie reached her door. She didn't look back. A crack of light, a swirl of hair, and she disappeared. The darkness covered an undefinable sadness.

Two alcoholics. One was unstable.

I turned and tramped to my room on the other side of the motel. The piece of paper in my pocket rustled with every step.

Johnnie Walker slept in my saddlebag, in my room. A sleeping monster I dared not wake. The day had both strengthened my purpose and weakened my will.

I dreamt of Maureen.

———

Papua New Guinea 2007

'Michael, he's gone. Richard's gone.' Maureen's voice became a shrill command: 'Faster.'

We reached the hospital. In an instant, Maureen told me later, that nurses, doctors and paramedics had assembled around my lifeless body like a rugby scrum.

An oxygen mask was pressed hard against my face. It didn't work. I wasn't breathing. Maureen pushed the nurses away and pressed her mouth onto mine. Maureen's lungs filled me with life. An anaesthetist needed to be found.

'He needs intubation,' Maureen shouted. 'Now!'

Maureen kept me alive. My throat swelled as fast as my windpipe constricted.

A local anaesthetist arrived in a flurry of white. His mouth tightened. The window of opportunity was closing fast. The oxygen tank stood ready. But my airway refused entry. The anaesthetist started to sweat. My throat ballooned to twice its size; my airway a thin straw. The anaesthetist persisted. Thirty seconds. A lifetime.

The tube entered my throat, metallic air found starved lungs, and my life kickstarted into motion.

'One minute later,' the anaesthetist told Maureen, 'and it would have been impossible.'

Ashen skin showed embers of life. My chest rose. I breathed. Maureen cried.

'Thank you,' Maureen said, still shaking and unsure of the cause of the calamity. 'Thank you.'

'What happened?' the anaesthetist asked.

'I don't know …' Maureen said. 'I just don't know.'

Twenty minutes later I surfaced. Alive, but shocked. An umbilical cord connected my lungs to the oxygen cylinder beside my bed. I blinked. Unsure. Of why. Of what.

Maureen held my hand. She whispered words I didn't understand, her voice gentle, her soothing breath a sedative.

Realisation rose like a volcano. I felt steel smash my throat. My eyes stayed shut while my body trembled. Vomit erupted from my mouth. Blood had flooded my stomach; now my gut rebelled and threw it back. Puke and blood filled my throat in a direct attack against the oxygen tube blocking their exit. A nurse vacuumed my throat. I breathed again. To vomit was to choke. I fought the urge but didn't win. I retched as my stomach spewed its poisons, and my lungs screamed for air. My eyes bulged. I sucked air like a flapping fish waiting to die. The nurse and her vacuum kept me alive.

Maureen's parchment face showed her fear. 'Stay still,' she said.

Weak, limp, unfocussed, I did as she said. Nausea bobbed and weaved like whisky screaming an unwanted return after a long night. I discovered later that the internal throat lacerations had bled profusely, most of it into my stomach. The shrilling vacuum met every retch. I eyed that machine like a fevered junkie eyes his stash; it never left my sight.

I lay still. Broken and smashed. I couldn't speak. Maureen held my hand, while the doctor, the anaesthetist and the two nurses stared in sympathetic silence. Something had almost killed me. But what? And how?

Strength came slowly. Then, in sudden agitation, my right hand scribbled the air.

'He wants to write ...' Maureen said. 'Please... pen and paper.'

A notebook appeared by my side and a pencil pushed into my hand.

In crazy cursive, I told my story: *Weight fell on my throat.*

Light filled the room. Maureen told me I had stabilised. I would live. Medevac had dispatched a doctor and nurse from Australia. Their plane would arrive soon. 'Everything will be okay,' she whispered.

Another violent vomit was countered by a vigorous vacuum.

Now my neck merged with my shoulders. I lay there unable to comprehend tomorrow; I was a disgusting toad spewing up filth worse than a swamp.

Hours passed and morning moved to afternoon. The medical team from Australia had landed. Maureen said they would fly me to Brisbane on a chartered jet. She would have to fly separately on the next commercial flight. She squeezed my hand, kissed my cheek, then left. I wanted to speak, to say sorry, to thank her, to tell her I loved her.

Hospital staff hefted me onto a gurney, clamped my body tight with straps, and hauled the ugly load onto an ageing ambulance that bounced, smashed and swerved across pot-holed roads to Moresby's airport. Then a porter picked up the relay baton. My gurney pushed ahead ploughing through waiting passengers and corridors of bureaucracy until it stopped on the tarmac, where this sad and sorry toad waited under a blazing sky. Jet fuel fanned the air while the nurse stood tense as a gunslinger with her vacuum cocked and loaded. She would need to be fast on the draw. The sun flared behind the nurse's head; her shadow hid my fear. Sweat ran into my eyes. I couldn't move. I couldn't speak.

An eternity passed before being hoisted onto a plane. The private jet hurtled across the Coral Sea on its two-thousand-kilometre flight to the Princess Alexandra Hospital in Brisbane, where the cold hit me worse than the heat.

My nightmare had started seventeen hours earlier. Now I waited for surgery, strapped down like a lunatic from Bedlam, staring at the sterile lights, surrounded by beeping machines, shaking from the cold. Until an anaesthetic darkness descended.

VOCAL CORDS

Melanie's yellow Beetle had gone.

Darwin next stop.

Today started both with a sigh and a *praise be*; there was an Amcal pharmacy in Katherine. After 1,100 kilometres, the pharmacist filled my faded prescription for Celebrex: an anti-inflammatory that kept the ol' fella's joints oiled and free. *Praise be.*

The Stuart Highway carried me north towards Darwin, the Northern Territory's largest city and Australia's smallest state capital. The isolated outpost sat near the tip of the Territory where it poked its lonely presence into the Timor Sea. There was only one road in and one road out. Once in Darwin, Yammie would pirouette and retrace the same 325 kilometres she would cover today. Six hundred and fifty kilometres and I'd be back in Katherine where a right turn would take me towards the west coast of Australia. But for the next two days I'd ride north, then south, across a sliver of the Northern Territory. Just a sliver. This Pom's brain boggled at the sheer size of the Territory, then boggled again at its population: enormous and empty. NT's headcount is 226 times smaller than England's, but its land mass is eleven times bigger. To the Aussies, my ride over the next two days was little more than a bug's pissing distance.

Sixty minutes and ninety kilometres later, I crossed the Edith and Fergusson Rivers. At Pine Creek I stopped at the Mine Lookout: a small viewing platform high above the reservoir. The lake rippled, hiding its darker past. In another life it had been a gold pit. After exhausting its yellow wealth, the mining corporation diverted Pine Creek to beautify the ugly crater. It took fourteen months to fill the sore, but now the water-filled mine sparkled under the morning sun. As I walked to a second, higher lookout, chattering black cockatoos fled from the cover of a solitary tree, screeching across the lake to find shade and security.

I rejoined the Stuart Highway and soon rode the Daly River Route. Seventy kilometres of raw beauty: grass trees and ghost gums, towering termite mounds, billabongs and creeks. A dying bushfire spoke of a recent rage. Smoke drifted across hundreds of square kilometres of bush, isolated eddies still spiralled, embers still pulsed, but regeneration would come from those black, charred ashes. And despite the huge bushfire, luminescent green sprouts sprung from the sooted and smouldering bush. New shoots looked towards the sky, and another chance – a 'life-after-death' spectacle. Gangajang's hit song said it all: *This is Australia* ...

A warm day. No cars. No people. Nothing. I was alone, at peace.

My thoughts turned to Maureen. My mobile couldn't scare up a signal. With the long blackouts, Maureen would worry and if disaster were to fall, a passing car would be the best I could pray for. A collision with a kangaroo or wallaby would be fatal. I conjured up images of road carnage, bloody scenes: me and a kangaroo wedded together in muck and guts. No hope of help. Delusion and time would be all I had ... five days later ... perhaps a passing car with Mum, Dad and the kids in the back.

'Oh look, Mum. Another roadkill,' says the young daughter, 'Looks like one of those bikie persons.' And after a pause, 'Must have been there a few weeks already.'

'Yes, dear, just hold your nose and look the other way.'

Two hours later I rejoined the Stuart Highway.

Whuummmpp, shake, rattle and roll. Whuummmpp, shake, rattle and roll. Two road trains passed in tandem. I countered advancing machine monsters with a tense grip on my handlebars.

A car dulls the senses; a motorbike frees them. Grass, honey-damp earth, ploughed fields, jasmine, wood smoke. And roadkill too, often smelt but unseen, but always a pungent reminder of life's fragility.

The road raced under my boots. Long distances made the mind wander. Mileage, isolation and the sun were stewing my imagination. Complacency broke with a bang.

WHUUMMMPP, but no shake, rattle and roll. 'Fuck!' I screamed. My speed had dropped to 135kph, but a car blazed from behind as though Yammie ticked over at walking speed. A black Porsche, late for yesterday's funeral, sped past at over 200 kph. I hated shocks from behind. Scared the shit out of me. My screamed profanity activated my Bluetooth helmet sound system: 'Service not available,' said the calm female voice. 'Fuck!' I screamed again. 'Service not available,' she replied with sanctimonious serenity. But it took this pants-shitting moment to discover my helmet intercom system included a voice-controlled personal assistant. But she only responded to screams.

The Northern Territory's maximum speed limit of 130 kph has exceptions. The government conferred an open speed limit on two chunks of highway: one, a 200 kilometre stretch between Alice Springs and Barrow Creek, and another seventy-two-kilometre segment from Barrow Creek to the Ali Curung rail overpass. This road, however, was 1,000 kilometres north of the Wild Bill Hickok stretch. Road trains, stray cattle, perhaps even a surprise willy-willy were understandable, but a black bombshell up my arse was another matter.

The Adelaide River War Cemetery offered a convenient, tranquil stop. The impeccably maintained cemetery commanded attention and respect. A silent stroll among its 434 bronze plaques blazing in the afternoon sun was a poignant reminder of the debt 'of so much owed by so many to so few'. *Lest we forget.* I sat in peaceful reflection under the shade of a huge fig tree.

Onwards.

I reached the outskirts of Darwin at 4.30 pm. As soon as I was in range, my mobile rang. A premonition of danger had hit Maureen too.

'Are you okay?' Maureen said, her voice betraying her anxiety.

'Great.'

'Where the bloody hell are you?'

'Just approaching Darwin.'

A two-minute rant hit me with six strokes of the cane. I should have called. I know that.

'I've been so worried,' she said.

My explanations wandered like my thoughts. Another place. Another time. In this expanse of nothing, it was easy to forget. Everything.

'I miss you.' And I did. It was the best I could say.

My excitement soon overtook guilt. My words flowed like rivers in flood. Drowning. Incoherent. Dry tanks and deep gorges, pink panthers and black Porsches, cemeteries and serenity, bush fires and billabongs, eternity and emptiness. Maureen's anxiety increased.

'I've ordered a satellite communicator for you.'

'A what?'

Maureen explained. Her fear was real. To mitigate the lack of phone signals, Maureen had bought an InReach Explorer Satellite Communicator. The gizmo awaited collection from an outback camping store on the edge of Darwin. Maureen had paid for it over the phone and ordered the salesman to have it charged and ready to go. The shop closed at 5.30 pm. I noted the address in Google maps.

'Be good,' Maureen said, as we ended our call.

I had forty minutes to get there. 'Proceed to the route,' said the Bluetooth lady in my helmet. *And beware of black Porsches.*

Forty-five minutes later I thanked the salesman for his help. This amazing piece of kit would monitor my every movement. Maureen would know exactly where I was – anytime, anywhere. The device boasted an SOS facility that alerted emergency services to, well, emergencies. I just needed to press the button.

'But be careful,' said the salesman with a grin meant to both alarm and assure. 'I heard that an old camper sent out an SOS call in error. His stupidity cost him $12,000 in fines.'

'Thank you,' I said, pondering the three core components of the message: old, camper and stupid.

'Take care,' said the salesman.

A chopper *whoop-whoop-whooped* overhead.

'A customer of yours?' I said, striding back to Yammie.

The 'Tracker' throbbed in my hand: safety secured, anonymity annulled.

Twenty kilometres north I found a caravan park – luck, not design – and exhaustion hit me like an old man who had ridden a motorcycle all day.

I asked the girl at reception about camping costs. She took pity on Don Quixote.

'There's a special on,' she replied.

'What's that?'

'Well, you can have a portacabin for fifty-five dollars which includes a single bed, TV, shower and toilet, Wi-Fi and AC.'

'Deal!' I said.

The satellite tracker sent Maureen my GPS coordinates and monitored my movement. I needed to stretch my legs. I walked to the ablution block with no doubt the urinal's location would be pin pricked for all to see.

———

Brisbane 2007

My body lay inert in a hospital bed. Clean, crisp, contemporary. Three bright balloons – red, blue and yellow – bobbed on the ceiling of my white sterile room. *Get well soon*, they read. A male nurse sat reading, head down, at the foot of my bed. Sunlight flooded the room from a large window behind my head. A winter morning blessed with promises of a hopeful day. I floated in the misty sunlight – rested, relaxed, peaceful.

Tubes snaked from my throat, my nose, my arm and a bottle of fluid hung over my head. Machines beeped, lights flickered, and strong white sheets squeezed my body.

Then yesterday's memory bucked like a mule.

I saw sixty kilos rush towards my head and felt the sledgehammer smash my throat. I remembered why I was here. My body convulsed, tubes shook, and the drip teetered. The male nurse leapt from his seat.

'Easy, easy,' he said. 'You're going to be okay. Everything's okay. You're in the Princess Alexandra Hospital in Brisbane.'

I tried to speak. My hands, now unrestrained, moved towards the mask that smothered my face like a squid, its tentacles spreading over my body.

The nurse held my arms. 'Easy,' he said. 'Relax.' The nurse knew I needed answers. 'You were in an accident, in a gym. Do you remember?'

Yes, my body affirmed. I remembered.

'A surgeon has opened a hole in your throat … a tracheotomy. To allow you to breathe. You're going to be okay. Lie still. Try to relax, a doctor will be here soon.'

I couldn't relax, but I lay still and stared at the balloons: *Get well soon.*

Minutes or hours passed, I can't remember, sunlight dappled the curtains shielding other inmates, each with a nurse station at the end of each bed. Specialised attention. My personal nurse rose to the sound of an approaching gown.

A young surgeon stood by my bedside. He told me his name. Got to the point. 'Richard,' he said in an American accent, 'you've had a tracheotomy. We needed to open the airway. Your throat was badly smashed by the weights. You're going to recover, but there's been a complication…' He paused. I tensed. 'Your voice box has been damaged. You may not be able to speak again. This is my present assessment. It might take several months before we know for sure.'

My body tightened like a neck awaiting the guillotine. I needed a million answers but was unable to ask a single question. Dumb and mute, I absorbed the facts.

'The nurse will bring you a pen and paper. Write down your questions. I'll pass by later today,' the surgeon said. 'I'm sorry.' Mission accomplished, he turned and walked down the corridor, past rows of beds of damaged people and broken dreams.

You may not be able to speak again. No voice, no job, no future. But I was alive.

Surgical emphysema had ballooned my head into a caricature of an ugly toad. My neck had spread across my shoulders. I felt like a grotesque gargoyle. A mirror said I looked worse.

Surgical emphysema is a medical oddity occurring when air is trapped under the skin. Veteran and trainee doctors alike wanted to touch me, feel me, push my skin. 'Crisp snow,' they said. 'It's just like pushing fingers into crisp snow.' My skin crunched and shifted under the pressure of a gentle touch. 'Amazing,' they said. 'Thanks.'

Each day the doctors and interns would come, alone, in pairs, in threes, at odd hours, day or night. 'Could we just …' they would begin.

Sure, said my hands, *help yourself.*

The junior medical staff prodded, pushed and listened. My body responded: *snap, crackle and pop*: Rice Krispies in the snow.

Wow! said their faces. 'So sorry' said their words. Frowns of empathy did little to mask their professional excitement. 'Bloody amazing,' they muttered among themselves, ambling off to other wards, other oddities, other notable experiences. Word spread like a Facebook meme. More medical students returned. *Snap, crackle, pop.* And the 'Likes' soared.

A beautiful student doctor walked shyly towards me. I nodded before she asked her question. *No worries.* She smiled a thank you and touched my skin. Beauty and the Beast. *Pop, pop, pop.* 'So sorry,' she said.

Days turned into weeks, and weeks turned into a fucking long time. After four days, the hospital transferred me from intensive care to a general-purpose ward. Miserable and low, I often hated my selfishness. I would recover. Other patients, I had learned, were terminally ill. They could check out any time, but they could never leave.

Maureen sat by my side. Discarded notes littered my bed like leaves after an autumn storm. Scrambled thoughts and scratched etchings said what needed to be said, and often what didn't. The pile of crumpled paper became a testament to my frustration and fear. At the end of each day Maureen scooped up my streams of scribbled consciousness and dumped them in the garbage. Until the next morning, when the melancholic Shakespeare would take to his pen again. Silver linings never saw the light of day. Lows followed lows, and lower lows descended into depression.

Each day I asked the same question: *Would I speak again?* 'It will take time,' they said. Time I had in spades. Hope I did not. Slowly, my physical health began to improve, but my mental health got worse.

The memory of steel weights crashing onto my throat segued into images of car wrecks. My gym accident nightmared into a collision. A car crumpling from the onslaught of a truck. My son, daughter and wife were with me. Dominic and Heather died. My daughter survived. Again and again my nightmares replayed the horror of the head-on. A flash of light before the darkness. But I was never in that car. They were.

Somewhere in my mute darkness, I had a startling revelation. A ray of sunshine. If I removed the plug from the hole in my throat, and pressed a finger gently over the hole, I could speak like Mickey Mouse high on helium. Maureen and Gabby laughed. Me too. Maybe Mickey was my mask; maybe hope hid somewhere behind the smiles.

Two months later the hospital deemed me fit enough to discharge. I could speak in raspy whispers. After ten days of home-based recuperation, I returned to Papua New Guinea. But I needed a microphone to communicate – no problem – but its power plant was. To stay 'on-line' I carried huge battery packs strapped to my waist, accepting that my fashion accessories could be considered suicidal.

A speech therapist helped me strengthen my voice and with her help, four months later, I trashed the microphone in ceremony of triumph. It was a miracle to have survived. A blessing to speak.

Post-traumatic stress attacked often. Still does. I saw the crashing weights every day, every night, and felt them hit with the ferocity of a truck. I tasted the bloody cocktail of rust and mucous. Nightmares attacked like unexpected artillery – grief the perpetual victor.

The weights had balanced on the hooks of the rusted Smith machine and it was the vibration of my body moving from the bench that dislodged the killer bar and its throat-crushing load. No-one

believed me. Sceptical faces showed their theory: I became too
exhausted; I couldn't finish; I tried for a push too far; I dropped the
weight. 'Sixty kilos would never balance on hooks,' they said. But they
did. I was there.

To stay sane, and against Maureen's wishes, I returned to the crime
scene – the gym. With Maureen at my side, I examined the gym like a
CSI detective. The horror of that morning was sharp and clear. The
sound of the throat vacuum hummed in my memory as a fitting
soundtrack. I stood in the hot and humid gym – a cave squeezed of air
– now decorated with safety notices plastering every wall. The
apartment block managers had neatened the area. Old junk and
obstacles had been removed. Too late.

The Smith's machine remained.

Replaying the scene revived my fear: the weight balanced on the
hook, my body beneath it. I did not drop it. Fatigue had not been the
cause, but I needed proof.

The Smith machine looked exactly as I had left it. I tried to position
the weights to balance on the hooks. Maureen helped. We couldn't. A
Sisyphean task: we tried and tried, failed and failed, and still it did not
balance. Maureen looked at me.

'Maureen,' I said, shaking with frustration. 'It happened – exactly
the way I said it did.'

'I know,' she said, not sure of anything. 'Let's keep trying.'

Defeat followed defeat. Until we won: the weight balanced *on* the
hook, not *in* the hook.

We held our breath and time stopped. The weight stayed in place,
poised, teetering, threatening like a ticking bomb. A minute passed …
and then slowly, softly as though our life depended on it, I removed my
phone, started the video, and gently touched the framework.

The weight smashed with a sickening thud against the leather
cushion of the bench.

Maureen's hand flew to her mouth. 'Oh my God,' she said. The
dust settled, calm returned, and Maureen's face regained some colour.

'One more time,' I said.

PISTE

Today I would backtrack 300 kilometres south, down the same long road to Katherine that I rode yesterday. When I reached Katherine, I'd take a right turn onto the Victoria Highway towards the pearling town of Broome and the Indian Ocean, 1,500 kilometres west. Maybe three days ride.

But first Yammie took me to the Darwin beach suburb of Fannie Bay. I wanted to see the monument dedicated to Ross Smith and his crew, winners of the 1919 Great Air Race. The race demanded one simple rule: complete a flight from England to Australia in under thirty days. Six crews entered. Ross and his co-pilot (his brother Keith), took off from London on 12 November 1919 and landed at Fannie Bay twenty-nine days later. The second 'finisher' took 237 days. Three planes crashed, two fatally, and one crew landed up in a Yugoslavian jail. Ross and Keith shared the £10,000 prize money equally with their two mechanics. Fourteen thousand miles in twenty-nine days. An outstanding achievement delivered with grit and determination. Smith and his crew became the inspiration behind the founding of Qantas the following year. An inspiration for me too. My 15,000-kilometre circumnavigation of Australia had two rules: finish in sixty-two days and keep Johnnie locked up. The former goal was looking good and the latter had stayed incarcerated. Day 11 and my odometer had racked up 4,000 kilometres – 1,250 kilometres ahead of schedule. But a certain fat lady always hovered in the wings …

Black coffee concluded my pilgrimage to Fannie Bay. Now Katherine. Exhaustion squeezed my body just one hour into the ride. I needed coffee, strong and often. I'd slept well, so perhaps my flagging energy resulted from the psychological effect of retracing the same stretch of highway. A welcome break at the Adelaide River War Memorial and a barra from the nearby roadhouse helped. I ate the fish under the shade of the same fig tree I had sat under twenty-four hours before. This oasis of peace fortified my reserves. Refreshed, I headed for Katherine.

Yammie powered south. Strong, consistent, trustworthy. She had been a powerful performer, a loyal companion. Eleven days and she hadn't skipped a beat. Yammie delivered. Day in. Day out. I'd been lucky to find her. Perhaps she found me. Love at first sight. I patted Yammie's flanks and blew Maureen a kiss.

I reached Katherine, refuelled, drank the last dregs of my coffee, then hesitated. Call it a day? Or try for Victoria River Roadhouse? I did the latter and turned west. The roadhouse, and my bed for the night, still lay 200 kilometres away.

The late afternoon sun dappled treetops in soft golden light; roosting birds flitted through ghost gums; and grass, tall as wheat, hedged the road in a wall of burnt orange. The light faded and deep in the trees, shadows burst into sudden skips and quicker silences. Roos.

After 150 kilometres the land opened into expansive paddocks and open bush. Mountainous escarpments horseshoed the horizon like castle parapets. A damp mist settled across the road as the Victoria River Roadhouse loomed from the dusk where wallabies dotted the paddocks still as statues. Too tired to camp, I took a six-by-six tin cabin next to empty fields filled with shifting shadows.

Ten minutes later I hooked my digital devices to my wall socket and my batteries sucked like leeches. My iPhone came back to life, then my laptop took its turn. I started at the escarpments spread across my window, darkening to silhouettes as the sky faded under the colour of smouldering embers. Memories rose like mountains.

Italy, The Matterhorn - Christmas 1987

The first piste hooked us all.

In 1985, Citibank moved me from London to Italy: my first overseas posting. I lived with Heather, my first wife, and our two sons, Jamie and Dominic. We rented an apartment in a small but modern suburb, twenty-two kilometres south-west of Milan. I worked in the old city centre, Foro Buonaparte, a wide, cobbled, tram-lined street overlooking the old fortress of Castello Sforzesco, and almost under the shadow of the Duomo, Italy's largest church. I could see the Alps from my office.

After many months in Italy, we were still apprentice expats. But once Heather had overcome her initial nervousness about a life abroad, we started a more earnest exploration of everything Italian with more confidence. We wanted to immerse ourselves in the culture. Well, at least we tried. But more than anything else, and there was a lot of everything else, Italy's Alpine lakes drew us back again and again. We made excited excursions almost every weekend: Lago di Como, Lago Maggiore, Lago di Garda, and Lago di San Giulio. We trekked in mountains, ate in rustic villages, marvelled at the vistas and swam in ice-cold Alpine lakes, all in our first hot Italian summer.

We enrolled Jamie in the American School of Milan soon after we arrived. He was almost five years old. After just a few weeks, Jamie started to replace English words with their American equivalent, and soon after adopted an American accent. The following year we started Dom in a preschool for Italian kids in the nearby village of Basiglio. He was three, but soon spoke Italian like his peers, and within six months his Italian was almost fluent. Heather immersed herself with the ex-pat wives' club. We both tried to learn Italian, Dominic helped us all.

Our second winter reached down from the mountains and crooked a finger. Jamie's American friends skied. Heather's expat friends skied.

My work colleagues skied. And Dominic's Italian friends skied. But so far, we had not.

'When are we going, Dad?' Jamie asked every day in November. 'When?'

'Next month.'

'Next Saturday?' he said.

'Three weeks.'

'*Fra pocco?*' Dominic said.

'Yes,' I said. 'Soon.'

The boys bubbled with excitement. Heather remained hesitant.

We chose a December trip to Cervinia for our baptism of snow, a two-hour drive from Milan. Cervinia nestled in the shadow of the Matterhorn. Monte Cervino, as the Italians call it, straddled Italy and Switzerland. We hadn't skied before, but I knew the longer runs trailed high across the mountains to Klein Matterhorn in Switzerland, twenty kilometres to the north. But one day at a time. Baby steps first.

I hired a ski chalet for a week, twelve days before Christmas. So, on an icy Sunday, the family's goal was simple: gentle glides down a nursery slope – without injury.

Madonna songs and Christmas carols echoed across the lower slopes from a nearby skating rink. '*Papa Don't Preach*' blurred with '*Tu Scendi Dalle Stelle*' and the squeals of festive skiers. The village sparkled under a canopy of blue sky, snow and tinsel.

I paid for three days of tuition: one hour a day for all us and ski passes for the week.

By 8.30 am on our first day, we had hired everything we needed, and more. Dominic's skis were a little wider than a twelve-inch ruler and about the same length. Jamie's were twice as large. Heather and I had skis as long as railway carriages. We had everything except the know-how to use them.

'*Lyka deeece*,' said the ski instructor. The West family copied. With skis angled in embarrassingly wide Vs, we snow ploughed to flat ground and salvation. On our third run, Dominic broke ranks and sped to the bottom, skis pointed like miniature javelins at the people gathered below. Jamie followed. My pride prompted me to do the same. We made it.

The instructor looked sour as the boys broke into smiles wider than the valley. Dominic escaped a second time, while Jamie and I watched Heather painfully pick her way down the nursery. Heather made the bottom ten minutes later as Dominic hurtled towards us like a missile from another slope. No-one had taught him how to stop. He didn't care. '*Scusi! Scusi!*' he shouted with a grin as he smashed through the three of us into a throng of unamused Italians.

And that was that. The kids took to skiing like eagle chicks on their first fall from a mountain eyrie. Naturals. I wasn't bad either. Heather remained hesitant but her bravery rewarded her with passable capability. Fast forward four weeks, and my salary evaporated before being earned: we bought our own gear and all the must-have accessories. And then, in a wild act of weakness, I rented a small apartment in the nearby village of Valtournenche for the rest of the season. Every weekend thereafter, with vacation weeks scattered in between, we skied. And skied. Black slopes soon became our go-to preference while Heather stayed on the nursery. Like all kids, Jamie and Dominic copied the stylish skiers. The ones that knew what was what and who was who. I followed the kids and tried to quell their speed. My goal was to mitigate risk; I couldn't teach them a thing.

Jamie and Dominic both excelled, but Dominic radiated star quality. The lack of fear helped, and a cheeky grin added to his colourful charisma. We neared the end of the season shortly after Dominic's fourth birthday. His skis were now twice as tall as he was.

In 1988, my last year in Milan before re-locating to Saudi Arabia, Jamie's American school had arranged a ski weekend for its students and their families to celebrate the New Year. Jamie wanted to go. We all did. I paid the money and signed up. It was the first time we had skied with other families. Everyone was astounded at Dominic's skill and bravery, Jamie's too. The weekend included fun events and competitions for the kids and the adults. It was the finale though that held everyone's breath. A 500-metre downhill slalom with Olympic starting gates and digital timers. There were two student categories:

under twelves and over twelves. Jamie entered. His seven-year-old excitement affected us all. Except Dominic. He was crestfallen. Too young. The organisers said the school's liability insurance stated all participants had to be over five years old. Dominic was still two months short of his fifth birthday. His disappointment hit me too.

After a week watching other children ski, it was clear that Dominic's ability equalled or exceeded kids twice his age. I took a risk and decided to speak to the organisers. They sympathised, and didn't question Dominic's competency, but insisted 'rules were rules.' Insurance restrictions tied their hands. I untied the ropes. 'What if,' I said, 'I give you a personal, handwritten waiver that absolves you from any liability?' They raised their eyebrows, hesitated, then agreed. 'The risk is yours,' they said. 'Good luck. Dominic has talent.'

Four kids went before Jamie. His turn came, and we held our breath. Jamie reacted to the starting buzzer with good speed. A fine start. But he took the second gate too fast and lost control as he weaved past the third. He crashed in a heap. Shocked, he picked himself up, shook his head and skied with skill to the bottom. The fall had ruled him out of contention. But despite the stumble he achieved a decent time.

Dominic went last. At the starting trigger, Dom rocketed out of the pen like a bullet. He hit the first gate at speed with a grin wide enough for all to see. Second gate. Third gate. Fourth. He disappeared into a cloud of snow at every turn, but his cheeky smile always emerged before he did. We stood near the start of the ski run, not the end. The roar of the appreciating spectators told us he had made the finish line. His time flashed on the screen. *Third!*

Out of a field of forty kids, many of them close to twelve, Dominic, at only four years old, had come third. We were all proud of him, Jamie, as well.

The American school closed the weekend's festivities with a gala dinner. A small speech opened the evening. The head teacher, Mrs O'Rourke, offered thanks to the parents, and the students, for taking part in a memorable week.

'And now,' she said, 'I'll announce the results you've all been waiting for.'

I didn't know what she was talking about. Neither did Heather.

'The annual American School Trophy for the best skiing family goes to …' – the room held its breath – 'the Wests.'

We were dumbfounded.

'Please,' she said, 'will the West family come to the stage.'

We sat still. Everybody clapped.

I leant forward and whispered into Dominic's ear. He jumped up and skipped to the stage. Roars of applause. Mrs O'Rourke pushed the microphone to his mouth as he reached for the trophy. Dom's huge smile attracted more applause. 'Bravo little fella. Bravo.'

'Don't you want to say something?' Mrs O'Rourke asked as the ruckus died down.

Dominic put a coy finger to his lip, just for a second, then laughed. '*Grazie,*' he said as he grabbed the trophy and ran back to our table. Dom's grin broke hearts.

23 JUMADA II 1422

An early morning drizzle settled over the roadhouse where a dozen wallabies sat twenty metres from my window. I opened my door to low cloud and the pungent smell of paddocks. The wallabies stared but stayed statue still: wet and forlorn. No riding today. Instead I decided to climb the escarpments hiding behind the rain. My body needed exercise regardless of the weather. My map showed a trail, two kilometres along the road, leading into Judbarra/Gregory National Park and its bluffs that rose 250 metres above the Victoria River. Breakfast first.

A three-minute walk, and I was the first to arrive in an empty roadhouse diner. Bacon and eggs and strong coffee never tasted better. The dismal day looked brighter.

Dafydd greeted me outside. A solemn face hosted a red beard still speckled with yesterday's dinner. Sodden ginger hair escaped from a yellow bandanna tied above brown eyes. Dafydd's yellow boots matched his yellow bicycle. As I watched, he cleaned his teeth in the water bucket provided for drivers to wash bugs from windows. Spare inner tubes of lipstick-red curled snake-like on a rear parcel rack under a yellow and black bedroll. Two bulging yellow saddle bags hung from each wheel. The man and his bike resembled a two-wheeled bumble bee. A once yellow T-shirt was stained the same shade as his beard. The sight was dazzling; the smell daunting. He looked up from the murky bucket and caught my eye. Unperturbed, Dafydd turned back to the dirty water and the business of cleaning his teeth.

Humbled by his *serious traveller* credentials, my curiosity pushed me to strike up a conversation

'Hi,' I said.

He nodded but his eyes stayed focussed on the bucket.

I tried again, 'How's it going?'

He shrugged.

'Where you headed?' I asked, thinking he might be speech impaired.

He raised his eyebrows and thrust his jaw toward the escarpments to the west.

'Me too,' I said, 'but I'm on a motorcycle.'

No response. I attempted another tack, 'How far have you travelled?'

Dafydd looked up and stared at me with eyes that moved like beads on an abacus. 'Two thousand, one hundred and fifty-three miles,' he said in a strong, proud Welsh accent.

'Wow!' I said. 'Can I ask your name?'

'Dafydd.'

'Richard.' I held out my hand.

We shook. He said nothing more. Ablutions completed, he turned and walked to his bicycle where he continued to ignore me. Dafydd checked the paraphernalia covering his machine like a sailor inspecting the rigging of a yacht before an ocean crossing.

'Well, good luck,' I said.

Dafydd looked up from his bike and held my eye for what seemed like an eternity. He nodded again. My optimism did the translation: *You too.*

Two thousand miles. Dafydd was inspirational. A Welsh warrior on a journey to wherever in a whatever way without a wasted worry about what people might think. Eccentric? Maybe. Brave? Indubitably.

The rain eased but damp mist hung over the roadhouse like a shroud.

I loaded my backpack with my camera, a beef sandwich, coffee flask and the satellite tracker. And started hiking towards the escarpments. Maureen would be watching.

The roadhouse lay among the huge red cliffs of the Victoria River section of the Judbaraa/Gregory National Park. The area is an ecological transition between tropical and semi-arid zones, and at 13,000 square kilometres is the Northern Territory's second-largest park. It's one tenth of the size of England.

I hiked along the verge of the highway looking for a trail. A yellow Beetle passed and stopped five metres ahead.

'Hey,' said Melanie.

'You following me or am I following you?'

'Hop in,' she said.

'Where you headed?'

'Kununurrara. I stayed in Katherine last night. The same place we stayed before.'

'I took a cabin back at the roadhouse you just passed,' I said. 'Kununurra tomorrow. Weather permitting.'

'Where to now?' Melanie's question sounded both metaphorical and literal.

'I thought I'd hike the escarpments.'

'Can I join you?'

Her wild blue eyes showed her independence and adventurous spirit. Melanie was small in stature, big in bravery. A woman running from her past on a solo journey around Australia to find her future. *Yellow Beetle, white daisy, blue-eyed, bloody courageous: a synopsis of a woman and a wild story.*

My reply was slow. 'Sure,' I said, not sure of anything.

We found a place to park. Melanie dug in the back of her car for a jacket, and we were ready to go.

The trail began easily enough, as did our conversation.

'You're ahead of your schedule,' she said. 'Sixty-two days you said.'

'I did. And unless I hit mechanical problems or bad weather or …'
I paused. 'I think I'll be good.'

'Impressive.'

The drizzle started again as we followed the trail to the escarpments now hidden behind the weather.

'What about you? Three months, you said.'

'I've been thinking about that. I love it out here. Three months isn't long enough to reshape a lifetime. I'm considering options. One says I stay much longer. Two says I stay longer still. And three says I find a job. Work my way around. Maybe take a year or two. Maybe travel forever.'

'Wow!' I said. 'I never asked what work you do.'

'I'm a nurse.' She gave a wry smile and a shrug. 'I work in addiction clinics.'

The irony slapped me in the face.

'Oh, I didn't start out that way. I was a theatre nurse. Blood and gore. That was me. But events,' she said, 'changed my outlook. Now I help those with the same problem I had.' She paused, 'The same problem *I have*'. Melanie understood the present tense.

'You're one big surprise.'

'I surprise myself,' she said. 'Sometimes.'

'But would you find work like that, here?' I said, waving my hand around to encompass the Northern Territory and the nothingness surrounding us.

'I doubt it,' she said, 'but I'll do anything. Barmaid, cleaner, roadhouse manager.'

'I believe it.'

'Maybe I'll meet the man I should have met thirty years ago.'

'I hope you do.'

The drizzle turned to rain, and the clouds sunk lower, sandwiching us between a grey wet blanket. Breathing became more difficult as our ascent steepened. Now the rain fell from a black sky like a solid sheet. No pitter patter today, just the roar of sky-fall. I looked for cover. The trail ahead wound close to a deep fracture in the escarpment.

'Let's wait it out a bit,' I said, nodding to the shelter. It was deep enough to offer protection. We huddled together unsure of what to say. A short silence segued into a long one.

'It's nice,' Melanie said. 'Cosy.'

And it was. Melanie radiated heat and talcum powder, but the closeness created an alarming intimacy. I leant away.

'You okay?' she said.

'I'm thinking we should move on.'

'Why? It's raining.'

'It won't kill you. Come on. I'll race you to the top.'

I stepped out into the downpour; Melanie followed.

We hiked upwards towards the escarpment looming above. The rain continued to batter the trail in a fortissimo roar while I stayed quiet hoping to hide my embarrassment.

The trail steepened as it cut through a narrow gap in the rock to the tabletop summit. It was not an easy climb, and the rain didn't help. I held out my hand to Melanie to pull her up the last few metres. Mountaineers we were not, but we punched the air as though we had just conquered Everest.

The rain eased. Far below, the highway thread like a silver hair across a black bolt of barren bush. A mute road train slid slowly towards Kununurra, a plume of spray trailing its progress. Several kilometres to the east, the roadhouse I left three hours earlier lay among greyed paddocks. I couldn't see any wallabies.

'We made it,' I said. 'Coffee?'

Melanie smiled. A pair of white cockatoos circled nearby. It was just us and them. I handed Melanie my flask.

'So, you'll stay in the roadhouse?' Melanie said.

'I'm not riding in this,' I said, arms spread wide to indicate the weather. 'Anyway, it's too late to move on. I'll be staying another night if it continues. I have a cabin. Small. Cramped, but warm. You're not going to camp in Kununurra? Not in this rain.'

'Of course.'

'Of course,' I said, repeating what I knew she would say.

'It's a four-hour drive with a coffee break.' I looked at my watch.

Almost one o'clock. 'I doubt you'll get there before dark.' I already knew her answer.

'I have a torch.'

'We'd better get going. It'll take an hour to get back to the road. We should go.'

'We should.'

We finished the coffee.

'Are you okay?' Melanie asked.

'Sure,' I said. 'Let's go.'

The trek down was easier and thankfully faster.

Seventy silent minutes later, Melanie's yellow Beetle appeared from the mist. We stood by her car, both thoughtful.

'I'll drive you back to the roadhouse,' Melanie said.

I wanted to accept. 'You have a long drive. I'll walk.'

Melanie was about to protest but stopped as quickly as she had begun.

'Okay,' she said. 'You have my number. Take care.'

Melanie surprised me with a hug. She touched two fingers to her lips, then pressed them to mine.

'Thank you,' she said. 'See you when I see you.'

I smiled, said nothing, and watched her leave. Melanie hunched behind the wheel of the Beetle. The white daisy looked bright and cheerful despite the weather. She looked in her mirror and held up a hand. The yellow bug rumbled west to Kununurra leaving exhaust fumes hanging in the mist.

It would take an hour to walk back to the roadhouse. I didn't see another car. I didn't see wallabies. Or kangaroos. Just rain.

Kuwait 2001

I had landed a position in Kuwait. A big win for a fucking big loser. I lost my job in Saudi Arabia some years before. An extended business trip to London while in a depressed state during my divorce had caused me to hit the bottle. Big time. Seeking shelter and security, I checked myself into a London rehab clinic. I exhausted my welcome three days later. Temporarily sober, I took the Saudia flight back to Riyadh and the inevitable end of my career. The Kuwait job surfaced as a lucky break: head of audit for a local bank. I started rocky and finished a wreck. Depressed and unwell, I began a tough job in an alien culture with no family, no friends, and a marriage in meltdown while living in a claustrophobic country smaller than most farms in the Northern Territory. At least the blokes in NT could drink beer.

Demanding work drained what little emotional resources I had left. A steep learning curve wound uphill through the organisation's internal politics, allegiances and animosities. Diplomatic dexterity did not appear on my CV. And although I may have been the new boy, I never bent a knee. I attacked confrontation with confrontation and poured alcohol onto the fire.

My office overlooked Kuwait Bay and the Persian Gulf. An azure sea sparkled across the straits that led to Iraq and Iran. Sleek ships, rusted tankers and old fishing boats trailed streams of effervescence across the harbour. Leisure craft lined orderly pontoons in a lavishly wealthy country. The serenity belied the rape of Kuwait ten years earlier when Saddam Hussein had brutalised the city during his invasion. The Iraqi retreat incited the viciously vindictive Hussein to destroy 700 oil wells across Kuwait. The desert landscape had looked like a vision from hell.

Fate had returned me here. I had lived and worked across the border in Riyadh ten years earlier when Saddam launched his missiles to attack me and a million others. My billion-dollar office view hid the horrors of 1991, but long hours, stress and anxiety started to amass an entirely different assault. The black dog would soon begin to swallow the beauty on the outside, while it ate away my sanity on the inside.

Kuwait prohibited alcohol, bars and public entertainment. No cinemas, theatres, clubs. Even the restaurants were split – families one side, single men the other. Solitude began to destroy my soul; depression did the rest. A colleague persuaded me to attend bible classes. Loneliness works in strange ways, even for irreligious people like me. The meetings kicked off with readings, followed by discussion. Then tea. I was both curious and argumentative, but real people attended. Friendly people. Nice people.

One evening the group debate focussed on divorce.

'It's a sin to divorce,' said a pastor.

'But …'

'It's a sin.'

I wanted to shout. To argue. To resist. But didn't. Instead, I just shook my head and left. Bible classes didn't cut it for me. Loneliness was better.

For my wife and my family, the period leading to divorce was tough. *Divorce*: a sharp, two-syllable, razor-edged, shit word. Terminal failure. The cause? Me. Alcohol reared its guilty head as the mitigating factor. But excuses are just that: excuses. I, me, and my drunk self were responsible. Now here I was – alone, dry, and in Kuwait.

'Alone,' I couldn't change. 'Dry,' I could.

Dry countries were never really dry. Deserts were never sober. Alcohol's illegality didn't stop its production. Or its consumption. The USA tried for thirteen years. It failed. Canberra tried for seventeen years. Australia's politicians didn't do dry either. They failed too. I tried. Several times. And also failed.

A small, musty store 500 metres from my hotel sat like a mediaeval trading post. It reeked of possibilities. The desert-dusted shelves offered everything: cigarettes and cucumbers, hookahs and honey, saffron and Slurpees, shisha and shampoo. And if they trusted you, really trusted you, maybe a bottle. My suit said money, my shirt sleeve showed desperation. Simple words to the right people sugared with a premium market price would most likely guarantee a successful transaction. Risk and reward. Supply and demand. Universal trading standards from Australia to Azerbaijan, from Katherine to Kuwait.

An old Kuwaiti man sat behind the counter. Dark, unshaven, unsmiling. Sharp eyes surveyed his shadowed shop under a flickering neon light like a carpet bagger ready to fleece a starving beggar. Dust swirled and settled with every movement. On the far side of the shop, a black ghost in a hijab moved in silence, searching the shelves, while an ageing Arab in dusty thobe shuffled toward the counter. He placed a 200-pack of cigarettes next to the ancient Burroughs machine and handed over a stack of dirty notes. *Ka-Ching.* The shopkeeper snatched the cash with his left hand and clicked beads of an abacus with his right. Double accounting. The former, I guessed, kept official records; the latter a personal tally. Blue eyes with the intensity of sapphires looked in my direction. Stone sharp. He knew.

'Scotch?' I asked.

A grimace and a furrowed brow said he either didn't deal in contraband, or he didn't understand. I tried again.

'Whisky?'

The man nodded. Quick and furtive.

'Two days,' he said. 'You come back. Two days.' He dismissed me with a nod to the door. *Now fuck off.*

Two days later I returned.

The man looked at me, shook his head, and showed his disgust. *Leave* said his body language, as he turned away and registered another transaction. *Ka-Ching. Click-click.* 'Tomorrow,' he said, without turning his head.

The third, fourth and fifth days ended like replicas of the second.

On the sixth day, he nodded and disappeared into the dark shadows at the back of his store. He returned carrying a black plastic bag scented in cardamom and turmeric. I paid. Fifty dinars. I did the mental arithmetic. Two hundred and fifty Aussie dollars. The black market didn't come cheap. No *Ka-Ching* for my transaction. Just the abacus – a private transaction: *click-click-click.* No words. With an imperceptible nod, he folded the money, turned his back and placed it in a belt around his waist. He pulled a curled notebook from beneath the cash register and recorded the trade. I left. Humiliated. He knew I would be back.

Empty streets. The muezzin had called Maghrib prayer one hour earlier. Dark streets. Almost seven o'clock. A lonely city. A deserted country. My pace increased; my stride stretched; my hotel room waited.

AA has many rules, clichés, tricks and mantras. A good one is the rule of HALT. The strategy says that the alcoholic should not become too hungry, too angry, too lonely, too tired. These conditions create dangerous risks and temptations. Desert-thirsty dryness pushed a risk too far. Every day, every week, every hour recorded a tick against A, L and T. Tonight, H got a tick too, and I racked up a full house, but food would have to wait.

The bottle roosted in my briefcase brazen as a bastard cuckoo in an illegitimate nest. In the hotel elevator, I hugged my case like a convict with a reprieve letter. And in a manner of speaking, that's what my briefcase contained: a temporary reprieve from stress, from depression, from … It was a ticket to a few hours of freedom. The cost, an irrelevance. I reached the door of my room, took a furtive look left and right. All clear. I stepped into the air-conditioned sanctuary, then discovered a swindle.

The old Kuwaiti had sold me vodka. Not whisky. He knew it didn't matter. My desperation told him everything. He was right. It didn't matter at all. I didn't give a fuck.

Two warm gulps tore into my throat straight from the bottle. The third gulp screamed: *slow down*. The warmth created time to think. An iced Coke from the minibar would serve as a mixer. Traffic lights. I needed to ease off. A shower would help while the buzz took hold. I placed the precious bottle back in the black plastic bag and buried it in my suitcase. I didn't want the bottle exposed to suspicious eyes: room-service, bed turndown. I hung a Do Not Disturb sign on my door.

My heart skipped a beat at the sudden wail of a muezzin. The call to Isha prayer. A mosque stood across the street; harsh lights lit its minarets. With the drop of a baton, a thousand voices erupted in mournful unison, beckoning the faithful to prayer. Beautiful voices, hypnotic voices, mesmerizing voices ricocheted across the canyons of the city, echoing down dark streets: calling, compelling, commanding.

'*Allahu Akbar*.'

I froze.

'Hurry to prayer,' demanded the muezzin. 'Hurry to salvation.'

The haunting intensity of their faith burned into my room.

'There is no God but Allah.' With these words the voices stopped. Isha prayers had started.

Long hours, stress and poor sleep had left me exhausted. After a hot shower, I laid down on the bed pleasantly plastered, but I knew the next swig would mean another, and before tomorrow, the bottle would be empty. I fell asleep knowing I needed to make the bottle last. Tonight's slip would be my first since my arrival in Kuwait three weeks earlier.

The phone rang. I panicked, shook my head, rubbed my hands over my face … and lifted the receiver.

'Dad? Dad…' I heard my eldest son say.

'Jamie?'

'Yeah, Dad, it's me. Turn on the TV.'

I picked up the remote. 'What's up? How are you? I've not heard from….'

'Just turn on the TV.'

'What channel?'

'Doesn't matter…'

The TV came to life: 'What do you mean it doesn't matter? Which …'

Smoke and flames billowed from the Twin Towers.

'Is this a movie?' I said, echoing the cliché used by millions.

'It's real, Dad. It's really happening,' he said as one tower crumbled. 'Dad … Dad?'

'Yeah, Jamie … I'm still here. My God. I can't believe it.'

'I can't believe it either,' he said. 'Nobody can. I've gotta go.'

I looked at the TV still holding the silent phone to my ear. The room rippled like a dream while the screen shifted from smoke to people to planes to media to mayhem. A woman jumped. A man followed. They fell to their death from sky-scraping floors to the rubble below.

'Oh my God,' I said to an empty hotel room as I edged towards my suitcase. My teary eyes stayed fixed on the smoking Towers as I opened my case. I smelt the alcohol before I found it. My clothes reeked of vodka. I hadn't screwed the cap back on properly. The bottle was empty. Three thousand people were dead. And I didn't understand. A. Fucking. Thing.

After 9/11, the world would never be the same; the world would never forget. The Islamic Hijri calendar lay on my hotel desk: 23 Jumada II 1422.

THE WORLD ENDS

Another cold morning – cloudy, but dry. The heat of the previous four days had made gloves unnecessary. Today, I needed them. Yammie took me west on the Victoria Highway towards Kununurra. The Victoria River ran parallel with the road. I sped alongside the slow river that would feed the Joseph Bonaparte Gulf at the end of its 560-kilometre journey. Ancient red sandstone outcrops, towering escarpments, valleys and ravines, bush and scrub conjured memories of childhood movies. 'Injun country,' John Wayne would say. Except it wasn't. It was croc country. Community leaflets scattered in the Victoria Roadhouse warned in large red letters: Don't Risk Your Life – Be Crocwise. Crocodiles lurking behind boab trees replaced Apache warriors and smoke signals.

Northern Territory wildlife rangers pulled 290 crocs from their waterways last year. The biggest measured a mighty 4.38 metres. Fourteen fatal attacks had occurred in the previous ten years. Not bad for a country with the highest river densities of saltwater crocodiles in the world, and a population that spends a lot of leisure time in the water. Not a risk Don Quixote would take.

A four-wheel drive appeared trailing a caravan fifty metres ahead. The registration plate gave no doubt about the *raison d'être of the* two occupants: GR3YNOMAD. I tipped my helmet. Old people. You gotta love them. Three years ago, Maureen and I went to Brisbane to see Santana, my favourite band. Carlos had been a teenage idol. As we arrived at the theatre, I realised it was the wrong band, the wrong night, or the wrong venue. 'Damn,' I said to Maureen, 'everyone's a sexagenarian. We've come to the wrong place.' Maureen gave me that look. She told me not be so stupid.

'They all look just like you,' she said.

'Funny.'

Maureen was partly right. But sixteen-year-old me remembered the first time I saw Santana: Lyceum Ballroom in London, June 1970. And in the forty-six years that followed, many more concerts would play a major part in my shape-shifting memories. Queen and Freddie Mercury topped the list in December 1979 with a live performance at the Lewisham Odeon in South London, one of England's largest cinemas. Freddie's performance electrified the young 25-year-old who sat in awe of the musical legend. I worked at Citibank just across the street and was lucky enough to get tickets. I saw Paul McCartney and Wings in the same month. 'Let It Be' moved us all.

The Fab Four reminded me of another Beetle. The road ahead was empty. No yellow Beetle, no white daisies.

I refuelled at Timber Creek where the store overflowed with curios. A wall framed with newspaper clippings and poetry offered insight into the surrounding area and its local history: The Ngaliwurru and Nungali Aboriginal people, the Victoria River, WWII, bush commandos, explorers and pioneers, crocodile photos and local yarns. The town and its 250 people provided the only civilisation in the 385 kilometres that lay between Katherine in the Northern Territory and Kununurra in Western Australia.

I discovered a bridge, a few minutes west of Timber Creek, with stunning views of the Victoria River. The Edmund Bridge carried a wide road and a pedestrian pathway across the river with a grand approach to … nowhere. The Bridge to Nowhere ended on the far side with gates barring any thoughts of going farther, as did several signs: Do Not Enter and Do Not Touch Anything – It May Explode and Kill

You. The dark side of the Bridge to Nowhere was a military firing range. Laser Hazard and Live Bombs added to the anxiety. I did an obedient about turn and marched back across the bridge hoping to grab a few photos of crocodiles lazing on the riverbanks. Despite all the warnings, the crocs didn't show, and the hazardous military ordinance didn't detonate.

Six kilometres west, traffic trailed to a halt waiting to clear Western Australia's quarantine border checkpoint. No bananas permitted. I had two. Feeling like smokers robbed of their cigarettes before a flight, I ate both with a cup of coffee at the side of the road. Refreshed and 'clean', I joined the queue.

'Anything to declare?' said an unsmiling customs office.

'No.'

He checked my panniers anyway. Johnnie stayed quiet.

WA highlighted three things of initial consequence. One, the speed limit decreased to 110 kph. Two, my watch went backwards by another ninety minutes. Three, I had already eaten my lunch, and it was only mid-morning.

I would have to watch my speed. Since leaving Cammoweal on the Queensland/NT border, the speed limit had been 130 kph. The two thousand NT kilometres that followed had seen me dutifully comply. Most of the time. But now twenty kph had been sliced from my speeding discretion. Vigilance was necessary.

The scenery continued to enchant me. Boab trees lined the road like bottles of bloated chianti. Boughs and branches sprouted from the top of trunks, five sizes too big for their limbs. Ents from the Enchanted Forest in *Lord of the Rings*. Old wizards peered from their twisted, gnarled trunks: a crooked nose under bushy brows, a gaping mouth, a stretched limb pointing west: *Kununurra – that way*. In WA, travellers didn't dress termite mounds, instead they carved inscriptions on boabs. Chianti-bottle graffiti. *PETER & PATRICK* was followed with two male gender symbols. And *JESS LOVES JOHNNIE* was circled by a heart. I loved Johnnie too: J Walker Esquire. A love/hate relationship. My Johnnie wore a top hat, red riding coat, white breaches and black boots. A tilt of his hat and a hearty wave with a walking cane never failed to invite a thirst. Perhaps he strutted behind the mighty boulders scattered among the ents. These gargantuan boulders looked like the aftermath of a rock fight between goliaths. The rocks, like the ents, bore evidence of contemporary society needing to scribble their presence. Thirty thousand years, ago stone-age travellers inscribed rocks with stories of their world; today's world travellers told us of theirs: Ban the Bomb.

Onwards.

Two hundred and eighty kilometres into the day's journey, a road sign shook me from my reverie. Lake Argyle. It sounded interesting. I looked at my watch. A ninety-minute gain to my day said I had plenty of time. Kununarra was a further forty kilometres west. Decision made. I turned south for a thirty-five-kilometre detour to Lake Argyle. The road passed through barren beauty and ended in a watery wonderland: Lake Argyle, Western Australia's largest freshwater reservoir. the Ord River is the principal contributory. The Miriwoong and Gajjerong people called it Goonoonoorrang.

The water spread below, immense and sapphire blue, surrounded by a billion-year-old landscape. The late afternoon sun cast a red hue across this Martian panorama. Mirrored clouds hung suspended in the water like clumps of cotton wool. The dam walls, on the lake's northern boundary, spread 335 metres across the outflow to the Ord River. I could have spent the entire day looking across the lake in dreamy meditation. But the sun sank lower and it was soon time to leave. I rode back to the highway and continued to Kununurra.

An oncoming four-wheel drive flashed its lights. *Shit! Police! Speed trap!* I shut the throttle and stayed alert. Three lazy steers ambled across the highway. Thank you, 4WD.

I camped at the Lily Creek Lagoon by Kununurra Lake and the River Ord. Twenty-five bucks secured my patch of heaven. Spent but satisfied, I crashed in my tent. Yammie had taken me 5,000 kilometres across Australia. Ten thousand to go.

Sleep. Then thirteen years of nightmares attacked.

———

Australia – May 2003

I sat in my office on a tired Brisbane Tuesday morning. Dark clouds greyed my window to a city just beginning its day. Staff shuffled past in a haze of steaming coffees and *good mornings*. A normal day. Another day. But a baseless fear settled in my gut like a gathering storm scares a dog. The air stilled. Drizzle turned to rain. I felt alone in a building thick with people. And began to tremble.

My mobile rang.

'Dad!' Jamie screamed. 'Dad …' He struggled to continue. 'Mum and Dom ...' The call came from England. In the witching hour. Jamie wailed. I gripped the phone. Dominic, his younger brother, was twenty; Gabriella, his sister, still a child. They lived with Heather, my first wife. We'd divorced ten months earlier.

'Dad,' he sobbed, 'there's been a car crash …'

'Tell me!'

Jamie said nothing.

'Tell me,' I demanded.

'They're dead! Mum and Dom are dead.'

'Gabby?'

'She's unhurt,' he said. 'Gabby's okay.'

My daughter survived. Dominic and Heather had not.

'I'm coming, Jamie. I'm coming home.'

In England it was the fifth of May.

Jamie's words had smashed down the line like poisoned bullets: 'They're dead.' *Bang, Bang*! Two syllables. Two deaths. A primeval scream erupted from my throat. 'Head on,' Jamie had said. 'A truck.' Images of blood, carnage and destruction.

But Gabby had survived. Unhurt. I ran the two kilometres from my office to my apartment. Maureen was already at the door. Jamie had called Maureen too. A flight booked to London. Taxi on its way. Despair. Dread. Denial.

'I'm so sorry,' Maureen said. 'So sorry.'

'Tell me it's not true …' I said, already swigging wine to dull the pain. Like a child, I looked for hope where none existed. *'Please?'*

I had spoken to Dominic Sunday evening. A foreboding seemed to pervade my last words to him. 'Drive carefully,' I remembered saying as I hung up the phone after wishing him happy holidays. *Enjoy, take care.* Now he was dead. My twenty-year-old son gone forever.

The taxi arrived. Brisbane airport. Me. Concourse. Insane. Crowded. Alone. Bar. Check-in. Bar. Customs. Bar. Whisky. Raw. Another. Bar. Whisky. Harsh. Another. Bar. Whisky. More. Another. Bar.

'Gabby, unharmed,' I mumbled. 'Unharmed.'

A nightmare flight took me to a reality I couldn't believe. A refuelling-stop? Dubai? Whisky. A change of planes? Whisky. Seatbelts. Whisky. Another.

Shadow memories of Jamie at Heathrow. Hugs and tears. Then a dark, painful, heart-wrenching, two-hour drive to the house where I once lived, in a life not long ago.

Now Dom was dead. Heather was dead. Gabby survived. Jamie didn't take the trip. Two blessings. Two curses. In my heart I knew Dominic had died holding his mother's hand.

BLACK DAYS

The Lily Creek Lagoon at Kununurra was 105 kilometres behind me. It was a bright day, but cold. The wind smashed my bike in random gusts; a seething southerly refused to let the temperature rise. My body felt like a slab of meat but I knew the cold waiting for me at the 'bottom-end' would be far worse.

Long ride today. A pinprick on my map said Fitzroy Crossing, my goal, was 647 kilometres south-west. Strong winds buffeted Yammie in erratic bursts. My arms, neck and shoulders took the stress. I decided to stop. Doon Doon Roadhouse offered fuel, food and rest. I hoped the break might see the blustery conditions calm.

A television perched high in the corner of the roadhouse had attracted a small group of travellers like moths to light. Seven sombre people gathered around that TV – a crowd in the outback. The transmission was weak but the images of shattered people wandering in shock at a seaside resort were clear. Hysterical, numb, grim, broken. Words snaked across the bottom of the screen:

Nice, France - Bastille Day: A terrorist truck killed 84 people, including 10 children, when he crashed a truck through a crowd celebrating Bastille Day in the southern French city of Nice.

My God. Charlie Hebdo. Bataclan. Now this. I shook my head. Innocents killed by extremist fanatics. The world was exploding like volcanos on a fault line of madness. People killed and maimed. Children slaughtered. So tragic. So sad.

I left the roadhouse and walked into the outback, into another world and another time.

The wind hadn't changed, but I needed to ride. The evil of man had the power to penetrate anywhere, anytime. No-one and no place were immune. I needed to leave the carnage of Nice behind. I didn't care about the wind.

I cocked my leg over Yammie, fired her up.

We gonna make it, Richie? Yammie asked.

'Hell knows,' I said. 'Just hold on to your hat.'

And that's how it was for most of the morning.

Roadkill ahead. A wedge-tailed eagle was feeding on a wallaby. The distance between us narrowed but the eagle didn't budge. I expected it to fly from the roar of my approach. It didn't. As I sped closer, it looked me in the eye, tore off another piece of flesh, then drifted into flight. The eagle played chicken. And won. But as it lifted, a wind gust steered the eagle into my path. 'Fuck me,' I screamed. 'Service not available,' said my headset. I ducked. The wedge-tail cast a shadow as its wing tip brushed my helmet.

I spoke with a park ranger the following day. He told me motor vehicles often hit wedge-tailed eagles. The eagles were too interested in their prey, not their safety. They can weigh up to five-and-a-half kilos. I could picture the newspaper headline: 'Chicken Rider Killed by Eagle.'

My bike didn't have a fuel gauge. I found the absence of this key instrument bizarre. I mentioned it to the riders back at Midge Point. They couldn't believe it either. One guy checked my bike, 'It has to,' he said. It didn't. But I did have two trip meters. At every refuelling stop, I reset Trip 1. This meter, therefore, would display the number of kilometres covered since my last fill-up. I used Trip 2 to record the distance ridden since Coolum Beach, the start of my journey. Two hundred kilometres was about my limit before a red light warned of a fuel drought; translated, that meant three point seven litres remained in my tank – fifty kilometres. More. Or less. I filled up at every opportunity I had, but Trip 1 was God, my petrol manager.

I arrived at Halls Creek, fuelled Yammie, coffeed myself, and continued my journey.

Somewhere west of Halls Creek, the Victoria Highway became the Great Northern Highway. Both were single lane with about nine inches of red rusty earth for the hard shoulder. At 3,195 kilometres, the Great Northern Highway is Australia's longest – about five times longer than the distance from England's south coast to its northern border with Scotland. On this 'great' road frequent signs warned of upcoming hazards: Slow Down Single Lane Bridge and Be Prepared to Stop. Riding increased the risks in different ways. Motorists no longer flashed lights to warn of cattle or horses. It was futile because there were so bloody many. And if it wasn't the kangaroos or the wallabies, it was the cattle or goats, road trains or willy-willys. But the biggest risk was me. Exhaustion and vigilance didn't tango. I would need to take care.

The single lane highways were both Beauty and the Beast. The beast we know, but the beauty of the narrow road was its power to suck a rider into the essence of the outback. I hurtled past cattle close enough to run my hand down their flank. I could smell, touch, see, hear and taste Australia's beautiful, untamed wilderness. Few highways in the world possess the same raw appeal. When I stopped, the silence, emptiness and isolation of the outback was immediate. There were no edges, no boundaries – just an immense nothingness.

Fitzroy Crossing next stop: 287 kilometres west. I would need to use my jerry. Safety said I should arrive before sunset. The abundance of roadkill painted a graphic reminder of the risks, but there wasn't much I could do, except park up. And I couldn't do that. I had a long way to go.

The termite mounds changed their architecture. The structures were huge, both in height and girth. Fat, wide, undressed like Michelin men. Western Australia, it seemed, preferred their termite mounds naked.

I stopped for a coffee alongside what looked like a meteor crater. It stretched for several kilometres like a horseshoe, open on the far side. I marvelled at the beauty spread before me, sad Maureen wasn't here to share the moment. The sun began to drop. I needed to get moving.

Pockets of cattle gathered close to the road. Twos and threes. Sometimes a loner. I slowed, very aware that daylight, and my fuel, were running low. The sun nudged towards the end of day and the road pointed directly into its descent. My visor helped to shade tired eyes from the blinding light. Soon termite mounds and rock formations began to take the shape of cattle and goats. I was tense. And tired. My fuel warning light flashed.

Low clouds streaked across a cobalt and crimson sky like a beach furrowed by the tide. Dusk bruised the white cirrus underbellies a purpled peach. Creatures of the day readied for its end; creatures of the night readied for its beginning. The changeover created risk. Thirty kilometres to Fitzroy Crossing.

Exhaustion hit me hard, but I didn't want to stop. I didn't want to waste time or light to refuel from my jerry. I pushed on. The shadows played tricks, and termite mounds moved like animals. Clumps of bush morphed into cattle, ready to bolt. Long charcoaled caricatures of trees, telegraph poles, and boulders stretched grotesque shadows towards me. Tension, muscle cramp and stress weighed heavily in my arms and neck.

The smell of wood smoke meant I was close. Two wallabies skipped across the road ahead. *Fitzroy Crossing.* I scraped home with a thimble of petrol and my jerry untouched. A hidden tail wind must have given me a big push up the backside. I took the first campsite at the Fitzroy River Lodge. Yammie could get her fuel in the morning.

It was dark: campsite mutterings, clanking pots, the thump of a mallet, a hammered peg, sizzling sausages. Civilisation.

I erected my tent by torchlight. Then hunger dragged my boots back to the pub near the entrance: The Fitzroy Lodge Lounge Bar. A lively Friday night crowd thronged the interior and spilled, loud and raucous, onto the verandah. Most of its clientele were Indigenous with pay packets to spend. The chalk-boarded menu boasted the best meat pies in Oz. They were. Mine sizzled in its own earthenware bowl and shouldered a huge serve of mashed potatoes and veggies. I took my pie to the verandah where two Aboriginal men and a woman offered a seat at their table. I joined them. My dinner acquaintances were friendly and polite. One engaged me with boozy banter. I didn't understand a word. I ate my pie, nodded and shook my head, using his body language to prompt my responses. The man's wife appeared frustrated. Too often, I think I nodded *yes* when the answer should have been *no*. She began to interpret. Her husband was a ranger. I understood a little more but not much. My bad hearing impeded understanding. The dialect didn't help and after several hours of Victoria Bitter, their strong accents had gained a drunken lilt. The other guy, she said, was an artist. As I finished eating, he produced a painting with the flourish of a magician. He had kept it hidden under the table, wrapped in cloth.

The painting was bait; I was the fish.

Dots filled the canvas in ornate designs. Its beauty hid a deeper purpose and, no doubt, disguised sacred meanings I didn't understand.

'Good price,' the artist said. 'Very good price.'

'I ride a motorcycle,' I said, mimicking hands held to handlebars, my right revving an imaginary throttle. I think I added *brrooom, brrooom* for unnecessary clarity. 'No room on my motorcycle.' I put my hands in the air in surrender. 'Sorry.'

'Cheap,' he said

'Sorry,' I repeated.

His disappointment was clear. Rightly so. He took another gulp of beer. And shrugged. But he was right: it was good, and it was cheap.

The pub became rowdier with each swig. I looked at my watch: 7.45 pm. Exhaustion crept over me like the last whisky before a blackout. I needed to sleep. I held out my hand to the artist, the ranger and the wife. Good shakes. A sincere farewell.

The ranger said something as I stood to leave. I smiled and nodded. His face suggested a headshake and a grimace were more appropriate. Their collective body language was clear: *Crazy guy.*

———

Worthing, West Sussex, England 8 May 2003

Dawn, the day after …

Fog and pain. Dom was dead. Heather was dead. Gabby was alive and Jamie was distraught. Two orphaned children had been left with the ghost of a father.

My old home smiled with memories of happy families. Photos hung from walls: Christmases and birthdays, holidays and beaches, family and friends, children playing in the snow. Confused and alone, I weaved from one room to another. I was alone. I was guilty. I was a Murderer.

Gabby's bedroom did not have Gabby in it. Jamie slept on the top bunk in the bedroom he had shared with Dom. The bottom bunk was empty. The bed cried for the young man who had warmed its blankets just two days earlier.

I gently touched Jamie's shoulder.

'Where's Gabby?' I said.

'Dad?' Jamie replied, eyes red and swollen, his face still in shock.

'Where's Gabby?' I repeated.

'Dad, you passed out. She's scared. She's at Nan's.'

'Why?'

'Dad, you were drunk. Crying. Screaming. You frightened her.'

I nodded and shuffled downstairs to the lounge where a small faux bar sat secluded in a corner of the room with four spirit optics lined neatly in a row: whisky, gin, vodka and cognac. My own mini pub. A small refrigerator laboured with a sad hum. Three cans of Tennent's Super, my choice of poison, still remained in the fridge – ten months after divorce. The sun was yet to rise, but I knew, it would never rise again.

I snapped the ring off a lager and held the frothing beer to my mouth. With my other hand I held a glass against the whisky optic. The Murderer acknowledged his guilt as he numbed the pain.

Gabby needed help. Jamie needed help. Both needed love, but the Murderer could barely help himself. His daughter's horror was unimaginable. Emergency services took two hours to cut her from the car. Her brother dead behind the wheel, her mother dead in the passenger seat. Her brother's girlfriend, Jodie, to her left. She, too, survived but remained critically injured. A second to destroy Heather and Dominic; a lifetime to torment Gabby and Jodie. An off-duty nurse held Gabby's hand through the window. Two hours later, the firemen cut her free. She survived. Gabby was brave. I was not.

'Dad? No!' Jamie shouted.

Too late. The whisky disappeared in the first gulp.

And another day started as the last had finished.

MURDERER

I t was warmer today and a short ride brought me to the Fitzroy River. Its thin and reedy stream wove like a small vein through a wide, sandy bed. The Top End's dry season would starve the river; the wet season would bloat it. In four months, Northern Australia's tropical monsoon climate would unload rain that would swell the river by up to thirteen metres. Now was the time to ride. The wet season would build in October with heavy clouds, often without rain. Practice runs. The heat and humidity and the weather's unpredictability for violence was all but guaranteed in the months that followed. The floodway markers at the sides of the road were evidence of the waters that might come. The beauty and power of the wet season would be something to behold.

I left the river and rode to Geike Gorge, or Danggu, as the Bunuba people named it. The Aboriginal ranger I met at dinner the previous evening suggested a visit; or rather, his wife who acted as an interpreter did. Trails led me deep through limestone cliffs and boulders carved by rains 400 million years ago. It was once a barrier reef. The wet season would drive the Fitzroy River much higher; its abrasive floodwaters would scour the limestone walls to a chalky white. Barramundi and sawfish and freshwater crocodiles apparently abounded. The latter, I was reliably informed, are harmless unless annoyed. I left them in peace and walked along the riverbank lined with tea trees, gums and mangroves until a screeching colony of fruit bats concluded my four-kilometre hike.

A hot day. Broome lay a long ride ahead.

Kilometres ticked by like sand in an egg timer. Grain by grain. The road shimmered under the heat. Woop Woop appeared as a mirage, then evaporated as fast as it had materialised. A nowhere place. A nowhere town.

The Willare Bridge Roadhouse provided fuel and food and steel 'donga' containers for accommodation. The roadhouse had been constructed from remnants of the dismantled town of Talgarno, originally built for post-World War II British soldiers. Talgarno had been a tracking station for the Blue Streak Missile Project near Willare. It closed in 1960. In the dry cattle grasslands, it's just as likely you'll find a rocket fragment as a fossil.

Broome was 185 kilometres north-west. I arrived after sunset and took the first campsite I found eight kilometres outside town. My tent sprung to life under torchlight, but a supporting wishbone fractured. Bugger. My $49 tent would need replacing. I'd need to find a camp store on Monday and buy another.

My tent light cast a yellowed canvas around the silhouette of an old man writing his journal. I left Maureen sixteen days ago in Coolum on the east coast of Queensland on the Coral Sea. Tonight, 6,000 kilometres later, I had reached the west coast of Western Australia and a gem on the Indian Ocean: the old pearling town of Broome.

––––––

Worthing, West Sussex, England 9 May 2003

'They're dead, Dad,' Jamie shouted into my nightmare. His hand rocked my shoulder. 'Dad?'

I woke to stark reality, emerging from under the bed covers that kept the bedroom as dark as my heart. Jamie's face folded into sadness and tears.

'Dad,' he said, 'it can't be, it can't.'

I pulled Jamie close, my breath heavy with alcohol, and hugged him tight. Two men destroyed by grief.

'Where's Gabby?'

'At Nan's,' Jamie said. 'Dad, she's in shock. She's scared.'

'Let's go.'

Jamie drove the five-minute drive to my mother-in-law's. Gabby sat on the settee. A ten-year-old child cloaked in sadness. Raw grief stabbed my heart as I held my daughter. Jamie put his arms around both us. Time stopped. Tears fell. Grief sucked air from our lungs and memories from our hearts. Smiles of a twenty-year-old, a loving smile from a proud mother, laughter from a time gone forever. A family wrecked. My ex-mother-in-law had lost her only daughter. My father-in-law hung his head low. Never speaking. Never raising his eyes. He couldn't look at the Murderer.

'Gabby should stay here with us,' said my mother-in-law.

'She's coming with me.' And the three of us left. Jamie drove back to our house: a family farmhouse, at the foot of the South Downs, and a home that once bubbled with laughter.

We opened the door and stepped into our private worlds of despair. I did my best but 'best' never rose above worst. Gabby's strength shone the way.

Days passed. Whispers. Phone calls. People. Shadows. Condolences. Police. Coroners. Undertakers. Newspaper headlines: 'Horror Crash Kills Mother and Son.' And tears. Always tears.

Twenty days disappeared in a river of sadness gushing headlong towards a day no-one wanted to see. The Funeral. Men and women from three fire crews were in attendance – the two who had rescued Gabby, and the third, Dominic's co-workers from his job as a part-time fireman. They formed an honour guard of respect for Dominic, for Heather, for their family: grandmother and grandfather, father and mother, friends and football mates, uncles and aunts, cousins and friends, brother and sister. The Murderer too.

I shuffled down the aisle of the crematorium. Jamie on my left arm,

Gabby on my right. Two coffins lay together, shoulder to shoulder. A sad and sombre service added lead to our loss.

'We are gathered here today …'

A short sermon.

A touching eulogy from Dom's best mate.

A final prayer.

A pause.

Then heads hung lower until a conveyor belt hummed to life and carried two coffins towards the fire that would burn Dominic and Heather into angels. Robbie Williams sang Dominic's favourite song. Scattered sobs echoed around the chapel as two lives disappeared behind velvet curtains.

The three of us left first. I put my arms around Gabby and Jamie, hugged them tight, then we shuffled through the crowded congregation. So alone, so together. We stepped out in bright sunlight, our loves behind us forever. Grief opened his arms and we cried into his robes. Grief was here to stay. For now, for a long time, for eternity.

I cried for Dominic, for Heather, for Jamie, for Gabby, for myself. The sun shone the next day, bright, but never right. It would never be right. Each day bled into another. Each night was a fog of whisky and sadness. Sleep rarely came, but lying in my bed, Robbie's voice did: rising, falling, thoughts ran through my head, echoes from the chapel, love was dead; 'Angels,' the minister had said.

Three weeks later we all left for Australia. Maureen would be our salvation.

IF

A warm Sunday morning and a gentle ride brought me to Broome's town centre. And a 'village' cricket green. Rural England alongside the Indian Ocean. *Craaack* – the unmistakable sound of willow striking ball – followed by blurred whites, muffled shouts and scattered clapping. One minute of calm until the bowler ran with purpose to make another delivery. *Craaack*. Rural England dissolved as the ball headed in the direction of the mangrove-peppered Dampier Creek.

The glorious Sunday afternoon beckoned locals and visitors to the beach, to the cafes, to the Mangrove Hotel. I was drawn to Pearl Luggers Museum. Restored wooden pearl luggers spoke of a history driven by adventurers. They had hoped to find overnight fortunes reaping the aragonite and conchiolin secretions of oysters. Pearls drove a 'gold' rush. A wild frontier town followed. Dreams of fortune brought immigrants: Chinese, Japanese, Malay, Filipino, Javanese and Pacific Islander. Dark times, too. By the late 1800s, America and Britain had abolished slavery. But here in Broome it had been rife. Indigenous men, women and children brutally enslaved and forced to dive for pearls. Hundreds died in the depths of Roebuck Bay. Artefacts and exhibits lay in the museum's backyard, a pearl shop too. Broome had been a wild frontier town: gambling houses, opium dens, brothels, slavery, profanity, drunken nights and brutal murders.

Craaack. Willow hit ball.

Fish and chips at the Mangrove Hotel returned me to civilisation.

All too soon the day ended, and an early night begun. I wrote in my journal. I thought about freedom. And pearls. I thought about the outback. And eagles. I thought about '*IF.*' And 'keeping my head.' I thought about Dominic. And tattoos.

———

My dad had not been a disciplinarian. He had not been one to dictate rules and boundaries. Dad had not been one to express his love. Quiet and introspective, but unpredictably explosive, he alone had managed Mum's alcoholism. Alone, my Dad bore much pain that only now, as a man older than he was at the time, could I understand. At fourteen, drinking was a lark for me. A rite of passage. A rebel's right. But my mutiny remained unquelled, maybe because I did well at school, at sport, at most things. Everything except the things that mattered. My achievements blinded my parents to my many failures. But one day, Dad gave me a poem the morning after a bunch of mates had dragged me home the night before, drunk as a skunk. I was sixteen. My Dad didn't read much, mostly the racing form, and he never spoke of poetry. 'Read this,' Dad said with disappointment and sadness as he handed me a poem written by Rudyard Kipling. 'It's called *If*. You'll do well to remember it.'

I did remember it. But I didn't learn. I failed Maureen, Jamie, Dominic, Gabby and Heather. My family. My friends. My employer. And myself. No-one deserved the toxic damage from alcoholic fallout. But Maureen gave me a chance. A new love, and another life. Too late to change yesterday's history, too soon to think of tomorrow's mystery, never too late to thank today for its gift. But it was Dad's poem, Rudyard Kipling's poem, that underscored all the strengths my weaknesses sought to aspire. Despite this, my compass held its course: self-destruction. IF only …

———

Dom was *Mr Cool.* He was *Dom the Don* – not my description, but the description of his admiring army. *Mr Handsome.*

'What do you think?' Dom said, flexing a tanned, muscled bicep.

A blue tribal tattoo curled ornately over his upper arm, still glowing from the grease protecting the ink that had scarred his formerly virgin skin just two hours earlier.

'Jesus!' I said, shocked. 'You're just nineteen. Why didn't we discuss it?'

'Cool, eh?' he said.

'Dom?'

'Dad, you would never have approved anyway.'

'That's not the point.'

'But don't you think it's cool?' he said with a smile he knew would charm. Testosterone and young men.

'Dad, it's not like in your day. It's different now.'

'How so?'

'It just is.'

It just is. And with these three words, he meant to explain the ideology of teens who were men. The philosophy of the young. The realism of youth. *It. Just. Is.*

'It just is?' I said in frustration.

He grinned, disarming, taunting. 'Warriors,' he said.

'Warriors?'

'Just joking.'

He smiled again, 'I thought you were a rebel too.'

Rebel, I thought. Once, in a land far away, in a time long ago, we were all rebels.

'I was.'

'Then get one yourself,' Dom said.

'Too old.'

We often fought. Not in anger, but in spirited father/son competition. We wrestled. Hard. From when he was fourteen or so, we'd arm wrestle or roll on the floor grappling for a killer hold until the loser submitted. Often the battle would be intense, but I had the weight and the strength, and I won. Until he was seventeen. At seventeen, I conceded more than I won. At eighteen, I gave up.

'Yeah, I guess you're right. Over the hill,' Dom said, his smile even wider.

I smiled too. 'Let's go,' I said.

'Arm wrestle?'

'Tattoo parlour!'

'You're kidding,'

'Let's go,' I repeated.

'Nah ...' he said horrified. 'Not a good idea.'

'Let's do it.'

And we did.

Four hours later a bald eagle perched proudly on my upper arm: white head, yellow beak, blue feathers. The artist got carried away and added a blazing crimson sun against a backdrop of blue pine trees.

'Cool,' Dom said.

Ten months later he was dead.

And I was to blame. On that day, in that moment, Dom lost focus. And control of the car he drove.

IF... I had been a better father, IF... I had been more disciplined, IF... I had taught responsibility, IF... I had been there, IF... I had not tempted fate, IF... I had given him a poem. Then his would be the Earth, and everything that's in it. And – what's more – I would have been a father, my son.

BAGZY

Dawn had yet to break but strange sounds rapped my tent. Pecking. Scratching. Pecking. *Tat, tat, tat, tat.* Bewildered, I crawled to the zipper and opened the flap. A fluffy chicken eyeballed me from a mess of white feathers. A Mexican stand-off ensued until I stood down and shrank back into my tent. The chicken eyed me menacingly while its gang of six hustled behind their leader's shoulder. The chicken didn't speak. 'Okay, take it easy,' I said. I knew what they wanted. My eyes held the chicken while my right arm fumbled in the rear of my tent, trying to find the remains of yesterday's bread roll. My nervous fingers rubbed the roll into crumbs before throwing them at my attackers. The chicken's blood-red comb wobbled as it turned, eager to join its gang and the crumbs, but not before it threw a contemptuous look over its shoulder.

The caravan park owner told me later she had bred these silkies. They were her babies. I shared my embarrassing vision of the local newspaper headlines: 'Outback Rider Held Hostage by Chicken Gang.' She laughed, but I knew she knew. Crazy guy.

The fracture in my tent wishbone needed attention. I didn't want to end up in the middle of nowhere with a duff tent. I took a short ride to a camping shop in Broome.

'A new wishbone will take about two weeks to get delivered,' the guy said.

'Forget it. I'll take a new one.'

I walked out of the store with a fifty-nine dollar tent.

Today I would head for Port Hedland, but it would be a late departure.

Fifty kilometres south of Broome, a huge herd of cattle kicked up thick clouds of dust about a kilometre from the road. I stopped, a long distance from the action, but grabbed my camera anyway. Aboriginal drovers corralled between 200 and 300 steers to drive them to muster. Two of them stood by a ute near the road. They saw my excitement.

'You wanna get closer?' one said.

'Sure,' I said surprised.

'Hop in,' said the other. And he started up the ute.

They took me to within twenty metres of the herd. Aboriginal riders worked the cattle. A bullwhip cracked like lightning among the bellowing steers. A horse reared with flaring nostrils and a wild whinny. Its laughing rider took minutes to rein in his mount. But not for a second did he doubt himself. I took my shots and captured the moment.

'Thanks,' I said.

'Pete,' said my driver, by way of introduction.

'Richard.' I held out my hand. 'It's a beautiful thing.'

'It is man, it is,' he said, as he squeezed my hand in a vice, 'but I love your bike. Wanna trade?'

We both laughed.

I continued south. Eighty Mile Beach and the Indian Ocean spread to my west and the Great Sandy Desert – 285,000 square kilometres of nothing – spread to my east. The GPS in my helmet spoke, 'Continue on this route for 645 kilometres and then make a right turn. The destination is on your left.'

Sandfire Roadhouse sat a daunting 297 kilometres south. I wouldn't make it.

Two hundred and sixty kilometres later, I pulled over to refuel Yammie from the five-litre jerry strapped behind me. Thirty metres ahead, a shrine had been erected by the road. I took a look. *BAGZY* read the words on the simple, white wooden cross. Bleached seashells surrounded the base, and inside this circle was an assortment of beer bottles and cans. A lump rose in my throat. This was a straight road. Straight, straight, straight as far as the eye could see, but already two dead cattle and a handful of roos had made my roadkill count for the day. Roos made a straight road dangerous. Mates must have made a pilgrimage to this spot where I assumed Bagsy had died. The bottles and cans were full. Perhaps an offering on a final journey. Maybe something that Bagsy would have wished to take with him. I mounted Yammie a little choked and continued south.

Sandfire Roadhouse had a museum in its backyard. Many roadhouses I'd encountered on the road offered glimpses of local history. Sandfire exhibited press clippings of the damage caused by Cyclone Lawrence. In 2009, it smashed Eighty Mile Beach with 280 kph winds. I filled Yammie and ordered a 'Ned Kelly': a meat pie with bacon and an egg in the middle. An Irish lady took my money. Early sixties. My age.

'So, whereabouts in Ireland you from?' I asked.

'Belfast. Ever been there?'

'Yes,' I said, surprising her. 'I was there in the early eighties. Just for a few days. I found the checkpoints and soldiers depressing.'

'Yeah,' she said, 'it was.' With a grim face she continued, 'The Troubles brought soldiers. And soldiers brought roadblocks. Security was a huge issue. The soldiers often stopped us. Once in our Fiat 850, they ordered us to open the bonnet. The sergeant looked shocked. "Shit," he said. "Someone's stolen your engine."' The woman threw a theatrical sigh. '"Yes," we told him, "but we've got a spare in the boot."'

I laughed.

A truckie ate lunch outside. I took my Ned Kelly and joined him. Blue eyes shone from a weathered face parked behind a Gandalf beard. I wanted to ask a personal question but felt it failed the political correctness of the day. A bit like asking someone with an accent where they were from, but I meant no harm. I did anyway.

'How many Ks do *you* do in a day?' I said.

'About eleven hundred kilometres.'

'Wow! Over what time frame?'

'The legal limit is seventeen hours, but my company sets a limit of fifteen hours.'

'How do they keep track?'

'Mate,' he said, 'if we put a foot wrong, they know about it. Our cab systems tell the boss boys if we don't take our breaks. The systems tell them everything. Mate, our vehicles even dob us in if we so much as stray across white lines. And if you fart…'

'Me too.'

'You?' he said. 'Ain't you on the bike?'

'Yeah, but my wife has given me a tracker. Tells her where I am every minute of the day. My limits are six hundred and fifty kilometres or seven hours, whichever comes first.'

The truckie looked incredulous. 'What happens if you go over the limit?'

I ran my finger slowly across my throat.

'Then youse better do what the boss lady wants,' he said.

Sandfire sat in the desert 170 kilometres behind me. The sun, now amber beneath the horizon, cast the bush in a glow as comforting as a campfire. Pardoo Roadhouse shimmered ahead, its neon lights flashing red and white like the welcome of a chequered flag at the end of a Grand Prix. Port Hedland lay on the ocean 130 kilometres farther south. Too far. Too risky. Yammie refused to go further. Pardoo it would be. I struck a deal for a donga: a partitioned steel shipping container – true luxury with a proper bed, and no chicken gangs.

BROTHERS-IN-ARMS

The outback dawn prepared to explode. Orange fire spread across the horizon. Pardoo Roadhouse was ghost-town quiet which offered a special time to walk and reflect. I found a trail that skirted the bush behind the roadhouse where a fenced paddock imprisoned a wrecked bus. It had been charred by fire, brightened by graffiti and battered by weather. The decaying hulk looked like an offering to the outback. An eagle perched on its roof eyeing my approach. I came too close and he didn't like what he saw. He rose to meet the sunrise with a single flap of his magnificent wings.

The food in the roadhouse was good. Very good. The night before I'd dug into homemade pumpkin soup followed by salt-and-pepper calamari. Two Indian men and a Brazilian woman managed the Pardoo Roadhouse. For breakfast I had homemade meat pie washed down with black coffee. Port Hedland waited across the desert, 122 kilometres south.

But I still lost weight. My belt had broken that morning as I tried to hitch it up another notch. I would need to buy another.

Port Hedland arrived before noon.

'What can we do for you today? The woman asked as I tripped through the door of the shop with my trousers around my ankles.

'A belt for starters.'

I had the purchase sewn up in minutes and walked out of the store with my head high and my trousers tight around my waist. I rode to the docks to view the tankers from faraway places. The sky remained cloudless as I headed towards Karratha.

A rest stop 100 kilometres farther south afforded another coffee to ensure I revived and survived. I sat alone at a shaded picnic table. Coffee steamed from my flask. A man of age – weren't they all? – watched from under his caravan awning until he couldn't contain himself any longer. He ambled over to my table. A predictable conversation-opener followed.

'G'day. Where you headed?'

'South,' I said. I gave him the full nine yards.

'Why sixty-two days?' he asked.

'Because I'm sixty-two and it seemed like a good number,'

'Yeah, well, I'm seventy. And reckon I might make eighty.'

Not sure how to respond, I said, 'And where you headed?'

'Fuck knows,' he said.

'Uh, uh…' seemed a safe answer.

'Don't know what the fuck I'm looking for, but I reckon I got ten years left to find it.'

'Sure,' I said, not really sure of anything but certain it was time to leave. 'Okay. Gotta fly. Good luck. Hope you find what you're looking for,' I said.

'You too.'

I threw him a wave and whispered my Na'vi allegiance, 'I see you.'

Yesterday I didn't make Port Hedland. Today I was tiring and wouldn't make Karratha. I stopped at the next town. Roebourne. The campsite lay on the eastern bank of the Harding River. On the western side, a small octagonal stone-walled gaol glowed peacefully in the late afternoon light. My map labelled the prison as a tourist centre. In 1900, three Aboriginal men were hanged there for the murder of a local doctor – a triple execution to mark the end of a dark century and the start of another.

I sat in my tent later that evening and looked at the gaol across the river. I held a cup of instant noodles in one hand and forked up steaming pasta with the other. Dark now, the gaol hid its sins in the shadows. One hundred and sixteen years ago… yesterday.

––––––

London, England circa 1996.

A mandatory health check with Citibank's doctor identified glaring problems no-one had ever seemed game to share. The elderly doctor diagnosed what I knew, and what I didn't. Alcoholism and depression. A psychiatrist confirmed it. Both recommended rehab, insisted actually. No other avenues were open to me. Refusal would likely result in a dismissal letter that began, 'It is with deep regret …' I needed to stop drinking.

The day before check-in, I left work, and ambled to London Bridge Station. Numb best described how I felt. Emotionless. Neither happy nor sad. I was a shell functioning on autopilot coded with a flight path to disaster. Somehow my job had stayed intact albeit frayed at the edges.

That night I drank at the railway station for an hour before I caught my train. Pleasantly plastered, I sauntered to the platform to take the two-hour journey to Worthing. As I opened the door of the carriage, I think I said something like, 'Fuck it,' before slamming the door and walking back to the bar on the platform. My seat was still warm. I took it and consumed as much as I could in as little time as I could. Not a minute to waste. I left, barely able to stand, and must have made it to a supermarket where I bought six cans of Tennent's Super. My kinda beer. At nine per cent ABV, it was a wicked brew. *How do I remember this*? Because I found an empty can and a receipt in my briefcase the next day. I was found slumped in the sleep of drunks at the end of the line. My first wife, Heather, was called to come and pick up this sorry-arsed bum – a disgraceful husband, a shameful father, a Murderer.

Next day, hangover still intact and a small suitcase in hand, I boarded the train back to London for rehab. The reception desk was discreet. A nurse escorted me along an empty corridor to my room where I would sign the forms granting a travel visa into a brave new world of abstinence. Huxley's words hit hard: *I am I, and wish I wasn't.*

I put my suitcase on the single bed and jumped as the nurse reached over to rifle the contents.

'We have to check,' she said with strength and sympathy.

'Check?'

'Just to make sure you have no alcohol.'

I waited. And watched. Humiliated but clean.

This was where I spent the next six weeks. I loved it. No doubt the first week of withdrawal had been tough, although much easier for me than most of the other inmates. But the sense of security eclipsed all else. I met others who felt the same. The enemy lurked outside the walls. Inside we were safe. The inmates were a strange slice of society: rich and poor, male and female, straight and gay, blue collar and black pinstripe, religious and atheist, HIV positive and negative. It was boot camp for my fellow alcoholics and other animals. Lectures, meetings, guest speakers, group discussion. The clinic was a re-education centre, where days merged from one classroom to the next. A sixth form college for addicts, all working towards their Abstention Certificate. There was coffee, cigarettes, and a mountain of chocolate. I didn't smoke but we all consumed our alternative addictions in a kitchen cloudier than a London smog and, despite the high risk of lung cancer, I began to feel better.

Rehab was a circus for outrageous extremists. Introvert or extrovert, we got where we were because of extreme behaviours. I drove my path to sobriety by leveraging my extremist traits. Nothing I did was done in moderation. Everything I did was done in excess. I don't have a middle name, but if I did, it should have been XS. I figured that the same extreme behaviour that got me here was gonna be exactly the same extreme behaviour that was gonna get me out. And stay out. Counsellors and group talk helped us see all the light we couldn't see, or refused to see. We laughed together. We cried together.

We made friends. We made enemies. We fought. We made peace. And some made love.

My first group counselling session half-mooned around Nurse Hatchett. This mixed group of sorry-arsed students of sobriety looked like they would rather be playing in a schoolyard. All of them stared at the floor, out the window, or looked at the ceiling. Except Dotty. And me.

'Who would like to go first?' said Nurse Hatchett as she beamed a slow smile around her flock. She lingered as she looked into our eyes, willing us to speak, to share, to confess to unspeakable thoughts and naked emotions.

The group studied its feet.

'William, what about you?'

Silence. Hatchett's sharp eyes swept the half circle like searchlights looking for rabbits.

'Henry?'

Henry intensified his examination of liver-spotted hands, long dead in his lap.

'Dotty?'

The sixty-year-old London cockney believed her cure still awaited discovery. She had arrived two days before me. Dotty didn't pull punches: 'There ain't nuffin gonna beat a fag in me left hand, a gin in me right, and a bloke between me bloody legs.'

The group nodded in silent assent: *Dotty's addictions would be tough to beat.*

Dotty stared at Nurse Hatchett, at all of us, daring anyone to battle.

Nurse Hatchett declined with a slow smile and a raised eyebrow. Then she looked at me.

'Richard?' she said sweetly, 'You're new too. Welcome. What do you think?'

'Interesting …' I said before gushing into a ten-minute torrent of gibberish punctuated with nothing but a drowning man's gasps for air. I made no sense. To me. Or anyone else.

'Thank you so much for sharing,' said Nurse Hatchett.

Abstention? That's what we voted for, but we were politicians who campaigned on truth but delivered in lies. Promises? Guarantees? *Fugheddaboudit*!

A few days into the program, I discovered another inmate who, like me, worked for Citibank. He was a vice-president, also like me, except he worked in the prestigious investment bank. We didn't know each other before admission, and now we became part of the same small world, made smaller by addiction. Cocaine was his habit, alcohol an afterthought. Together we built relationships; we built bonds; we moved forward as a team; we were a fighting unit battling a common enemy. We had the same goal: survival.

I became obsessed with the addiction of abstention. I would listen to the stories of others and accept their honesty. Often bizarre and mostly insane, they had the same themes as mine – 'unique' replicas. I spoke truthfully about drinking for the first time, and that truth became the foundation for other truths. Truth bombs exploded like artillery shells. 'Sodium pentothal,' said one inmate, 'you know they put it in our coffee.'

We shared: our stories, our dreams, our worst nightmares, our heaven, our hell. We learned to walk naked in shopping malls. That's what it felt like – nowhere to hide. But you always knew you could walk down the stairs, out the door and onto the street a free man, anytime. A pub sat across the road, tempting sin. *Come in and see me some time*. Some did. But most stuck it out. And the bond grew. At least I thought it did. *Semper Fidelis*. Comrades. Brothers-in-arms. Ours not to reason why, ours but to do and die, into the valley of death rode the alcoholics, vodka to the right of them, whisky to the left of them, cocaine in the front of them … if only. At the outset we were told to look at the person on our left and the person to our right. We looked. 'Now hear this, now hear this,' said one counsellor parodying a military announcement:

'Two out of three sitting here today will enter rehab again,' he said.

'What?' I screamed from deep within my disbelieving body. 'No fucking way.'

Two weeks later, the vice-president from the prestigious investment bank disappeared. AWOL. He crashed and burnt in the hotel across the street; worse still, he took another inmate with him. She ditched her platoon too. Both ended up in bed smashed on cocaine and booze. I felt wounded. Traitors all. Fucking deserters. How naïve was I? Little did I know that four months later, I would also become a defector. Two out of three. We were pussies.

THIRTY DAYS TO DIE

Kilos slid from my body like water from an ice block in the sun. My hollowed-out cheeks and diminishing belt holes were proof. Muscle cramps attacked anytime, anywhere. Stomach muscles during the day. Hamstrings at night. I controlled the former with tyre-screeching stops and a burst of strained stretches. The latter, well, the latter was another thing entirely. Hamstring cramps attacked in the dead of night with the shock of a mortar strike. A particularly vicious assault exploded in the wee hours of a calm and unsuspecting Roebourne campsite. My hamstring snapped tight like a line that just hooked a marlin. I sprang upright, screamed, forgot I slept in a tent, smacked my head on the roof strut, fought an unseen ninja, and rolled screaming in my sleeping bag like a lunatic in a sack race to hell. I kicked the ninja's arse but not before my death struggle moved my tent two metres to the east. As quiet once more settled on the campers of the Roebourne caravan site, the curtains of an adjacent caravan fluttered. A white-haired couple peeked out in panic. *Crazy guy.* No doubt they checked *DunRoamin's* locks before venturing back to sleep after resolving to move to a safer site first thing in the morning. I didn't sleep well. When I woke, my elderly neighbours had pulled stumps and moved on. *DunRoamin* had hit the road in a dawn escape.

In the preceding two days, exhaustion stopped me from reaching my chosen destination. Today, I would ride on the North West Coastal Highway. My goal was Carnarvon, 670 kilometres south-west. My longest ride to date, and this time, I hoped, not a town too far.

The weather squeezed my mood and sapped my strength. Clouds spread ominously from the south, the first since Victoria River. Exhausted and filled with doubt, I questioned my twenty days: a clean sheet and no major problems. But my inner pessimist said this was the lull before the shitstorm. The fat lady still waited to sing.

Hazy escarpments rose in the distance, blurred by rain. Clouds were moving across my route, but not towards me. The highway cut between the escarpments like a chisel blade through old wood. I rode through without hitting a single raindrop. The far side of the escarpments opened to clear blue skies and a Martian landscape. Red sand rippled into rifts and drifted into an infinite desert horizon. Two hundred and eighty-five thousand square kilometres of it. Western Australia's Great Sandy Desert.

My mobile phone sat in a holder bolted to my handlebars. Networks were rare. Particularly between towns. Music tracks flitted across the screen as I fiddled my Bluetooth helmet selector and flicked to my music of choice. iTunes had a wild array of genres, most of which I didn't understand, but my choice of music had always been clear. I had two preferred two genres: the one I liked and the one I didn't. Tracks from *Peaky Blinders* blared through my helmet speakers. Nick Cave spat his words with venomous vigour: 'red right hands' and 'black coats' and 'gathering storms'. I opened the throttle. 'In the border fires, in the humming wires ...' And road works.

A ghost in fluorescent jacket jumped onto the road. In his right hand, dusted in red sand, was a STOP sign; he thrust it into my path like a pike. I sat on my steed, helmet tilted down ready to charge. He brandished his pike, demanding acquiescence. Yammie sped her rear tyre, but the man stood his ground.

'Mate, you got a wait of about fifteen-to-twenty minutes,' he said with an English accent.

'Bugger.'

I dismounted and approached his pike. He lowered it with magnanimous chivalry.

'So, where you from?' I asked.

'Southampton,' he said in an English accent. 'That's in ...'

'I know where it is. I lived twenty miles away. What you doing here?' I asked.

'Widening the road,' he said. 'Seven metres to twelve.'

'Right-O.'

Ten minutes later, another vehicle pulled up behind me. A converted bus towing a small Suzuki Vitara. *Nullarbor Warrior* was writ large across the vehicle. The driver jumped out. He had a shaved head, rolling jowls and a frog mouth. Five feet tall and five feet wide. He stretched out a browned, hairless arm with a pudgy hand anxious to grab mine.

'Jaffa,' he said.

'Jabba?'

'Jaffa,' he said more loudly. 'Jeffrey. Everyone calls me Jaffa.'

'Right,' I said. 'Richard. Everyone calls me Rich.'

Our hands met, and we both reached for the STOP-GO man.

'Malcolm,' he said as we shook his hand. 'Everyone calls me Pom.'

And now, like all men in the world, we spoke about footy, weather, petrol prices and road works. Two hundred kilometres of the latter lay ahead, Pom told us.

Deep in conversation, unaware we stood in the middle of a red desert planet, Pom's two-way radio buzzed, interrupting our discussion. Pom listened. Then nodded.

'Good to go in a few minutes,' he said with a smile.

We shook hands, said our goodbyes and 'saddled-up'.

'So long,' I said, opening the throttle as my wheels spat out a plume of red sand.

———

Worthing, England 1989

Mum told me Dad would sit me on his motorcycle tank and take me places. She said I was three. 'Your dad was crazy,' she said. 'Crazy.' No helmets, no regard for risk, just the joy of the moment. And me, just a baby. Today, the cops would lock Dad up and throw the key away. I don't remember the tank rides, but I do remember the little guy that had gotten bigger and progressed to pillion. Dad loved the horses when he could afford it, which was never. We rode to the horse races on his Triumph, just Dad and me. I'm not sure how old I was, maybe five. On this particular day, I must have been getting tired because I remembered Dad stopping that old bike somewhere in the English countryside. It was a summer's day. He had found an open field beside a copse of beeches and bluebells. We lay down in the grass and I slept. I remember the warm afternoon, the breeze, the grass, and the smell of my Dad's sweat.

Fast forward a quarter of a century to my office in Riyadh, the capital of Saudi Arabia. After a telephone call with Mum, I discovered Dad was in hospital with stomach pain. This wasn't a surprise. He had had problems for some months, but like many men of his time refused to go to the doctor. Now in acute agony, he had been in hospital for nearly a week. Without diagnosis. Mum was frantic. I ended her tearful call and telephoned the hospital in Worthing. I needed to speak to someone in charge.

'We're still not exactly sure what the problem is ...' the doctor said. 'We're still conducting tests.'

'But what do you think it is?' I persisted.

'As I said we're not exactly ...'

'Damn it,' I said. 'I live in Saudi Arabia, my mum is losing it, my dad is in pain, just tell me what your experience suggests.'

'Cancer,' he said. 'We'll know more in a few days.'

I took a flight to London that night.

The next day I met the consulting surgeon without my mother.

'It *is* cancer,' he said. 'And I'm sorry, it's inoperable.'

I couldn't breathe. I sucked in air. 'Inoperable?'

'I'm sorry.'

'How long?'

'It's difficult to say … we're not sure … we…'

'As a surgeon you see this every day. Please, just tell me. How long?'

'Thirty days. Maybe a little more, maybe less.'

'Thirty days! Jesus. Does he know?'

'We thought it would be best if you tell him. It's better coming from family.'

'Shit,' was all I could say as the tears rolled down my cheeks.

Dad lay in a hospital bed cocooned in white sheets. He looked dreamy, distant. In a regulation inmates' gown, he resembled a concentration camp victim, swathed in a semi-white sack. *So quick. So, fucking quick,* I thought.

'Hey, Dad,' I said, shocked at how much weight he had lost. I squeezed a faint smile onto my horrified mouth. 'How you feeling?'

'Okay. You?'

'Good.'

'How was your trip over?'

'Long … look, Dad … I don't …' I stuttered and my eyes teared up.

'Just tell me how bad,' he said. 'It's okay.'

'Dad, I don't know how to break it any other way. It's cancer. And it's terminal.'

Dad swallowed, nodded, and took a deep breath. 'How long?'

I opened my mouth, looking for brave words I couldn't find …

'How long, Rich?'

'Thirty days,' I said. The words smashed him like a volley of cannonballs.

We looked at each other. Then he hugged me, just for a minute.

'Okay, okay …' he said. 'No use us getting all worked up. That's how it is. Now I want you do something for me. Today. Right now.'

'Tell me.'

'Put a fiver on Ghost Rider. Two o'clock at Sandown. To win.'

My expression froze. My mouth tight as a clam.

'To win! Okay? To win,' he said.

An each-way bet had never been Dad's style.

'You'll have to be quick. Better go now,' he said. 'And just a fiver.'

Dad nudged me with a gentle punch to my shoulder.

I stood and looked into his face … seconds slowed. Dad snapped his fingers like a hypnotist demanding a return to reality.

'Okay, I'm on it,' I said turning towards the stairs that would take me to the crowded street below where no-one knew my dad was dying.

'Oh …' said my dad to my retreating back, 'and don't tell Mum.'

'About the thirty days?' I asked.

'No, the bloody fiver.'

I drove to the nearest betting shop and placed Dad's bet. Fiver for him and fifty quid for me. The surreal moment seemed like an omen. Dad gambled with religious fervour. Horse racing was his life. I hoped in imminent death he would win. Fifty pounds from my own pocket cemented my belief in his faith.

'And they're off …' The radio static cackled against the commentator's drone, rising and falling as the horses clambered over the hurdles, excitement as a new leader hit the front, sadness as another filly fell at the fence. Up and down. Up and down. In the anonymity and safety of a smoke-filled betting shop, I was just another faceless punter. The commentator's words blurred into a single, breathless stream: *anastheycomeintothefinalfurlongits NeverSayDieanosein-frontofDeadCertaaaaannd* … Never Say Die has it.' Dad's horse didn't get a mention until after the race ended, '… and bringing up the rear by *three* lengths is Ghost Rider.' It sounded like a eulogy. Dad's horses always came last.

———

The day darkened with cloud and time.

I pulled into a roadhouse to refuel 130 kilometres from Carnarvon. A meat pie and a carton of milk satisfied my hunger. I thought about staying. Each day brought less strength. A Welsh girl served me in a singsong, get-along voice. I pushed on.

The evening cooled; the weather signalled rain.

I made it. Six hundred and seventy kilometres. My tent almost erected itself at the first campsite. Numb automation now enabled me to pitch my tent in darkness. When complete, I'd scratch my head. *How did I do it*? It's like finding yourself in your kitchen with a steaming mug of coffee, dressed in underpants, not remembering even entering the room, let alone who made the cuppa.

I wrote in my journal as the rain arrived. And a text followed:

Melanie: *CALL ME*. The time stamp read 2:54 pm. Another followed in seconds: *URGENT*. 4.49 pm.

The sun had long gone. I sat in the darkness of my tent. Two missed messages, two hours apart, two hours ago.

BIG C

The day exploded over my tent in an orange blaze bloodied with cottonwool clouds, but the sun did little to ease the cold still lingering from the night before.

I had sent two texts and made four calls the previous evening. Two more this morning. None were answered. The yellow Beetle had a day's lead on me. Melanie left me at the bottom of the Victoria River escarpments nine days ago. Her daisy had bobbed on the dashboard as she waved farewell. She had headed for Kununurra. Two-and-a-half thousand kilometres in the past. I had ridden out of the Victoria River Roadhouse eight days earlier, one day after Melanie. Either I had overtaken her, which was more likely, or she was still ahead. My ride from Victoria River didn't shed any clues: no accidents, blown tyres, breakdowns, police, ambulances or Beetles.

I interpreted *CALL ME* and *URGENT* as though Melanie were behind me. If correct, it would be better to wait. I called again. No answer. If I didn't receive a reply by tomorrow, I would let the police decide what to do. A woman alone in the outback, maybe in trouble was cause for concern. The best scenario would be the cops proved me a fool. The worst didn't bear thinking about. Twenty-four hours.

The morning turned, and the thermometer headed south in sympathy. I thought about the next leg of my ride: Augusta lay 1,200 kilometres on the most south-westerly tip of Australia. I guessed that would be another three-or-four-day ride. After Augusta, I would turn east – homeward bound. Then the cold would become severe. But more pressing problems took the form of a front tyre that was looking like a bald head after a fresh shave. I needed a new one. Fast. Perth would be ideal. New tyre, oil change, air filters and a general check-up. I had twenty-four hours to kill.

I rode to One Mile Jetty, six kilometres away. The 120-year-old jetty poked a wooden finger one-and-a-half kilometres into the Indian Ocean. Hard jarrah wood supported a structure that shouldered a single-line rail track for the Coffee Pot train. Tourists could walk or ride in the Coffee Pot. I walked with my camera in hand as storm clouds blustered from the south. Historically, the jetty gave farmers a lifeline to export wool and import supplies. Today, it creaked and groaned as the Coffee Pot eased its way across its spine, saving tourists a one-kilometre return walk. The glory days had long gone; a token trip for curious holidaymakers was all that remained.

The rain would arrive soon, but there was still time for a few photographs, a coffee and a sandwich before the short ride back to my tent.

I called Melanie. No answer.

I called Maureen.

'I've missed you,' I said.

'I miss you, too.'

'I'm in Carnarvon. Storm's coming, but I'm good.'

'I know,' said Maureen. 'It looked like you were in the ocean earlier.'

The global GPS tracker had worked its magic. Maureen knew where I was and knew I was safe.

'One Mile Jetty, actually,' I said.

'Call me tonight. Are you sure?' Maureen said.

'Sure? Sure of what?'

'Are you good?'

I knew what she meant.

'I'm fine,' I said, saddened I had to be asked.

'Call me tonight.'

'I will. Love you.'

'You too.'

I called Melanie again. No answer.

The rain finally arrived as I coasted to a stop next to my tent. My dirt patch soon turned to an island of mud. I looked to the skies and asked only that I stay dry.

CALL ME. Melanie's text had sat unread in my messages for fifty minutes.

I followed her instructions. Not possible. No reception.

———

Worthing, England 1989

I walked into the hospital with Mum. Dad's diagnosis devastated her with the strength of a nuclear bomb. Life, as she knew it, was over.

Dad didn't ask about his horse. The newspaper on his bed had already reported Ghost Rider's emphatic loss.

'Hey, Dad,' I said, as my mum bent down to kiss my father's head.

'Been thinking …' he said, 'I want to come home. You understand what I'm saying?'

We did.

'Of course, darling,' Mum said. The doctor had already organised a hospice. The arrangements were in progress. But I could fix this. It was probably the only thing I could fix. 'Right, Dad,' I said. 'I'll sort it.'

The following day, Mum and I drove to the hospital to collect Dad. The night before, Mum had lost what little control she had and drank herself into oblivion. Dad could see she had had a bad night. But then he would not have expected less. Despite the challenge, Mum made herself look pretty, wore her Sunday best, and lipsticked a big smile. Dad had dressed early, eager to go. I don't recall much about his medication other than a huge bottle of morphine, although I do recall the dosage. 'When he needs it,' the hospital had said, 'give it!'

And that's what we did. Dad did not want to do anything that might trigger pity. He didn't want visitors. Or fuss. All I remember is that he spent each day studying the horses while he drank tea. Gallons of tea with morphine chasers. The tea flowed in, flowed out. Toilet, armchair, toilet, armchair. His trips to the loo were timed with the TV ads. In the beginning, before the morphine really took hold, he could do his stuff unassisted. After ten days he couldn't.

Citibank, my employer, had generously allowed me compassionate leave. No date agreed to return to work, but the clock was ticking. Heather, Jamie and Dominic had stayed in Saudi Arabia. My family waited back in Riyadh. I didn't want it any other way.

Dad set his daily routine calibrated around the TV and the horse racing. After one trip to the loo, he did his usual shuffle into the lounge, but as he reached the middle of the room, his trousers fell to his ankles. Hairy, bony legs sprouted like weathered twigs from the pile of trousers at his feet. Dad looked at me, at Mum. Then he laughed loud and long, and we all cracked up together.

He deteriorated quickly. The morphine took over. He floated, slept, dozed and rarely surfaced to consciousness. The pain increased and the morphine bottle began to empty. At night, his instincts sent him for trips to the toilet. Unaided. I only realised this when I heard him fall. I'd pick him up, carry him to the loo, and lay him down afterwards.

Down, down, down he went until one day: 'Rich,' Mum said in a raspy whisper, the ubiquitous fag between her fingers, 'I can't do this.'

'Do what?'

'I'm sorry, but I just can't bear the thought of waking up tomorrow, the next day or the day after and finding Dad dead. Next to me. I can't do it.'

'But we told Dad we would.'

'I can't,' she said through a tear, a cough, and a cloud of smoke.

I didn't argue, but I didn't agree. My Dad was no longer my father. Not anymore. Mum's emotional needs trumped mine. Dad no longer recognised us. His spirit had gone; a shell remained. My mother had lost all strength. I couldn't help myself either. I cried.

'If that's what you want, I'll arrange it,' I said, my selfish distress clear as I remembered Dad's wishes: '*I want to come home.*'

My mother had the right to decide. Dad didn't know where he was. Collectively we decided a hospital would better manage his pain. We felt he would be more comfortable and experienced staff would do better. We felt lots of things. All of them lame excuses. Dad went back to hospital. Mum went into a black hole.

Mum and Dad lived close to the stony, pebbled seaside town of Shoreham, fifteen kilometres from the hospital. When my mother arrived home after a day at the hospital, she would drink. Me too. Except I would grab a six-pack of Tennent's Super, walk to the beach, and swig the heavy brew with my head hung between my knees. Surf pounded the polished pebbles, sucked them into the ocean and spat them back. I sat there long into the night, in my special place, with my thoughts and selfish sadness, and my supply of honey-thick lager close by. Each night I drank. Each day I drove to the hospital. Mum lost all control because the man who controlled her lay dying in hospital. Dad had been her restraint, her keeper, her quartermaster. He held the keys. Without Dad all bets were off. In the drinks cabinet, the booze gathered like a crowd looking for direction. Now the Blue Nuns, Harvey's, Cockburn's and Gordon's waited. In another time, in another world, a saner man would have emptied the bloody cabinet. But in this moment of sadness, sanity seemed too severe.

Citibank and my boss began to pressure me to return. I had been away from work for thirty days. Mum and I were at the hospital for about sixteen hours a day. My younger sister, Jackie, too. We split the shifts. Dad's estranged younger brother made one visit. They'd not spoken in years. Too late to mend rifts. Too late to say goodbye. Dad didn't even know he came.

Dad's life hung on a thread. The doctors thought he would die yesterday. They said the same thing the day before. 'It's close,' a nurse had said that day. 'It's close.'

'Thirty days,' the senior consultant had said a month ago. 'Maybe a little more, maybe a little less. You appreciate this is an estimate,' the consultant had said, concerned perhaps I might mark a date in my diary.

'Yes, I understand,' I had said.

'We cannot predict the timing. There are too many factors to consider.' He hesitated, then qualified his forecast, 'but barring major developments, I believe your father will pass within those parameters.'

'I understand,' I said, again not understanding anything at all. Neither did Mum.

Day 31 and Dad's hospital graphs descended through the floor.

Mum's respites at the hospital were filled with smokos. Two-minute escapes. Lots of them. Dad drowned in morphine. Mum choked on ciggies. She coughed and wheezed legally in the cold car park, illegally in the locked hospital toilet. The nurses smelt the smoke and heard her sob, but they looked away, and Mum stayed out of jail.

Dad's old army photo looked at me from above his bed. I'd stuck it there on Day Fifteen. Every doctor, nurse, carer and cleaner commented on his Hollywood good looks. *Frank Sinatra* said the older nurses with a memory. *Kevin Costner* said the younger ones. Whoever. He had been a handsome man. My dad had been an athlete, a gymnast, a champion swimmer, a motorcyclist, a daredevil risk-taker. The photo and the dying man were as similar as hope and despair.

Dad had stopped recognising us ten days ago. Now he slept and woke in a muddled mess of morphine and confusion. Tubes pumped life in; tubes pumped waste out. In. Out. In. Out.

Each day more pain, each day more morphine. It was a 'two-man race' for the winner's ribbon. Neck and neck. In the last week, the morphine streaked ahead; Dad's brain trailed far behind. Dribble oozed from his mouth in a snail stream beaded with bubbles. A weak pop confirmed he was still breathing.

In neat cursive, the photo above his bed read: *Burt (Germany – August 1949)*. It was his birthday. Dad was twenty, a radio operator in the occupational army of a defeated land. A young, dashing man who didn't smoke nor drink. The former vice would later suck him into an addiction that would kill him. Forty a day, every day. A habit he shared with Mum. As for the latter, well, Dad only dabbled in drink; Mum had been addicted to both. So far though, she hadn't smuggled miniatures into the toilets, just ciggies.

Day 32.

Dad died.

Lung cancer killed Mum four years later.

MURDER IN MILAN

The rain didn't stop until dawn the next day. The pitter-patter of water on stretched nylon had persisted throughout the night. I stayed dry in my fifty-nine dollar tent, but my mobile phone battery had died. I slushed through the mud to the camp kitchen. Wet benches and picnic tables sat in a puddle deep enough to swim in. I put my phone on charge and set the kettle to work.

A text kicked in within a minute.

ALL gOoD. Sent 1:22 am

IM OkAY. NO WOrRieS. Sent: 3.13 am.

But I was worried. I called. No answer. I texted: *Where R U?* No answer. Erratic reception and the weather didn't help. The kettle boiled and hot coffee followed. The texts suggested that whatever problems my imagination had created were no longer a problem. To contact the police would be stupid. To stay felt ineffectual. Leaving made most sense. I would try to call later. I needed an explanation; Melanie didn't need a white knight on a Yamaha.

Geraldton next stop.

As I left the caravan site, I stopped and entered the camp reception office.

'A silly question,' I said, 'but have you seen a yellow Beetle?'

'Blonde, convertible, white daisy?' he said. 'She left the day you arrived.'

Melanie had maintained a day's lead despite the speed at which I rode. Time on the road rather than kilometres per hour must have allowed her to stay in front. Now she was two days ahead.

'Thanks,' I said.

The sky had cleared; the sun shone, but the temperature dropped. The cold would become more challenging as I rode south into Australia's true winter. The cold meant real fatigue and genuine worry. But so far, so good – silkies, kangaroos, wedge-tailed eagles, wallabies and willy-willys notwithstanding. Now wild goats and emus sprang into the fray. The goats gathered in flighty families of threes and fours. They posed no risk, but clusters along the road forced me to keep my right hand and right foot hovering over the brakes. I stopped a couple of times to take photos, but the goats quickly skittered into the bush. Two emus stood statue-still with eyes that didn't miss a beat.

Wooramel, Overlander, Billabong and Binnu meant fuel and coffee. At Overlander, Monkey Mia and Shark Bay offered an attractive 155-kilometre detour. The World Heritage region was tempting, but the weather from the west whisked dark clouds towards me. I continued to Geraldton. The road punched through red earth while the land sped past in a blur of dense bush. Straight and undulating like a swell of ocean, the highway rose and fell towards the horizon where the rain had decided it would meet me. Closer to Geraldton the sun disappeared, the cold intensified, and the rain caught me in a squall that luckily ended as soon as it arrived. The scenery and the weather transported me to England's south-east counties. Sheep grazed across gentle hills alongside patchwork fields of yellow rapeseed and green lupin, stitched together by hedgerows of gorse and flowers. The cold wind bit through my jacket and underlined the Englishness of the vista.

Cold, wet, hungry and tired, Geraldton met me with the comfort of the Wintersun Hotel. Tonight, I decided, I would have a real bed, with a giant TV, an empty minibar and multiple power outlets. I put my equipment on charge and headed to the bar and restaurant.

'Rump steak with wedges,' I said to the waitress.

'No worries ... and to drink?'

'Soda water,' I said, watching for hesitation. 'Please.'

'Sure!' she said without a question mark.

The steak arrived, circled by mountains of potato wedges. A large bowl of aioli added to the calorie count. I needed every kilojoule. My trousers looked like they belonged to my big brother. My belt holes marched ever inwards and had now reached the end of the line. I was a skeletal sixty-five kilos; the previous year the bathroom scales had said eighty kilos. The training, sweat and grunt poured into this adventure took me down to seventy-two kilos. Now another seven kilos had evaporated into the outback. My present weight was a record: my lowest as an adult. After three years of living in Italy, twenty years earlier, my weight had mushroomed to porcini proportions: ninety-six kilos. Fifty percent heavier than the man who sat eating steak and wedges in the Wintersun Hotel. In Milan, the Italian culinary *Mafiosa* pushed Negronis and pasta with offers I couldn't refuse. Gin, Campari and sweet vermouth, a twist of orange, and a handful of ice. Negronis packed a punch difficult to duck. The taste still lingered.

———

Milan, Italy – May 1987

'Congratulations, guys,' I said to my two Swiss colleagues.

The news of their promotions to assistant vice-presidents reached us from their home office in Zurich. Both had been posted to Milan 'on loan' to help me on a project for six weeks. Tonight, and just one week into our work, we would raise a glass to their rise in the ranks. *Celebrate* in Citibank-talk took on a meaning beyond *un piccolo bere*. Thirty-three years old, and after two years in Milan, my alcoholic apprenticeship soared to new heights.

The Swiss pair were chalk and cheese. Pierre Kiriakides had a mop of Afro hair crowning an unusually large head atop a short but heavy frame. Jean Colombara epitomised the Nordic image of tall, slim, blonde and handsome. The three of us had met several times during conferences and training courses across Europe. Pierre wore a permanent smile that offset Jean-Pierre's more reserved character. Situated in the centre of Milan, on Foro Buonaparte, my office had views of the Castello, and a few hundred metres from Brera, the Milanese answer to Montmartre. Bohemian Brera: cobbled lanes, bustling street markets, galleries, bookstores, rustic restaurants, trendy bars and a vibrant nightlife. Brera was the place to be. The three of us, with arms outstretched, could touch the blue-greys, ochres and pinks of the street walls. Negronis were a temporary relief from stress, but in recent times they had been elevated to must-have status, whatever my day delivered – pressure or peace. Tonight, all bets were off.

A spring evening, cool and pleasant, blessed our *celebrazione*. But first things first. *Un bar alla moda*. The bars in Brera converged old-world ambiance and new-world trendiness – an Italian rhapsody that only the Milanese could achieve. Brera was a perfect setting to celebrate two significant promotions.

Pierre's bubbly, smiling face is as clear today as it was then. Excited and proud. We all were. Two newly minted assistant vice-presidents and a baptism to senior management in Brera. I don't remember what Pierre drank, but I do remember it was on the rocks. Measures in Milan were poured with one eye on the potential for a marathon and the other on economics. The three of us were suggestive of a spending spree that favoured the former. The tipple sizes trebled. Exuberance followed. The evening blurred as quickly as the bars.

My acquaintance with Pierre was close enough to know he liked to party. So, at the height of the night, and at full swing in a lively bar, it came as a surprise when Pierre said he had had enough. My offer to order Pierre a taxi to take him back to his hotel was met with a polite rebuttal. Pierre insisted he wanted to walk. So, Jean and I slapped him on the back with more *congratulations* and bid him goodnight. Pierre, we both agreed, had made an unusual, but wise call. We all had early starts. Jean and I returned to the bar while Pierre wove unsteadily back down the same cobbled street we had entered four hours earlier.

My morning started with white light and a black headache. Memories of the previous night floated behind the fog of a blinding hangover. A thirty-kilometre drive brought me back to the centre of the city where my office overflowed with work. The smoky, dark anonymous bar two streets from my office began its role the year before as my *now-and-again* two-minute start to tough days. Now it was the obligatory start to every day. A *caffè corretto*, a strong espresso laced with grappa – *chiodo scaccia chiodo* (one nail drives out another) – had become my Italian hair of the dog. I popped a polo mint as I mounted the stairs to Citibank's Italian headquarters.

Steady and stronger, I opened my office door at 7.45 am. Jean sat at his desk.

'Hey, Jean,' I said trying to smile. 'A good night.'

'Yes, very good,' he said in French-accented English as he waved a hand feverishly at his head to show the damage of the night before.

'Where's Pierre?'

'I don't know. He didn't answer my call. We normally meet in the lobby.'

'Oh okay,' I said, my disappointment clear.

A big night is never an excuse to be late. Unwritten Citibank drinking codes categorically state that no matter what, you turn up, on time, and ready to work. Magnitude ten on the Richter Scale of hangovers didn't cut it as an excuse. It was still early; Pierre had time to save face.

A short work-related discussion with Jean concluded with me leaving to attend back-to-back meetings. I returned to my office late morning. Pierre had still not arrived. Pissed off, I called the hotel. Pierre didn't answer.

'Shit,' I said to Jean. 'Not good enough. Promotion or no promotion.'

My team and I continued to work. I called the hotel again at lunchtime. No answer. A tough day stretched to evening. As Jean left for the night, I asked him to check on Pierre.

'Of course,' said Jean. 'Certainly.'

Jean arrived next morning after my *caffè corretto*.

'Pierre?'

'He didn't answer my call,' said Jean, 'or my knock on the door.'

'Shit,' was as good a response as I could muster. Worry overtook anger.

I telephoned the hotel. Pierre's room. No answer.

Then I called again. And spoke to reception.

'Check the room of Mr Kiriakides. Please!'

Five minutes later I received a reply. 'The room of Mr Pierre has not been slept in.' Precise, accented English delivered a shock for which I was unprepared.

'Fuck it.'

'Prego.'

I killed the call. Jean understood. Bad news.

'Pierre has gone AWOL.'

'Never!' said Jean.

Accident or illness? It couldn't be anything else, Jean and I agreed. There could be no other explanation. I had my staff call local hospitals. Nothing. I decided to contact the police. A *poliziotto* took my statement as he pecked at a typewriter and smirked.

'*Una donna*,' he said. He believed Pierre had run off with a woman. 'Come back in a week,' he said with a wink.

With no alternative, I went to Citibank's most senior officer in Italy. His office sat one floor above mine. Deeply troubled, I explained everything. Within an hour, I re-entered the police headquarters with a senior Italian banker with influential contacts. Telephone calls to the right people had raised serious alarms. This time they understood. This time I sat in sober offices in front of senior serious policemen.

I made another statement. Officers questioned me about that statement. 'Everything,' I said, 'happened as I stated.' A translator translated my statements.

'A photograph,' they said. 'We need a photograph.'

Pierre had left his briefcase in the office. Thirty minutes later I pried it open. A lucky break: Pierre had tucked a photo of him and a blonde woman into the folds of his case. Pierre was a bachelor. The photo looked like it had been taken at a recent office party in his hometown of Zurich. I gave the photo to the police. A press release followed; Pierre's family were informed.

The next day I received a call. The police had found Pierre. In the morgue. They needed me to identify the body.

'Jesus,' was all I could say, 'I can't believe it. It can't be him.'

My boss, Ken Flynn, had already flown in from Germany early that morning.

'Ken,' I said, 'they've found Pierre's body.'

'Christ! You okay to do this?' Ken asked. 'I'll go with you.'

'I'm okay,' I said, not okay at all, but certain of what I had to do. 'I'll go alone.'

I took a taxi from Foro Buonaparte to Via Giuseppe Ponzio. A ten-minute ride, but long enough for my imagination to create images of what I might find, and who I might find. *Maybe it's not him,* I thought, but dismissed the idea because Pierre was, well, so damn identifiable. Short, Greek origin, head too large for his frame and a mop of curly Afro hair. In any event, he was Swiss, he would have carried his passport, wallet, credit cards, business cards. *What the hell happened?*

The morgue was classic Italian: faded ochre, nondescript, old. It looked more like a tired apartment block for the less affluent than a warehouse for the dead. Two nights ago, I celebrated with a bubbly, exuberant and happy Pierre. Now the police said his body lay in the morgue. A sombre woman at the reception desk asked me to wait.

'*Secondo piano,*' she said, five minutes later.

'*Grazie,*' I said, willing my legs to walk up the cold, concrete, disinfected stairs to the second floor.

'*Quaranta-due,*' a voice yelled to the morgue attendants waiting at the end of the corridor. 'Forty-two,' I whispered to myself, as my shoes clicked along a cold corridor of ascending numbers. *Quaranta-due.*

Two men pulled a trolley from a refrigerated container.

'Fuck.'

A large head with curly hair and eyes closed forever lay on a gurney. Dried blood covered his nose and mouth. Pierre's ripped and blood-spattered white shirt revealed a bare chest. His arm hung over the side of the gurney in a gesture of finality. One shoe covered his right foot. His left foot was bare.

'*E lei?*' the morgue attendant said in Italian.

'Yes … *Si* … *e Pierre Kyriakidis.*'

Later that day, I discovered Pierre's body had been found in a dark colonnade, close to Milan's Central Station, on the sidewalk that lined Via Vittor Pisani. Road works and scaffolding screened a passageway from passing traffic; floor to ceiling boarding had created a pedestrian tunnel – a cave. His body was found behind a pillar 100 metres from the roads that intersected each end of the sidewalk – the maximum distance from passing traffic. The perfect place to conceal a crime. Pierre's attackers had stolen his passport, ID, credit cards and money. Muggers had murdered Pierre.

The coroner's report concluded Pierre died of suffocation. He choked to death on his own vomit. Death by natural causes. The report dismissed robbery as the cause of Pierre's death but acknowledged his attackers ransacked his body. The 'mugging', the findings concluded, had occurred after he died. But a bloodied face, ripped shirt, missing shoe, and a dark and dangerous location said otherwise. *Mugged? After he died!* I think not.

I returned to the morgue two more times. Pierre's brother, his next-of-kin, flew from Switzerland to identify the body. I went with him. Pierre's death was devastating to his family and those that knew him. His brother flew back immediately. Several days later, the morgue summoned me back. The Milanese authorities would fly Pierre's body to Zurich that day. I had to sign another document to confirm it was indeed Pierre's body that lay in the coffin before the lid could be nailed down. It was still him. I signed.

For the next six months, I worked with Citibank's Italian Head of Human Resources to prove that Pierre had been murdered. This conclusion, although abhorrent, would have made a huge difference to his family, emotionally and financially. We didn't succeed.

RIP Pierre.

ALIEN

The weather warmed and smiled all the way to Cervantes. Two hundred and twenty-three kilometres south along the Brand Highway. Canola and lupin fields spread either side of me in a blaze of chequered gold and green. The bucolic patchwork spread far to my east, while towering white sand dunes lined the west. The Indian Ocean sat on the other side.

Today, I had purpose.

The fine weather had injected energy into my flagging body as I headed towards The Pinnacles in the Nambung National Park. Cervantes lay seventeen kilometres to the north of my goal. That's where I would hang my hat for the night. I arrived late-afternoon at a sleepy, clean motel close to the highway. Two minutes later, my kit lay across the floor as Yammie and I roared towards The Pinnacles.

The landscape exceeded my imagination. Thousands of limestone pillars spread across a dusty desert. A blustery wind whipped red sand across a landscape barnacled with pinnacles like columns from a ruined city. I imagined the toll of a distant bell. Wind and rain and erosion had created The Pinnacles, not human hands. Some pillars towered five metres high; others were the height of tombstones. A movie set on another world: Warrant Officer Ripley. Giant eggs. Extraterrestrials. In *1995, YouTube* captured an alien sighting. And the alien had a name: Mr Connolly. Billy to his friends. The Scot had danced naked around the ancient limestone pinnacles in an act of insane comedy to promote his World Tour of Australia. I wanted to promote Beyond Blue too. Raise money. I set my GoPro on my tripod, undid my shirt, unbuttoned my trousers, and began to kick off my shoes … but daylight faded with my bravery. I killed the idea before it killed me. Instead, I soaked up the majesty of a million pillars melting in shadow against the softening light of a fading star. It would be dark soon. I saddled up and rode twenty thoughtful minutes back to my motel.

Yammie eased into the car space outside my door. I checked my phone. A good signal but no texts. The room was spartan, spacious, solitary. Eerily quiet too. Complimentary tea and coffee sat next to the kettle; an uncomplimentary bottle of wine sat alongside. Two lonely glasses nestled neatly beside it.

Fill me.

An old but comfortable armchair hugged my tired body, an empty bottle of soda water sat at my feet, a hot tea shook in one hand, while the last of my cheese rolls stayed clenched in the other. I stared at the wine bottle two metres away. The mini fridge vibrated with a constant reminder to my lonely room of the life it hid within. Beer, wine, spirits. Bad spirits. I sat in the dark as the streetlamps threw yellow beams across the floor. Searchlights, looking for me.

I sipped my tea, chewed my roll, and trembled.

The room looked like a seventies movie set. The red wine grew large. I imagined the silky red liquid sliding down my throat, the warmth, its velvet potency. The promise of bliss. *Red, red wine, stay close to me, don't let me be alone.* The present tense smacked my forehead. I was afraid, like a peasant unearthing an archaeological treasure from a mythical people. The peasant understood the potency of the curse and instinctively sensed the danger. He sniffed around the object, fearful of its power to inflict pain, and understood it should be left well alone.

A text snapped into the room like a rifle shot.

CALL ME.

It was Maureen. My angel. My rock.

I called. 'Hey, it's me,' I said.

'Are you okay?'

'I am now.'

INCARCERATION AND RELAPSE

The sun shone in a blank sky of cobalt blue. Church bells. Easy on a Sunday morning. Freedom before a short ride to Perth where Fremantle Prison would incarcerate me for two nights. While 'inside', a mechanic would care for Yammie, change her oil, fit new filters, and check her health. I rode south along the Brand Highway determined to enjoy four hours of liberty before forty-eight hours in jail. At Lancelin, I would take the Indian Ocean Drive to Perth, then onwards to Fremantle, and my cell. Twenty-five kilometres south, I reined Yammie to a halt. Hangover Bay: it sounded like the place to go if your head hurt. Pristine sand, calm surf and a wide sweep of white shoreline. Waves from the turquoise waters of the Indian Ocean lapped onto virgin sand, where a man had to do what a man had to do. I punched the air with a clenched fist that no-one saw, and yelled a 'Yeah,' that no-one heard. I danced the dance of crazies and dared the waves, then ran a hasty retreat. Dance and dare. Advance and retreat. Only I could understand. The child had escaped the man, perhaps the alcoholic could escape the drunk.

Huge sand dunes capped with white sand, scrub, grasstrees, gorse and yellow flowers lined the west side of the road where short gaps offered sporadic bursts of turquoise ocean. The day warmed to pleasant but suggested a cold, crisp night was ahead. Comfortable riding weather would end soon, like my freedom. But the subtle change from nowhere to somewhere began to show. Urban life trickled onto the roads and hinted of a flood. Weeks of solitude and outback nothingness now evolved into cars, houses, people, police cars. Life, as I knew it, had returned.

First, lunch in Lancelin, but as I turned from the highway to enter the town, a police roadblock slowed all traffic in and out. I had paid for my petrol. My speed had been contained. No alcohol in my system. But no matter how dry, I would always retain a fear of such random stops, rational and irrational. Today, the boys in blue waved me through. My anxiety passed. No obvious reason for their presence. No vehicle inspections. No RBT. Nothing. But no matter, in two hours I would voluntarily check-in to my cell. But my last meal was the meal of kings. A pie floater. An epicurean feast loved or loathed dependent on which side of the tracks you stood. The meat pie floated on a bed of mushy peas into which the thick, soggy pasty square of pie would slowly sink. Two kilos heavier, I fired up Yammie. Only 140 kilometres separated me from freedom and captivity. After weeks of wattle and sand, Perth soared like a glass oasis. Yammie weaved her way through highways of six-lane traffic, emphysemic exhaust and preoccupied people, but always closer, ever closer to Fremantle Prison, now just thirty kilometres south.

Fremantle Prison had been welcoming visitors since 1850. Forty-four of them had taken the long drop with a hangman's noose. Martha Rendell, the child killer and last woman to be executed in Western Australia, plunged from the scaffold in 1909. Eric Edgar Cooke, the 'Night Caller', as he was nicknamed, confessed to a further two murders, on top of his convicted six, ten minutes before his execution in 1964. There was no certainty which cell they would assign me. I just hoped it wasn't theirs. My crime? Many. But this incarceration was about curiosity. A minor addition to my rap sheet that cost me sixty-three dollars per night. I had scheduled Yammie for a service and a new rear tyre first thing Monday morning.

A daunting gate bookended between two towers and imposing

walls welcomed me as I turned into *The Terrace*. The gates led to the main prison. The Youth Hostel Association sat in the annexed section of the jail fifty metres to the left.

'Hi, how can I help?' said the young receptionist.

'I've booked two nights in a cell?'

'Sure,' said the pretty woman whose lapel said *Sadie*. 'Solitary or shared?'

'Solitary.'

'Cool. We have a free cell with two bunks. Both are empty.' She handed me a map and key with a smile and marked my cell with a yellow highlighter. '*Take a left at the gallows, straight on until you reach the flogging room, then it's the third on the left. Cell two-oh-seven. Have a nice night.*'

Cell 207 was exactly where she said it would be. Orders of the day had been posted on the steel door: '*All ghost sightings to be reported at reception.*' The key opened a steel door that shut with iron-fisted finality. The cell had no natural light except for a barred window high in the corner. Coldness oozed from whitewashed walls. Sepia photos of executed prisoners were strung along dark corridors. Few escaped, many rotted. A cell door clanked from the depths of the corridor bringing history closer to the present. The prison forced fear into your soul. A convict had pencilled a poignant message onto the wall alongside my bunk: *Nolite te bastardes carborundorum*. Another inmate had scribbled a more recent plea: *My crime? Illegal music downloads. My hope? Prisoner segregation by music genre.*

I needed a hot shower. The ablution block deserved special mention. Five stars: two wardens fired high-pressure hoses while a third shotgunned delousing clouds of chemicals. Two minutes of intense defoliation ensured one exited the shower block feeling … cleansed. I laughed at my warped imagination.

My mobile rang.

'It's me.'

'Jesus,' I said reacting to the fear in Melanie's voice. 'Where are you?'

'Augusta.'

'What's wrong?'

'I'm …' she said, drawing one syllable into a long slur. 'I'm … not well.'

'What …'

'I'm drinking.'

'Fuck.'

STONES AND BELTS

Houston, we have a problem. Yammie's visit to the mechanic revealed a stone embedded in her drive belt. Surgery would be problematic; a transplant was the only option. Japan was the only donor. No Yamaha organs could be sourced in Australia. Houston offered two options. Wait for the organ to be delivered in approximately three weeks, which would mean another twenty-one days' incarceration in Fremantle Prison, or continue, knowing Yammie might bust a belt at any time. Patient and rider pondered … *Houston, we'll take option two.*

Yammie had new oil and filters and, except for the stone in her belt, she was healthy. She needed a new tyre though. There was another problem. *What's that, Houston?* We won't get the rear tyre until tomorrow. One more night in prison.

'Melanie,' I said into my mobile, 'did you get help?'

'No.'

'Why not?'

'I'll wait.'

'For what?'

'You said you'd ride to Augusta.'

'I am, and I will, but not until tomorrow.'

'I'll wait.'

'Shit, I mean, I'm not good at this, I'm…'

'You're sober. I'll wait.'

'Not a good – *CLICK* – idea,' I said to no-one.

Johnnie stirred in my saddlebag. I didn't need to see him. I felt him.

Twenty-five days. Twenty-five vertical lines each struck through with an aggressive horizontal line of abstention. Another thirty-seven vertical lines awaited execution. Thirty-seven days alone. Melanie's distress triggered my own. Ten years sober and she'd thrown it all away. *Why*? Melanie's sobriety and relapse echoed those of the millions who had gone before her. And the millions who would follow. Yet her familiar story seemed strangely unique. Melanie's strength had helped me cement my own. Tonight, cracks appeared in my walls. My cell constricted and squeezed my thirst. Twenty-five days. Eight thousand kilometres. *Fuck you, Johnny*. Melanie needed help.

CHECK-OUT BUT NEVER LEAVE

'You can check-out, but you can never leave,' said Fremantle Prison's slogan. But I did. Leave. Failed escapes such as those attempted by Peg-Leg Pete and Archie Butterfly went through my mind as I pointed Yammie towards Augusta. A last look over my shoulder revealed no-one was on my tail. I'd made it. But then so did the Postcard Bandit and he had had a five-year run before recapture.

Yammie had her new rear-tyre fitted, a wash and blow dry. She sparkled, but I hit the road $500 lighter. I tried to put the day's end goal from my mind. Difficult. Melanie was in trouble 325 kilometres south. Rich pastures, sheep, cattle, pine forests and vineyards. South Western Australia in all its glory. But it was cold, and getting colder.

My coffee breaks moved from luxury to necessity. I used the time to bake my gloves on Yammie's exhaust. The temperature sank with the sun. In the bottom end, winter acted just like it said on the packet. Fatigue from the cold trumped time in the saddle as a greater risk. Routine glove-warming stops proved insufficient without intense body movement. My body needed blood and warmth pumped to its extremities. It needed life. Long periods in the cold didn't cut it. So, coffee breaks now included workouts. I jumped, hopped and flapped.

My padded jacket swollen with jumpers bulged like a bear – a bear with a fly up his arse and a wasp down his shirt. Passing cars slowed; open-mouthed drivers stared.

Me and all my fingers arrived in Augusta just before sunset. A storm gathered. Rain would come with the dark. Malevolent weather. Melanie's lodge was two kilometres ahead.

A wood-fired stove burnt in the kitchen. Melanie sat cloaked in a blanket. A big mug of hot chocolate steamed in shaking hands.

'I'm sorry,' she said, 'so sorry.'

'Melanie, please, don't apologise to me.'

Silence with the gravity of post-nuclear fallout spread between us. Pine logs cracked in the stove. Smoke wisps leaked from its blackened cover. The rain arrived. Melanie's eyes spoke of pain.

'I'm okay,' she said. 'It's done.'

But I knew: 'Done' was never 'Done.' I waited.

'My mother …' she said. 'She's dead.'

'Jesus! I'm so sorry. What happened?'

'Heart attack. Sudden. Unexpected. She was seventy-nine.'

'So sorry.'

'I have no-one else. Dad was a bastard; she was a saint. It's a tough story. I let her down. In recent years she was proud. Of me. What I'd done.'

'Melanie, I expected worse. I expected …'

'You expected me to be paralytic.'

'I…'

'You were right. Two days, three nights. I was shitfaced. I leave tomorrow. The funeral is Friday.'

'But …'

'I'm driving to Perth in the morning. I'll ditch the car there. My flight leaves for Newcastle tomorrow afternoon.'

'Can you drive? Are you ...?'

'Tomorrow I'll be good. It's tonight I'm worried about.' Melanie pulled the blanket around her shoulders and sipped from her mug. 'Stay with me until morning.'

HELP: SOMEBODY, NOT ANYBODY, SOMEONE

Y ou ask yourself how. You ask yourself why. You ask yourself questions. But you know. You know there are no answers. *Help*: Melanie needed somebody. Not just anybody. *Help*: she needed the sober fraud with Johnny Walker hidden in his saddlebag. Me. Everybody had tried to help me get my feet back on the ground. But my toes never touched the deck. At least not until I met Maureen. And now that commitment to sobriety sagged like a blanket under a mountain. Relapse was contagious.

I had taken the remnants of Melanie's poison bottles and thrown them alongside the five empty bottles she had murdered in the two days before I arrived. The brave yellow Beetle driver now slept through her sadness and exhaustion. She shouted and cried as she nightmared through her blackness. Demons attacked her loss. Hunched in an armchair, I waited through the long night until morning.

I brewed coffee in the kitchen while Melanie packed.

Silent, sober, she sat and sipped her coffee.

The rain had eased to a misty morning that waited outside the window. Light rose from behind the clouds. Melanie had to drive 300 kilometres to Perth for a two o'clock flight. She had seven hours to do it. A long drive through clouds of tears and a hangover drowned in sadness.

'Thank you,' she said, touching my arm. 'I'll be fine.' Her words sounded as comforting as a wretch refusing a blindfold before a firing squad. Melanie raised a hand in a gesture signalling she didn't want me to follow. *STAY!* She hoisted her backpack, turned and walked to her Beetle. The engine cranked and fired in a base clef warble, gravel crunched beneath tyres, and the convertible headed north to retrace a journey she'd made three days before. A white, wilting daisy trembled on the dash.

I sat in that kitchen for painful minutes with a lifetime of memories.

My phone rang and my blonde saviour brought me back to reality.

'Hey, babe.' Maureen's voice warmed me instantly.

'Hey,' I said.

'What's up?'

'Augusta after the storm,' I said. 'I'm packing up. I'm tired, but ready to go and so happy to hear you. I miss you.'

'Are you good?'

'Sure,' I said. 'All good. Today I head east. I'm coming home.'

Bacon and eggs wafted from across the street. I stepped into the gravel tracks made moments earlier by a yellow Beetle. And followed my nose.

Satisfied and eager to push on, I checked out. Nine o'clock – a big day lay ahead.

'Make sure you check out Cape Leeuwin before you leave. The lighthouse is the tallest in Australia,' the proprietor had said. A faint smile of encouragement followed. 'She'll be right,' he said, with the suggestion that he knew or was at least aware of the last few days of drama. I hoped he was right. His support helped temper my swelling sense of unease.

A ten-minute ride took me along the coast road to Australia's most south-westerly point. The lighthouse stood proud and mighty at the junction of the Southern and Indian Oceans. A crisp morning offered a chance to reflect. I pulled Yammie to a stop alongside a ridge of sand dunes and walked through a cutting to the beach. I unpacked my Canon. The lighthouse rose from the Cape a further 500 metres west. Waves from two oceans crashed against the rocks.

On the beach, a beauty eclipsed the lighthouse. She danced in the sea in a white lace dress. Asian eyes looked at me with an embarrassed surprise that equalled my own. The young woman held her dress at ankle height, at the edge of shingle and sand, while wavelets washed over her feet, blued with cold. Her bare forearms held down a simple bridal crown of flowers that struggled in the breeze. My mouth fell open, as did the Asian man's when he appeared from the rocks with a cell phone.

It was a cold morning for a photo shoot. The man ignored me. He was dressed in a ninja-black beanie, scarf, overcoat, pants and white trainers. He pointed his phone while flailing his arms and corralling the girl-bride into ever more poses. This way, that way, forwards, backwards. The wind picked up and the girl shivered. *Left, right,* his hands gestured; her head obeyed, tilting demurely to the batons of his hand. He yelled a command. She smiled. He yelled another. She flicked her hair. It flew with the wind, long and black, flying this way and that. She was shivering. I waved my Canon at the man. His spread an arm with an open palm: *Be my guest.* I snapped a few shots, raised a wave in thanks.

'Congratulations,' I said. The man said nothing. The girl nodded. Shy and embarrassed, perhaps.

I ambled back to Yammie. Of all the lighthouses in all the towns in all the world, she walked into mine. But Cape Leeuwin looked grand in the background.

Two minutes and eight dollars later, I stood at the door of the lighthouse crowned with its name: CAPE LEEUWIN 1895. I strained by neck up towards the dome, thirty-nine metres above. The solitary sentinel looked out to a cold angry sea as two olive-green parrots roosted nearby on the dark rock. My Pommy eye couldn't reconcile the bleak cold with parrots and palm trees. A morning of surprises.

Mid-morning and Yammie sped towards Walpole. My compass

pointed towards home, 6,000 kilometres east. I pushed aside all concerns for Melanie, relapse, grief and funerals. Johnnie stirred in my saddlebag.

My motorcycle jacket had kept me warm as I roamed Cape Leeuwin's lighthouse and headland, but I began to sweat. Once on the bike, I chilled rapidly and now shook like maracas in a hurricane. Desperate and cold, I stopped at the first fuel station, stripped off my jacket and my damp T-shirt on the forecourt. It was an icy day. Bare-chested, I searched my panniers for a dry vest. Johnny sneered while the lady at the cash desk watched in horror. 'It's okay,' I said. 'I'm crazy.'

Less cold and with a belly full of coffee, I headed towards Albany. In a tick of time, my world had changed from open horizons and roads straighter than light to bends and loops that curled through a woodland of giant karri and tingle trees. These timber leviathans lined my route like a Brobdingnag guard of honour dwarfing Cape Leeuwin Lighthouse in both size and age. These beautiful giants ranked among the tallest in the world, some soaring over eighty-metres high with root systems deeper than Australia's tallest lighthouse. I rode through a tunnel canopied by a chaos of boughs and branches. Sporadic sunlight flickered across the road. A calm strength settled over me. I no longer felt cold.

The small town of Walpole shouldered the forest. My tired body welcomed the thought of a warm bed. I discovered an old hostel that offered a small, musty room that included an antiquated heater. I manoeuvred this lifesaver next to the head of the bed and plugged it in.

There was a lemon tree laden with fruit in a grassy backyard just outside my window. A hot shower hit the wish list first. Rusted corrugated-iron walls shielded the ablution block. I found a single shower and a single toilet inside – both as ancient as the old karris. The shower delivered a hot luxury, though the time limit printed on the wall forbade me from staying longer. Cheap and basic. I needed nothing more.

The hostel's kitchen was across the yard. Pots of all shapes and sizes hung from racks in the ceiling. Mugs and plates and glasses, all things necessary to cook, eat and drink lined wide wooden benches. A vase of assorted flowers sat under the window. The kitchen radiated heat. My body began to warm.

I had bought a meat pie at the last roadhouse; it was now in the microwave ingesting radio waves that would turn it from cold to volcanic in under a minute. With a fork in one hand and a bread roll in the other, I sated my hunger. Hot tea helped. On the kitchen counter, a slab of carrot cake was wrapped in Glad Wrap with a handwritten instruction: Eat Me. I did as commanded, then offered a silent prayer of gratitude to Unknown Samaritan Travellers.

Wood smoke drifted into the kitchen from under an adjacent door. A small sign read: COMMON AREA. Behind the door was a snug room with deep armchairs, a rug-covered sofa and a bookcase brimming with books. In the corner, a large, open-wood fire threw out a welcoming blanket of warmth. The two armchairs sat in front of the fire. A man in his seventies occupied the closest. He looked up from his newspaper and nodded. Coffee steamed from a mug on the side table next to his armchair. I sank into the armchair opposite. The fire crackled as flame flares spiked and receded. A small TV rolled out the evening news in a tone too low to hear but loud enough to acknowledge its presence. I watched with no interest. Heat from the fire crept into my bones and before long, I glowed with a warm calm. Time slowed and an hour passed. The man spasmodically ruffled the pages of his newspaper, flicking it with a starchy shake until it lay perfectly for the next few minutes. Until he shook it again.

The fire and the comfort pulled me into a trance. Eyes open, body asleep.

'*Huh hum*,' I heard the man say as he gave his paper a more robust rustle. '*Huh hum*,' he said again, nodding at my phone vibrating in my pocket.

'Ah,' I said. 'Thank you.'

ARRIVED! Funeral tomorrow morning, read the message. A sad-face emoticon with a single tear ended the text.

The man shook his paper again. The fire cracked.

I'm sorry for your loss, I texted back.

The clichéd weakness of my words did nothing to convey my emotions. Or my fear. For her, for me. My fingers typed another text, two more words that said nothing and everything: *Take care.*

I'm flying back to Perth soon. Check your wing mirrors, texted Melanie.

Jesus. I didn't know what to say. A thumbs up was all I could manage. I thought she should stay with her family. Her sons.

Tired legs and an aching back rebelled against my efforts to rise from the comfort of my armchair. I stood, arched my body, massaged my back. 'Night,' I said to the silent man opposite. He nodded and flicked his paper. A headline caught my attention: 'Japanese Man Knifes and Kills 19, Wounds a Dozen.' The world still screamed evil deeds deep into an enchanted forest. No escape.

I trudged, heavy with thought, across a cold backyard damp with dew, past the lemon tree to my small bedroom and the old heater. I slept embalmed in musty warmth, snug as Bilbo Baggins in his hobbit-hole. I dreamt of Maureen. Of lemon trees, ents, huorns, fanghorns, karris and tingles. I dreamt of funerals and sherry and port wine. I dreamt of the Valley of The Giants.

GRANDMA TINGLE

I woke early, warm and refreshed in an old room on the edge of an ancient woodland. Outside my window, the cold lemon tree sparkled with tear drops.

A forest of tingles twenty-five kilometres east offered a steel walkway to explore the forest where it weaved a 'sky bridge' 600 metres through its upper canopy. I rode east towards The Valley of the Giants. Thirty minutes later, I pulled Yammie to a stop in an empty carpark, save for an old white kombi with no occupants. Almost nine o'clock. Early morning mist still drifted through the trees. The tourist kiosk accepted my concession card and I parted with fifteen dollars and fifty cents.

The skywalk trailed gently upwards to reach forty metres above the forest floor where it wound a narrow path through the tops of the red tingles. Huge trunks towered alongside the skywalk as the steel trail led between gnarled boughs that stretched towards you, over, under, and around you. A man-made cocoon hugged by giants. The walkway sighed with gentle movement. A moving, living, forest of tingle and karri floated in a ghostly blue mist of honey and menthol: sharp, sweet and soothing. Centuries of forest. Birds whipped from branch to twig like shooting stars in a sky of green. On the forest floor, the buttressed bases of the tingles reached circumferences of twenty metres. Insect, fungal and fire damage created hollowed lower trunks that could be walked through, rather than around. At dusk, quokkas emerged from the undergrowth and possums crept from their hollows. The trunks and boughs of the tingles morphed into ancient ents with arms and faces. One old tingle took the form of a grizzled grandma. The old lady stared at me from hooded eyes sitting high above a warted nose and witch's chin. *Go east, young man*, said Grandma Tingle, *and you will find your princess.*

Onwards. Homeward bound.

Beyond the heavy shade of the forest, the day had warmed to an English spring. Yammie now sped into open pasture. We rode towards Esperance. My speed rose with my mood but was short-lived. A sober sign on the South Coast Highway blazed with three large crosses:

11 Fatalities in 2015

My hand eased off the throttle. But there had been times …

––––––

Athens, Greece July 1992

I sat in my office overlooking Syntagma Square on a warm summer's day. The busy streets hummed one floor below with tourists and traffic. Dirty lace curtains hung from the window that opened on to a narrow balcony; the lace gently rippled in the breeze. Paper and files were spread chaotically across my wooden desk. Untidy. Like me. Like the building and its old ramshackle offices. In the sixteen months since Desert Storm, Citibank had transferred me back to Italy where, after only six months, my boss moved me and my family to Athens. My role now included audit responsibility for both countries. I shuttled back and forth between Athens and Milan in a growing flood of anxiety. Five days here. Ten days there. The need for a relocation made no sense. Work overwhelmed me. Alcohol softened the sting, yet I functioned.

The smell from a mug of strong coffee wafted from my desk. I forced my bleary eyes to feed clarity to a brain that didn't want to dance. The week had barely begun.

Late nights and an early start had weakened my energy. The drone of the busy square settled into a mesmeric lullaby. My eyes began to close. I drifted. Gabby would be born in two months. I smiled. I daydreamed out the window. The Grand Bretagne Hotel was across the square. Tourists ambled aimlessly while presidential sentries slow-marched outside Parliament House: red caps, white tunics, white kilts, white stockings, red leather shoes and black pom-poms. Pomp and pageantry drifted through my window on the scent of summer, souvlaki and exhaust.

BOOOOOOOOM

Time froze.

It started again as a cloud of smoke drifted across the square. Screams followed.

My staff outside my office shouted words I didn't understand.

'Jesus! What happened?' I said.

'*Den xéroume.*'

'Speak English!'

'We don't know.'

It was a stupid question. No-one knew, and we wouldn't find out for several hours. A bomb? Gas explosion? Grenade?

An instant earlier, in a room of The Grande Bretagne, a curtain had eased across the open window where a rocket launcher had been pointed towards the western side of the square. The RPG hit the minister's car before we heard it. Marxist guerrillas, known as *17 November,* had planned to assassinate the Minister of Finance. He narrowly escaped, but a bystander was killed and five others were injured. From the Scuds of Riyadh to Marxist rocket attacks, it seemed explosive ordinance had unsuccessfully trailed me to do what alcohol was already achieving, albeit more slowly.

Two months later, the summer ended with a breakneck ride on the back seat of a staff member's motor scooter to reach the hospital, where my beautiful daughter had entered the world in a hurry. Heather had given birth to Gabriella. Then, like now, I felt blessed, but unworthy.

―――――

Forty kilometres east of Walpole, several hundred deer appeared in open pasture. They stared at the motorcycle roaring past that had interrupted their grazing.

A meat pie at Albany, then onwards to Esperance. It was good weather – cold, but not freezing, though my fingers still quickly numbed. I stopped regularly and warmed my gloves on Yammie's exhaust pipes. The temperatures would soon become much worse. The 'bottom end' would be tough. Long distances passed between truck and car sightings. My mind wandered incessantly to the stone in my drive belt. Would it snap? At the next bend? In the middle of nowhere? Ravensthorpe got the gong for the overnight stay. Cold weather, a huge walk with Giants, and a 400-kilometre ride had left me exhausted. My weight loss of seven kilos in twenty-eight days had weakened me too.

The first pub had no room at the inn. However, the bartender booked me into one of their single cabins a kilometre from the main street. A key and a map took me and Yammie to the end of a dirt road where forty single cabins were scattered. Ravensthorpe looked as tired as its historical gold and copper deposits. Sheep and wheat kept it turning, but I guessed it was mostly people like me that added a buck. My cabin was like a morgue.

BLACK NIGHT

Black. Cold. Nothing.
    If I wrote about it, if I did.
    What would I write?
The truth?
Would I tell you about the fairy tale?
It happened once upon a lifetime ago –
Or would I write about the horror …
In the last days of chaos?
Of a failed man…
Or would I tell you about the stories?
Of big cities in strange countries
Far from everything real …
Or, I don't know
Would I tell you about her?
The princess in Australia
Or maybe I would just scare you
With the truth and the facts
A story of love and loss
And the Murderer
Who destroyed it all.

. . .

Nightmares attacked a fragile body. The Murderer confessed to the crimes. Past crimes, present crimes, future crimes. Maureen had gone. Alcoholism the cause. Alcoholism filled the vacuum of separation. Loneliness lent itself to despair and self-hatred. Six years, and still the memory persisted, lit with an eternal spotlight that sucked the man's sanity. The poison still vivid in his darkest nightmares. Six years. And still. And still he saw the chaos of bottles scattered across the room. Sharp, murdered lonely bottles in a desert of discarded dreadful dreams. Dry bottles, emptied pill blisters, and a sea of empty notes swelled the room – a claustrophobic cemetery flooded with sadness and garbage. It was time. The past was too late, the present too painful, the future too criminal. It was time. The crimes must cease. It was time. Balcony doors opened to the blurry night. It was time. Late traffic still droned a distant forty-two floors below. It was time.

Days and nights had passed while he died. Camels and dusty plains and Bedouin tribes. An Arab hero galloped across light years of pain. Arabia and Rome. Drought. Desert Storm. A village, a minaret, a campfire, prayer and belief. Parched. A quest for redemption. My father, where are you? Islam, religion, strange chants, an ancient language. Jamie. Searing storms of blinding sand. Nights of fires. Days of blindness. Dominic. Voices. A cave. Richard, can you hear me? Voices from nowhere. Richard? Gabriella Sofia. Voices without faces. Richard? Voices without light. Stars and spaceships, medals and honours. Spies and freedom. Water. Dumb. Thirst. Mute. No-one could help. No-one could see. He was alone in the night, in the desert, in a goat-hair tent, rich rugs strewn across a mud-dried floor. Allahu Akbar. Allahu Akbar. A gentle hand. The Pope. Kind smiles. A dagger and thorns. Praise be. Christ. Jesus. God Almighty. Dry redemption. Ten days and ten nights. A dark temple, cool and damp, dying people, sick and injured, sari-dressed nurses. Walls that miraged with elephant men and snakes, moving, moulding, morphing, white walls, digital monitors, drips and beeps. Richard, can you hear me, said the saint in white. Yes, whispered the wretched man, I see you.

Maureen held his hand.

———

A cold morning killed a true nightmare. Shaking hands and wet sheets. Six years had passed. Since *that* day. Six years or 600 years, the memory would live for a lifetime.

My heart slowed. The horror receded, slowly, like an outgoing tide, like the morning after the storm.

I loaded Yammie, fired her up and left the darkness behind.

I headed for Esperance, Norseman the goal.

The weather had blessed me for twenty-nine days. No doubt about the facts, but every doubt about why. Luck didn't normally ride pillion with me. The afternoon approach to Townsville had been the only dangerous ride. Torrential rain and a tired body had been an unwelcome fight just three days into my journey.

Maureen's faith supported me.

Melanie scared me. Ten years wrecked by a single day. *Faith* – she needed to find it. *Relapse* – she needed to beat it. She would bury her mother Friday.

Canola fields replaced the forest. Yellow to my left, yellow to my right and yellow in front of me. Mellow yellow everywhere. My camera worked hard to capture the essence of what lay before me.

Onwards.

The day became warmer.

We going to do this, Rich? Yammie purred.

'Sure,' I said.

Give me a go, she said. *We're close.*

I pulled back her throttle. We pounded down the road spitting dust and grunts while the speedometer spun higher.

Give me more, she screamed.

Yammie surged. I followed.

More, she said.

I opened her up. No cops. We felt as one as we roared ahead.

'Nearly there,' I yelled.

I know, Yammie purred.

We both sensed the enormity of the moment. I had to slow down. The moment needed to be savoured, enjoyed. I wanted to watch ... 6 ... 7 ... 8 ... 9 ...

Yes, yes, yes, Yammie screamed.

'OOOH MY GOD!' Trip Metre Two hit 9999.9 ... then boom – 0.0. We both exploded with joy.

The 10K Club. I pulled over. If I'd been a smoker, I would have lit up. Instead, I sat on Yammie with a satisfied smile and a coffee. Twenty-nine days. Ten thousand dry kilometres. I started to whistle 'And I'm feelin' good.'

We arrived in Esperance a little after noon. Melanie texted ten minutes later. *I'M GOOD* – hands pressed together in prayer ended her message. I replied with the same.

I rode along Esperance's Esplanade and onwards through the town. Good luck rather than planning brought me to Ocean Lookout. A steel structure with spiralled stairs led to a circular viewing platform ten metres above the bush. West Beach lay to the west and Lovers Beach hid beneath the cliffs to the east. Powerful surf rippled across mottled turquoise waters until it crashed onto white sand. *C'est incroyable*. The French named the area Esperance after taking shelter from a storm 225 years earlier. 'Esperance,' I murmured. *HOPE*. I wound my way down the stairs and walked through the bush to expanses of flat rock that surrounded the look out. A good place to rest. An hour of reflection passed in a minute. More coffee, another meat pie and a packet of peanuts added a touch of elegance to this chance discovery.

A middle-aged couple approached.

'Hey,' said the man.

'Hey.'

The couple smiled.

'On holiday?' said the woman.

'Sort of,' I said.

'Sort of?'

I explained. The couple were friendly, genuinely interested in what I was doing and why. At the mention of *Beyond Blue* they offered a cash donation. Protocol meant I couldn't accept cash and directed them instead to *BB's* fund-raising platform: 'EveryDayHero'. A few clicks would easily find my page: *A Ride Around the Block* where they could glean more information about *the charity* and my project. I set my goal at $10,000. Generous people had already given $4,950. A tad below halfway. The couple donated fifty-five dollars, edging me over the midpoint. Kindness from strangers moved me. The email that accompanied their donation moved me more:

Hi Richard – It was lovely to have the pleasure of the halfway mark! Depression is a terrible issue – We have two daughters who have all battled with serious depression and who have learnt how to cope with it, but life has never been easily light-hearted for them. It can still be meaningful and worthwhile though. Our youngest (31) is a mental health nurse and finds that very rewarding. She has also just spent time with me in Uganda helping with a community development project started by a black Ugandan friend living in South Africa. She has fallen in love with the people and what we are doing. Being able to support others in the good they are doing is a privilege so I'm glad we ran into you – even though the contribution is small. I know how much even little things can mean to people in need.

I had been fortunate to meet good people who loved to help others, loved adventure and loved Australia. This support gave me energy to finish what I had started.

Norseman lay 200 kilometres north on the edge of the Nullarbor Desert. I took the Norseman Road and headed for the Coolgardie-Esperance Highway. Rain crept from the south. I opened the throttle and stayed out in front. Trees became sparser while a break in the scrub exposed a huge plain of mustard yellow stretching to the east. A glimpse of the Nullarbor. To the west, the fading light stressed the blackness of the land charcoaled by bush fires. Railway tracks paralleled the empty road, and the sun dipped from the day. Ten kilometres to Norseman.

The French may have named Esperance, but folklore says in 1894, Laurie Sinclair's horse, Hardy Norseman, stomped up a nugget of gold and the town's name was sealed. In honour of the Midas-hooved horse, a bronze statue grazed in a nearby park. But Norseman is not the only animal sculpted from history. Life-size metal camels – ships of the desert – populate a nearby roundabout: modern art dedicated to the memory of the old camel trains. Their long shadows would soon be lost to the night. The Norseman Hotel was the perfect place to rest for the night. Smoke drifted from a wood fire in the rear, another fire crackled in the pub's lounge. Forty bucks a night for a single room and the offer of the woodshed for Yammie.

Locals began to fill the pub's lounge while others congregated around the fire in the backyard. Friday night. A beer filled every other hand, wine the rest. The conversation amplified in direct correlation to the alcohol consumed. I quietly ate my salt and pepper calamari while a soda water warmed next to my plate. The Nullarbor Desert tomorrow. Melanie's mother was being buried today.

A young man ordered a round for himself and two mates. Three beers: XXXX Gold. Icy tears dripped down lager-filled glasses topped with froth. The smell, the taste, the cold, the buzz … all too familiar; all too dangerous. I took my soda water into the backyard where a wooden, black-painted sign alliterated a dedication: *Bobby Baker's Bar.* A framed print of a warrior with sword and shield looked down from an external wall: *VIKINGS.* Flames flicked high above the rim of a large open hearth punching warmth from the middle of the yard. An iron cauldron beneath the bell glowed with spent ashes. A beer would be good. Bloody good. I stood mesmerised by the flames, hypnotised with desire. My phone buzzed. Maureen.

'Where are you?'

'Standing by a fire.'

'Say again …'

'Norseman.'

'Are you okay?'

'Tired. Exhausted.'

'But are you good?'

'Good,' I said. 'And excited. The Nullarbor tomorrow.'

We spoke of the day, of Maureen's job, of our dog, of kind people, of home. Soon.

'I love you,' I said standing discreetly at the edge of the yard where the warmth didn't reach, and the shadow chilled me with foreboding.

'Good luck,' she said. 'Not long now.'

Five thousand kilometres to go.

———

Worthing Cemetery, 2009

The man had travelled from the other side of the world, and now he knelt by two graves, unaware of time or space. A scrap of newspaper blew damp and dirty across the cemetery, fluttering news of Sussex from the Worthing Gazette in the fields of the dead. No-one but the man could see its date: 15 March 2009. Overcome with grief, he hesitated, then gently laid both hands on the cold, polished gravestones. The heart-shaped headstones overlapped each other as though in an enduring hug. His frozen fingers traced across the inscriptions, touching each letter, each character – the spaces etched in stone. The man sobbed as the translations entered the darkness of his broken heart. Despite the cold, the cursive characters warmed under his touch. His fingers dwelt on the letter *H* and slowly traced an *E*. Pained, his fingers moved across each headstone as though reading braille. His fingers hesitated, continued and faltered. At *D*, the man stopped, unable to accept the horror he had caused.

The man had never been to this place. The man had never sat with them. Had never said a prayer. Heather and Dominic died six years ago, yet the man had not come. Until now. His heart too sad; his guilt too black. Even now he doubted his own sanity. The man's body trembled as he tried to comprehend their deaths. The man knew his pain would never heal.

The inscriptions affirmed his self-hatred. The man was not a father. He had no meaning, no substance. The man was nothing. The words burnt into him as he read the inscription for the first time. The man had given his parents-in-law consent to bury Dominic's ashes with their daughter. His mother-in-law had reserved a plot for herself and her husband and was she who had made the inscriptions. Dominic was a

Beloved Brother And Grandson – not a Beloved Son. Now he understood. The white space would be his epithet.

The late afternoon light faded. Dusk. Low scudding clouds darkened and wept. The man sank to his knees onto the icy, damp earth.

In loving Memory Of

Heather	*Dominic*
Ann	*Stuart*
West	*West*
5-5-2003	*5-5-2003*
Aged 48	*Aged 20*
Beloved Mother	*Beloved Brother*
And Daughter	*And Grandson*

Forever in Our Hearts

He cried for those he loved. He cried for the pain he caused. He muttered words of apology. Nothing could ever undo what he had done. He prayed Dominic heard him. With all his heart, he prayed they forgave him. Now he needed to drink. He needed to drown.

DO YOU FEEL LUCKY, PUNK?

E*arly Saturday morning, the man packed his belongings. A long ride across the Nullarbor Desert lay ahead; doubt would follow close behind. Norseman to Eucla. Seven hundred and twenty kilometres.*

The man had stayed in the finest hotels around the world: New York, London, Paris, Vienna, Rome, Copenhagen, Brussels, Athens, Beijing, Tokyo, Kuala Lumpur, Johannesburg, Istanbul. The list was long; the gratuitous luxury now a dusted memory from a dead dynasty of corporate pin-stripe black. A life lost. A son lost. The man thought he had lost everything that mattered. Perhaps he had. But now in a different life, he realised the present mattered more than the past, and everything that mattered, he had.

The man's helmet and swag sat on the single bed. He stood and held out his arms. His fingers touched each wall. The washbasin offered one functioning tap, the other had seized solid. Cigarette-scarred linoleum covered a wooden floor that creaked like a ship's deck. Power and antenna cables snaked up the corner to the ceiling and joined with a tiny TV. There was a frail wardrobe with two wire hangers in the corner.

The man looked through fresh white-lace curtains; the back door of his room led to a verandah that wrapped around the hotel. The street below was empty. Quiet. This had been his home for the night. A good home. The man stepped into the hallway of the musty corridor lined with rooms he guessed were like his. A narrow carpet, more bare than thread, snaked over the linoleum-lined hallway – a trail to the external toilet and two showers. As he walked past the bathroom, the man smelt the sweet, stale, addictive air of the pub: a musty cocktail of beer, polish, disinfectant, wood smoke and embers still smouldering from the fire that had warmed him the night before. The man descended the rusted iron staircase to the patio below, then followed the stone path to the woodshed where he had parked his motorcycle for the night. The man looked at his motorcycle and realised he loved it. She was ready. So was he.

A warm sun welcomed the day.

I loaded Yammie. We refuelled a few blocks behind the pub. Black coffee and a cheese kransky for me, ninety-five octane for Yammie. Cirrus clouds frayed like cotton threads across a blue morning. A blessed breeze rose from the west, promising a small push from the rear. My gloves stayed redundant in my saddlebags for the first time in 2,000 kilometres.

One hundred and fifty kilometres ticked across Yammie's odometer as we cruised eastward on a road as straight as a compass bearing locked on home. The early sun picked through the trees that lined the road and lit smooth trunks of white, grey, pink, silver and orange. A stopping point on the south side of the road opened to a huge plain of red sand already shimmering in an optical illusion. I stopped for a break and saluted the experience with a coffee.

Blue bush, mulga scrub, spear grass and spinifex swallowed the road, squeezing the Eyre Highway into a gossamer thread of inconsequence. I followed that thread as it stretched east. Nothing interrupted its journey save for a few roadhouses set several hundred kilometres apart.

'Emus,' said a local at the Norseman pub. 'Keep yer eyes open!

They're frigging dangerous.' I saw one, and the emu saw me. It didn't move.

The roadkill toll was less than expected, apart from a 500-metre stretch where seven or eight wallabies lay dead despite a million flies that said otherwise.

A road sign signalled an RFDS Emergency Airstrip was near – the Royal Flying Doctor Service. I passed the sign, looking left and right for the airstrip. Piano keyboard markings told me this was not Abbey Road. The highway *was* the airstrip. Another strip of white zebra crossed the highway one kilometre farther ahead – end of airstrip. I would ride through another three emergency airstrips before the day ended. Three hundred kilometres closed up behind me. All I could see was scrub grass and bush. A vast emptiness.

A road sign sped past in a blur. I pulled Yammie to a stop. We did a U-turn in a cloud of dust. *CLICK*. Iconic road sign and ol' boy posed for a selfie. The straight road I had just ridden just got straighter.

---

90 Mile Straight Road
Australia's Longest Straight Road
146.6 km

Boredom would be a battle; lethargy lethal. The road ahead disappeared into a vanishing point, a pinprick in a Goliathan bush, and for an eternity it never changed. The road was, well, straight, very empty and very long. I felt the need to open the throttle. Steady as she goes, but the captain's command was ignored. The outback, the beauty, the emptiness took control. Common sense evaporated; craziness filled the vacuum. My hand wound open the throttle. The acceleration was intoxicating … 120… 140… 160… 185 kph. The ol' boy danced in the saddle.

'Get your pistons pumping … born to be wild,' I sang as Yammie roared past solitary road trains, my hand raised in salute. 'Yeah.'

Waaaaaah, Waaaaaah, the road trains trumpeted in tribute (or tongue-lash). *Crazy guy,* I imagined the drivers shouting.

Stupid, twenty-one, and reckless … I crashed limits. Yammie could go faster, but at 185 kilometres per hour we hit our comfort ceiling. Fast enough for me. I confessed my sins and flicked my eyes to my mirrors like a Wimbledon zombie. *Thwak. Throk. Thwak. Throk.* Mirrors, road, mirrors, road. Rhythm and blues. *But ain't nothin' gonna come from behind.* The road ahead disappeared into a shimmering horizon. High, safe and focused, we sped toward Eucla.

Madura Pass approached where an immense dry steppe spread below. Roe Plain rolled off the horizon. Yammie screamed down the pass where we continued east across the plain. Moodini's Bluff: a great wall protected my north; emptiness lay to the south. Eucla 185 kilometres ahead.

Fifty kilometres to Eucla; 670 kilometres behind me. My energy melted like ice on a desert day. I slowed down, cruised. One hundred and forty kilometres an hour. The sun edged towards the horizon and the cold seeped across the Nullarbor. Thirty minutes to Eucla.

A car approached from the east.

A small grain … snowballing closer.

'Go man,' I said full of self-congratulation, 'yeah, nearly there.'

The grain became larger. Much larger…

'Fuck.' A police car. My eyes darted to the speedo. 'Shit! One-forty.'

I hit the brakes. *Too late.*

Two furious faces blurred past in an explosion of red-blue lights and sirens. The patrol car skidded to a halt one hundred metres behind me. I pulled over and dismounted. The police car's wheels spun and screeched, a manic U-turn … it geared up for a chase. I stood next to Yammie as the police car sped towards me in an intimidating squeal of rubber, smoke and strobes. It settled three metres in front of me, panting in a halo of lights and dust.

Like a scolded schoolboy I waited for my punishment. I considered raising my hands. I didn't want them to shoot me. *Don't be stupid*, said my saner self. I kept both hands at my sides, palms open. No weapons. *I'm clean.*

'Do you know how fast you were going?'

'Uhm, not too sure … maybe…' The officer cut me off.

'One hundred and forty-one bloody kilometres an hour,' he screamed, spittle flying from his mouth.

My face registered shock and horror.

'Go and check the reading in my car. Go and look,' said the policeman.

Radio chatter buzzed from the patrol car authenticating ugly reality with military static, white noise and urgency. I didn't need more intimidation.

'I believe you,' I admitted. 'I'm sorry.'

I couldn't explain. I had no excuse. Insanity didn't cut it. Speeding had a reverse correlation with age. The higher the speed, the lower my age. The Nullarbor made reckless delinquents out of mature men. My ageing clock had sped backwards, minutes measured in decades. But the cop would never understand. I apologised. Again.

A kangaroo court, no words, a proclamation, and the policeman dished out the penalty: three demerit points and a $400 fine: a death sentence. Devastated but deserving, I swallowed the punishment. I ransacked my brain, my recall hampered by age, fear and fatigue. How many points had I already lost? Eight? Or nine? I couldn't remember. Nine, and I would lose my licence –my road trip over – eight, and the game was still on. Whatever the tally, the Sheriff had nailed *The Nullarbor Kid*. The police had busted the ol' boy's balls.

'Sorry,' I said again, as the officer shoved the ticket into my hand. He paused for a second, discharged a look of disgust, turned on his boots and strutted back to his patrol car.

They turned off their strobes as the driver executed a slow three-point turn and headed west and disappeared into the sun.

I stood by Yammie while the day sank. The desert cold arrived faster than my ticket. My stomach rebelled; my heart raced.

The sky greyed, curdling into something darker; sour clouds whirled like banshees. Memories erupted with failures and fuck-ups. A torrent of guilt fell from the sky. Twenty minutes of a seeping dusk was all that remained of the day. I could stay here for the night. Pull into the bush. No-one would know. I extracted Johnny from my pack and held his weight. It felt right, like a pistol cocked to fire. I held Mr Walker like a lover before an execution. The bottle felt perfect: cool and balanced.

A road train roared past – one metre from my bike. The truck's dash lights flared across a twenty-year-old's handsome face. A flashbulb moment, but sufficient for me to see the driver throw an encouraging wave with a saintly smile – *You can do it.*

I bundled Johnny back into my saddlebag. Mr Walker snorted. The road train thundered east. I latched the saddlebag slowly while my urge to smash Johnnie subsided. *You can do it, the truck driver had said.* Johnnie's time would come. I straddled Yammie and eased her gently towards Eucla. Windmills evaporated like a desert mirage. Don Quixote rode Roccinante the final fifty kilometres to Eucla – limp and lame, desperate and dejected.

Black and purple clouds drew a curtain across the day. I paid for a room, a burger and a soda. Neptune-cold, I laid on my bed, and thought. Seven hundred kilometres, a speeding ticket, three penalty points, and a fucking fine. A huge ride, reckless speeds and a moment of madness had sucked every dribble of this ol' boy's energy. Existing demerit points still riddled my driving record. But just how many bullet holes had blasted my licence? Eight, or nine? Did I feel lucky? 'Well do ya, punk?' said Dirty Harry. 'Go ahead, make my day.'

But I didn't want to know. If I didn't know, well, I didn't know.

I collapsed on my bed and dreamt of prison cells, deserts and dust...

A 44 Magnum exploded somewhere in the ether.

DRY AS A DEAD DINGO'S DONGA

Sunday morning. Quiet and foreboding. The weather matched my anxiety.

Loaded and refuelled, I set off for Ceduna in South Australia. Dark, scudding clouds raced to greet me. The day looked foul. After ten minutes we reached South Australia's border. No quarantine officers held up a hand, so I sailed through but lost forty-five minutes of my life. South Australian time was ninety minutes ahead of Western Australia. Eucla had a time zone of its own. A forty-five-minute halfway house eased the inconvenience of workers flitting across the state line. My time in Eucla should have been euphoric, instead my licence looked like a lost cause.

The Nullarbor desert lived up to its Latin name: *Nullus* – Nothing. *Abor* – Trees. *No Trees.* The Ngandatha people called the plain *Ooondiri* meaning waterless. Yesterday at the Cocklebiddy Roadhouse, a truckie said the Nullarbor was as 'dry as a dead dingo's donger'. Today said otherwise; heavy, dark clouds obscured sky from land. The dead dingo's donger was gonna get real wet, real soon. 'Soon' came quickly. The rain fell like leaden sheets. Road trains still hit Yammie with a *whuummmmpp*, shake, rattle and roll, but now every onslaught smashed me with a slab of dirty water too. It's exhilarating to ride a motorcycle in beautiful weather, but nothing is more miserable in wretched weather. By the end of the day, bloody miserable became fucking miserable.

The Nullarbor Roadhouse had fuel, coffee, meat pies and shelter. I stopped, rested and ate. The Western Australian border was now three hours and 190 kilometres behind me. South Australia had welcomed me with the worst weather of my journey. I had hoped with a sixty-minute roadhouse respite the rain might ease, but it refused to reveal its hand. Better or worse? I rode on.

Twenty minutes later I took a right turn; the first I had seen for hundreds of kilometres. I had read about the baleen whales that came to the area to mate, give birth and socialise. The Shangri-La for whales lay ahead: The Southern Bight. A ten-kilometre ride. *Nothing*. To date, I had ridden 12,000 kilometres, but today the cold, the rain, and the buffeting winds won. I couldn't do it. I turned around and headed back to the highway in defeat. The next day a local newspaper article said the whale count was a mammoth 169. I'd missed it.

Nundroo: my next refuelling stop. Three German women served at the counter. The day remained grim, but I still had another 170 kilometres to go. The disappointment of the previous day pushed me further. My goal was Ceduna. The weather, fatigue, and foreboding demanded I stop for the night. But after forty minutes, I pushed on.

This next leg proved even more atrocious. Every kilometre ticked across my odometer like grains of sand trying to build a mountain. The road disappeared into the muddied waterfall of the grey horizon. Straight roads posed no risks, but slippery, unseen potholes did. I eased off the throttle, and crouched low behind my windshield as watery bullets smashed my helmet with the intensity of a wet desert storm. Hour after hour. The road trains got bigger and meaner. Dusk fell and truck searchlights snared me like an escaping convict. Glare. Blindness. Blackness.

Ceduna. Nearly there. Dark. Cold. My shoulders screamed; my back bellowed. Pain and tension strained every tendon. Lights appeared; civilisation had arrived. I was wrong. A South Australian quarantine checkpoint 380 kilometres east of the Western Australia border loomed from the night. A customs officer held up a hand. *STOP!*

'Any goods to declare?'

'I don't,' I slurred with cold and exhaustion.

He believed me. No searches.

Minutes later I pulled into Ceduna. The pulsing lights of the roadhouse were unattractive but comforting. *Beer, Pokies, Pizza.* A gaudy welcome after a savage night. Time to quit. They had one room vacant. Mine was at the back of the roadhouse facing south towards the ocean. Through the rain-lashed window, I saw nothing but black cloud and the scarring of angry surf as it edged across a lead-grey sea. I closed the curtains, took off my jacket and peeled leggings from my wrecked body. I shuffled to the shower. Hot water with no time limit. The heat eased the strain in my back and shoulders. Warm and exhausted, I fell into my empty bed and thought of Maureen: the spark in my cylinders. Sleep sucked me down like ink into blotting paper. Oblivion.

ONE MILLION CAMELS AND A FUNERAL

The rain had stopped but the strong south-westerly wind said it would be back. A bitterly cold morning, I didn't need an excuse to rest. No riding today. I ate a big breakfast in the roadhouse then went back to bed. The sun had been up fifteen minutes.

I gave the day a second chance at ten o'clock. An extra two hours of sound sleep and a belly full of bacon and eggs had injected me with renewed energy. I needed to walk to stretch my arms and legs still tight with tension and unwind from too much time spent in the saddle. Ceduna's town centre was a short ten-minute stroll.

A brick church, a little over three doorframes wide, looked familiar. I had never been here, but a sense of comfort invited me to try the door. Locked. I searched my mobile: the next AA meeting wouldn't be held until 5.30 pm on Friday. Four days. I had to leave tomorrow. A coffee shop would have to do.

Ceduna lay 800 kilometres north-west of Adelaide. But over a scalding mug of coffee, I decided to follow the longer coastal route. Tomorrow, I would head south-east toward Port Lincoln, then north-east to Port Augusta, then double back on myself and ride south-east again to Adelaide. My odometer would rack up another 1,100 kilometres.

Yesterday a road sign had piqued my interest, and my fears. Three images strung together: a camel, a wombat, and a kangaroo. The sign spelt out the dangers for the next ninety-six kilometres. The wombat looked like it was asleep, but the other two played havoc with my imagination: a kangaroo mid-skip and a camel at full gallop. I understood the dangers of kangaroos. But camels? A little research startled me. Australia's wild camel population is the largest in the world. Imported camels had supported Australia's early trailblazers to explore the continent's interior. Burke and Wills were among the first. Camels opened the outback. Particularly in the most inhospitable areas of Australia's desert regions. The domestic camels thrived. Just a few years before Burke and Wills died on their last fateful expedition, only a handful of camels had set foot in Australia. But their numbers grew. Trains, trucks and planes rendered the camels obsolete, and they were 'let go'. Freedom bred feral camels. By 2008, the wild camel population exploded into a million or more. Culling brought the numbers back to around 300,000 and the price of pet food dropped. That's still a lot of camels. A wombat would be bad enough, but a head on with a one-tonne camel? *Fugheddaboudit!*

I coffeed in Ceduna, took a long walk around town, then returned to my room. By mid-afternoon, I was back in bed. By early evening, hunger pulled me back to the roadhouse for more food. Then back to bed. Yesterday's weather had taken a big toll.

My mobile rested on my bedside cabinet. A text appeared.

I said goodbye to Mum. Arrived in Perth Sunday night. Two days earlier than expected. Sadness sits in my suitcase. I'm not good. But I am sober. I need to get back on the road. Leaving Perth tomorrow for Norseman.

Melanie's message demanded I reply. Was there an emoticon for: *I'm confused?* I didn't know what to say. Anything I did say would send a message I didn't want to send, and if I said what I wanted to say, I'd say something I shouldn't. I was headed for Port Lincoln tomorrow. Slow down or speed up? Run or stay? Melanie's yellow Beetle left Perth this morning. Despite the long drive, I guessed she might be in Norseman tonight.

I sent the thumbs up symbol, which said nothing and everything.

Minutes passed. Melanie was thinking.

Melanie: *Where are you?*

Me: *Ceduna*

More minutes.

Melanie: *Thumbs up.*

Nothing and everything.

My fingers hesitated on the keyboard … and that's all they did … hesitate. My phone dissolved into sleep. I tried to do the same. Despite a lazy day, a late morning and an afternoon nap, good food, and a warm bed, despite it all, I couldn't shake off the exhaustion. But sleep didn't come easy.

THONGZ

After the horror ride into Ceduna, I had forgotten to take my gloves from the saddlebag. Bugger. They were still wet. My hands would freeze. Despite the scattered clouds, it looked like the rain might give me a break. The cold weather wouldn't. Within minutes my fingers blued into digits of ice. I stowed my gloves in the cargo net that held my jerry. The wind would dry them. Until then …

Streaky Bay, one-hundred kilometres south-east, was a chance a to stop, get warm, and bring life back into my hands. I wanted to take some shots of the long jetty that stretched into the ocean. My numb hands reached into my saddlebag to pull out my camera. I dropped it. Johnnie laughed as my lens exploded into a mess of shrapnelled glass and plastic. The camera survived; the lens was a write-off. Port Lincoln – 300 kilometres south – would be the nearest town to buy a replacement. Much cheaper than my Canon, I chose a Tamron. I ordered it directly. The lens wouldn't arrive until tomorrow afternoon. So, no need to ride to Port Lincoln today. I'd stay somewhere else tonight. Somewhere warm. Somewhere close. Somewhere soon.

One hundred kilometres south of Ceduna, a sign piqued my curiosity: Murphy's Haystacks. The 'Haystacks' lay in a wheat field two kilometres from the road. Mallee scrub circled the riddle. Molarshaped boulders over eight-metres high towered from the middle of the field. Orange lichen dripped over the pink granite rocks in what appeared to be a dentist's surgery for giants. The rocks arrived 1,500 million years earlier than the man after whom they were named. From a distance, they could be mistaken for haystacks, but I rooted for Murphy's Molars.

The hike warmed my hands and reignited the flow of blood through my body. After ten minutes in the saddle, they were numb again. My ten-minute ritual would become a necessity for the rest of the day. I roasted my gloves on Yammie's exhausts while my hands slapped at the pipes. Five minutes later with hot gloves and thawed fingers, I remounted. Ten minutes later....

I'm in Eucla, said the text.

Jesus, that Beetle flew faster than a falcon chasing a swift. A reply would have to wait. Frost-frozen fingers made it too difficult to tap back an answer. Maybe an excuse. Best to wait and think. Only sixty kilometres to Elliston. *Melanie in Eucla.* I shook my head again. That yellow Beetle should race at Le Mans.

I needed a place to stay.

Elliston was close and as good as anywhere. The town hosted two towering silos that stood like sentries over its Waterloo Bay. Huge cliffs stood to the north. A steel jetty poked 500 metres south toward the Great Australian Bight – next stop, Antarctica. I took a cheap cabin at the caravan park – old and weathered – but it had a heater.

Where are you? Melanie texted.

A shower in the ablution block fifty metres away gave my body the warmth it craved. Then I hit the local bakery. Bread, pastries and pies. All a man needed. I took my peppered steak pie and a bottle of milk onto the street. An end-of-a-long-day satisfaction settled over me as I ate. I didn't send another text. And I didn't receive one. The coldness that tortured my body since early morning had gone.

Across from the bakery, a neat village green hosted a local town flag and a war memorial. Next to it sat a sculptured life-size whale's tail. It rose from the grass with the majesty of an imminent splash. Farther down the street, a solitary three-legged humanoid stood lifeless yet foreboding. This sculptured alien spoke of portent. A face without definition held my stare. Elliston looked different.

An old local walked past and looked at me with unblinking eyes.

'We surprise everybody,' he said. 'Check the Cliffs.' He pointed north and waved a nervous hand showing they were close. 'The Cliffs,' he said again as he fluttered fingers with both hands like he was shooing me towards salvation.

'The Thongs,' he whispered. 'The Thongs.'

I smiled the smile I reserved for lunatics.

'I feel like I'm fifteen again,' he added.

'Sure,' I replied. 'Good on you.'

Retreat and research sounded like a good option. *I feel like I'm fifteen again.* Whatever the man was taking, I wanted some. *The Cliffs.* Tomorrow.

Ceduna tonight read Melanie's text.

She followed with another text one minute later: *You?*

Should I stay or should I go? If I go, there will be trouble. And if I stay, it will be double.

Me: *Elliston*

Nothing.

Melanie: *Can I call? Tomorrow?*

I hesitated…

Me: *Sure*

It was a cold day, but short and slow. I was still exhausted. The little heater in my room worked overtime and my room soon burst into musty warmth. Sleep came quick.

MEET ME AT DOCS

My mobile burst into early morning dreams. Maureen's voice. Excited. Exuberant. My wonderful wife had booked a flight to Melbourne. She would meet me there. And it got better: she had booked a flight to Sydney too. Fifteen hundred kilometres to Melbourne. Maybe a four-day ride. Then a thousand-kilometre hop and skip to Sydney via Canberra. Maybe a two-day ride.

Doubtful lows now soared to ecstatic highs.

'I can't wait,' Maureen said.

'Me neither.'

'I love you,' she said. 'Ride safe. Be good. Be there.'

'I will.'

'I see your progress on the satellite tracker. If you leave the road, even for a loo trip, I see where you went. I see everything. Isn't that amazing?'

'Amazing!' I said. 'And I love you too.'

'Hold the line a sec,' I said pretending to check my imaginary appointment calendar. 'I'm free.'

'I knew I had to be quick to avoid disappointment,' Maureen said.

'Ha ha,' I offered. 'Book a table for two. Anywhere. Six pm. Your choice. My shout.'

'DOCS,' she said.

'What?'

'I'll see you there.' Then Maureen laughed in the way that only Maureen could.

I missed her. A lot.

Yammie carried me north to *The Cliffs* and Clifftop Drive. *I feel like I'm fifteen again,* the man had said. A gravel track snaked along the steep and rugged cliff edge. Anxious Bay spread out below. Then giant sculpted thongs appeared at the edge of the Cliffs. *Thongz.* A man-sized construction of a pair of flip-flops. A smile spread beneath my helmet while I searched for *I feel like I'm fifteen again.* A few hundred metres farther along the trail, another sculpture stood close to the cliff edge. I didn't need a plaque to tell me I had found it. A teenage caricature sat on a bicycle meant for a toddler. Skinny legs, monstrous feet and a surfboard tucked under his arm. My smile stretched. I kicked Yammie onto her side stand and put my helmet on the sculpture. My camera captured the moment. The local man was right: I did feel like I was fifteen again.

The track hugged the cliff tops; the seascapes were as stunning as the sculptures. Research told me I had discovered 'Sculptures on the Cliffs'.

Soon I saw a meshed-steel net enclosing a fish carcass of sculptured metal. The ocean rose and crashed through the open spaces between its skeletal structure. A vision of freedom trapped in a prison of bones.

MARA stared at me from a face two-metres tall. Latvians considered her the mother of Earth. Serene and sage. Her windblown hair looked like the sails of a tall ship: a ship of ghosts, of eighteenth-century immigrants. Later I discovered stories of mass slaughter: 167 years ago, a local posse threw Aboriginals over the cliffs. Men, women and children. Official records blur with the stories told by locals: *Two hundred murdered,* the Wirangu people said. A massacre.

Farther along, four faces glared at my intrusion. Neanderthal foreheads, large noses, hooded brows, big ears. Easter Island on Elliston Cliffs. From one-to-two-metres tall, they regarded me with knowing faces. Look on my works, ye Mighty. And despair! The antique traveller from a modern land didn't say a word. He took a photo instead, then sent those enigmatic sculptures searching for social LIKES they didn't need. It felt like trespass.

My phone rang.

'It's me. How are you?'

'Melanie! Hey, I'm good. But you, how are you?'

Clichéd introductions for a complex connection.

'What's the noise? Where are you?'

'Elliston Cliffs with Easter Island faces.'

'What?'

'Sorry, it's the surf and the wind. I'm standing on The Cliffs.'

'Cliffs?'

'Elliston. I'll call you later. Give me an hour.'

Sixty minutes to think.

Onwards.

My English blood could no longer tolerate the cold. Fourteen years of subtropical weather in Queensland had weakened my Northern-Hemisphere resistance. I could no longer 'do' cold. The impact of icy wind and long rides generated fatigue far beyond what I expected. I was flagging. My concentration had sunk to dangerous lows. My body shook within minutes of hot coffee and warmed gloves. Apparently, when the going got tough the tough got going. But the ol' fella couldn't remember 'tough' and didn't have a clue where he was going.

Rolling hills and herds of sheep reminded me of Sussex. Of England. Of another life. Fields of rapeseed blurred past in a haze of impressionist art. Summer images in an Australian winter.

A detour took me to Coffin Bay. Ninety minutes had passed. Cold and fatigue forced me to stop longer in this iconic location. A cafe provided fuel and food. Chicken, chips and peas with strong coffee. I began to feel my blood warm and life creep back into my hands. A large chalkboard behind the counter offered daily specials: oysters. I took a dozen for dessert, fresh from the bay across the street. I had never tasted better.

Now I needed to make a phone call.

'Melanie.'

'Hey,' she said.

'How are you?'

'I'm good. Look,' she said nervously. 'Augusta was a reaction. I'm sober. I'm grieving. And I'm sorry. But I had to move on. Newcastle was a bad place for me. My sons said to stay. But what I'm doing is better.'

'What *are* you doing?'

'Well … I decided to continue my journey. Like you, I'm gonna go the whole way.'

'The whole way?'

'Yeah, all the way around. Then, I'm gonna do it again. Slowly. And look for work. At least if I've done it, I'll know where to shoot.' She paused. 'Where are you?'

'Coffin Bay.'

'I'm two hours behind you.' Another pause. 'Can we catch up?' she said.

A yellow Beetle, white daisy, blonde hair and a courageous character swayed me to give the wrong answer. 'Sure,' I said, not sure of anything. 'I'm headed for Cowell. Too far?'

'No, not too far. I'll call when I get close.'

Melanie had a four-hour drive ahead of her.

I stopped in Port Lincoln for more fuel and the camera lens I ordered the day before, and a haircut. The barber gave me a seniors' discount. The sad part? I didn't have to ask. As I rode out of town, a statue of Matthew Flinders and his cat, Trim, sat humbly on the sidewalk. He had done it. They had both done it. Two hundred and fifteen years ago they sailed around Australia. I raised my hand in a silent salute.

Two hours to Cowell for me. Four hours for Melanie. Three days to Melbourne and a six pm date with Maureen. Nothing would stop me, not even the loss of my licence.

Two hotels on Cowell's Main Street had rooms for the night. Quietness had settled on the town as the end of the day hovered on the edge of night, when life appears to limbo. Nothing stirred. The Commercial Hotel hugged the first corner. The Franklin Harbour Hotel loomed from the next. I chose the former. The latter overlooked the land-locked harbour from which it had taken its name. A court had hanged four Aboriginals on this site thirty years before its construction. The stories said the Indigenous men kicked and struggled for some time, so the hangman hung onto their legs until they wriggled no more. The Commercial Hotel provided lodging over a pub, old like the Franklin, but without the ghosts.

Sixty dollars bought a snug single room, access to the hot showers down the hall and a common guest room to sit, make coffee and think.

I parked Yammie on Main Street. Nose-to-nose parking bays ran down the middle of the road. The town looked quiet, but an uncomfortable anxiety made me consider the gear in my panniers. My saddlebags had no locks. Yammie's rain cover was just that – a cover – and Johnnie would be left unattended. Mr Walker would need to spend the night with me. I walked down the creaky staircase while the aged oak squeaked in distress. *Stop. Stay. Staaay.* Johnnie leered with anticipation as I buried him under a shirt. Then my phone rang.

'Yes,' I said, quick and anxious.

'It's me,' Melanie said. 'Are you okay?'

'Fine.'

'Where are you? I'm in Main Street,' she said as her yellow Beetle appeared at the end of the road.

Shit.

'One sec. Stay there. I'll come down.'

Instead, I ran across the street, up the groaning stairs to my room and threw my shirt and its fucking fugitive onto the bed.

Back in the street, I saw Melanie's Beetle bathed in the light of the Franklin Harbour Hotel.

'Hi,' she said, stepping from her car.

'Hi.'

The stars betrayed the blackness between the clouds. A breeze from the harbour chilled the street, while the hotel threw out a soft yellow light. Melanie stepped forward and hugged me.

'Thank you,' she said.

I hugged her back.

'You good?' I said, not knowing what else to say.

'Sad but sober.' Melanie gave a wry smile. 'I'm sorry, I …'

I held up a finger and waved away the words that would follow.

'No apologies. It's done. You're okay. Augusta's forgotten. I'm sorry for your loss.'

Melanie's eyes began to tear. 'Where are you staying?' she said.

'There,' I said, pointing at the Commercial Hotel.

'Maybe I'll stay here?' she said, head nodding towards the Franklin. Her words teetered on the edge of a question; a statement a nose behind. 'Maybe' was a mistake. Maybe was meek and wrong.

'You should,' I said.

My phone rang. 'Hey babe,' I said looking at Melanie while speaking to Maureen.

Melanie turned and walked to her car.

'The tracker says you're in Cowell.'

'Yeah, I am. I took a room at the Commercial Hotel.'

'The tracker says you're in the street.'

I laughed. 'I am. I'm stretching my legs.'

'Just about to start a shift. I'll call tomorrow. Where will you be?'

'Adelaide. All being well.'

'Wow! Be good. Be careful. Talk tomorrow.'

Melanie walked towards the Franklin with her backpack.

'Maybe dinner in thirty minutes,' she said. Her inflection gave no doubt. Dinner was a given. Only the time was open to debate.

'Sure,' I looked at my watch. 'Seven?'

'Seven,' she said with a smile. 'Your place or mine?'

'Yours.'

I had conceived my ride around Australia for many reasons. Hidden in those reasons were sixty-two days to reflect. Sixty-two days to prove what I needed to prove. Johnny Walker lurked beneath my shirt, Melanie across the street, Maureen 3,500 kilometres away.

I picked up my phone and tapped the screen. *I love you.* Maureen would read my text at the end of her shift. *Lots*, I added.

We had pig on a spit. Wednesday night special at the Franklin Harbour Hotel. Twenty-seven days ago, I overtook a yellow Beetle as I headed towards Camooweal and the Northern Territory border. That evening I ate with its driver. Tonight, and a lifetime later, we ate together again. My soda water sat next to her orange juice. Alcohol surrounded us. Yet we had escaped to freedom. Recapture was not an option. Funerals and family, alcohol and addiction, sobriety and sanity: of these subjects, we discussed not a word. Excitement of the present. Intoxication of the future. Next adventure. Next stop. Tomorrow. Melanie had salvaged her Augustan wreck. Sleek and seaworthy, she was a different woman. She seemed at peace; her mother's death would hurt later.

My phone rang.

'It's my break. Where are you?' Maureen said.

'Having dinner.'

'Where?'

'The Franklin Hotel.'

'Who with?'

'Melanie.'

'Melanie?'

'Another traveller.'

Melanie was fine. Maureen was not.

Wednesday night required an articulate email. An honest answer. A clear explanation. A message of 600 words of 'Honesty' that Thomas Jefferson said was 'the first chapter of the book of wisdom'. Maureen was wise, I was not. Melanie was an alcoholic, me too. But my honest 600 words made no mention of my unmentionable mate, Johnnie. I ate with him every night. Trust in my strength pushed lies through omission, but willpower was a thing I sought, not a thing I owned.

Melanie was a brother. A sister in need. A friend. Nothing else. Johnnie was a bastard.

Sleep wouldn't come. I used the time to write in my journal. Day 34: Dear Diary. But I didn't write about my day. I wrote a story. A blurry piece about prejudice:

The Morning After

The train rocks the man with every sway, twist and jerk. His head rolls like a rag doll dancing to the strings of a silent puppeteer. The man's children, a girl of seven and boy of five, scream and shout, jump and holler. The man sits silent, his lifeless body animated only by the rhythm of the train. Unshaven, stained shirt: the man looks like a drunk. He observes his children; he witnesses their rampage, but like blind eyes staring into the sun, he sees nothing.

The carriage is empty except for an old woman perched like a stuffed crow in the opposite seat. Rigid, she fights the train to maintain her poise, and all the time, her wrinkled hands wield knitting needles that orchestrate grand flourishes, turning a chaos of wool into a well-mannered scarf. She raises her eyes above half-rimmed glasses at precise intervals and stares. First the man. Then the children. Then her knitting.

It's early Sunday morning. No-one gets on. No-one gets off. The train bounces along the track oblivious to the humanity of its cargo. The children suck energy from air and leap from seat to seat. Muddy shoes, snotty noses, sticky fingers – singing, laughing, dancing, yelping. The boy holds the remnants of a messy sandwich; its red sauce leaves a tell-tale track across the patterned seats. An empty can of Coke rolls down the carriage and stops at the woman's shoe.

Disgraceful, thinks the woman, Utterly disgraceful. She watches and broods as the children run wild. Brats. The man stares at his feet. Says nothing. Does nothing. The woman darkens her look. She tries to glare the children into submission. In my day...

The children pull faces, stick their fingers in mushy, sandwich-filled mouths and stretch their lips, corner to corner. Clown-like. This wildness is unwitnessed by their father.

The train slows.

'Redcliffe,' says a metallic, dead voice. 'Redcliffe, next stop.'

'Daddy, Daddy, we're here,' says the girl.

The train shudders, the man stays in his seat, and the carriage jerks to a halt. Doors swoosh; a shaft of sunlight fills the shadow. Icy air spreads along the passage. The man stirs from his trance. He looks up, nods, and with great effort, rises from his seat. He seems shocked as though woken from a spell.

Words spill like cold stones. 'Anna. Tom. Hold hands. Watch the gap.' As the man follows his children towards the doors, the old woman sneers her distaste.

'You should control your children,' she says.

The man is shocked to hear someone speak. She is talking to him. He glances at his children. He understands. 'I'm sorry,' says the man. 'We've been at the hospital all night. Their mother died five hours ago.' The man pauses. 'I'm sorry...' he says again as he steps into another world, his words trailing behind like guilty epithets.

A TALE OF TWO CONSCIENCES

A dry patch on Main Street the size of a yellow Beetle attested to Melanie's departure. My silent phone attested to Maureen's misgiving. And a full bottle attested to the truth Johnnie had not been touched.

Cold day.

My sad heart rode pillion.

Adelaide sprawled 238 kilometres south-east across the Jarvis Strait by ferry. But there were no ferries. Google Maps said there were, but a local told me the service had stopped. Instead, I should take the Lincoln Highway to Port Augusta 200 kilometres north-east to the top end of the Jarvis Strait, then do an about turn and take the Augusta Highway 300 kilometres south to Adelaide.

Cold, cold day.

A squall had gathered and dissipated as though in surrender. The day looked clear. But temperatures and fatigue stole my last dregs of energy.

Cold, cold, cold day.

Two hundred kilometres later, Port Augusta emerged with the hazy purpled-blue beginnings of the distant Flinders Range spread behind it. Civilisation took a different form. The road sign ahead said no drinking in public. *Hi, I'm Port Augusta and I'm a city dry zone.* But I needed to be warm as well as dry. My gloves didn't cut it and my fingers froze like webbed feet in an ice block. Operating the brake and throttle was like knitting with boxing gloves. My feet faired a fraction better. I had my boots to thank for that. But the cold from my hands snaked like iced tendrils into my brain. Exhausted and frozen, I stopped at a motorcycle shop and held up my gloved hands in explanation.

'Try these,' said the mechanic.

Huge, down-filled gauntlets dwarfed my puny digit-freezers that excused themselves as gloves. 'Done,' I said. Seventy-six dollars: expensive but necessary.

Thirty minutes in a warm cafe across the street helped. A hot coffee and a cheese kransky helped too, but it didn't cure. Fatigue should have made me quit. Killer cold weather should have iced a sensible decision. I should have stayed for the night but didn't. I had a date in Melbourne. Walking back to Yammie my phone buzzed.

Coober Pedy next stop. Can't thank you enough x

Melanie must have passed through Port Augusta just before me. She had a head start, longer than I thought. I didn't pass her. I was glad.

Another text, two seconds after the last

You have my number xx

A smiley face was my only reply.

Now like two atoms after a collision, we sped in opposite directions. She to the north, to an opal town where the residents lived in caves called dugouts, and me to the city of churches, 300 kilometres south.

So close. So far. So good. Melanie had been on the edge of freefall into a Relapse Ravine. People, networks, belief, support systems – personal bodyguards – we all needed help, but it was still so easy to drown. And so hard to surface. The reverb from my own colossal sobriety-cathedral brought a powerful peace. It hovered in the air. I sighed in its presence. Delicate and ephemeral. My private bunker was under constant attack. Alcoholic terrorists armed with relapse grenades lurked in the shadows. *Fire at will*, said the commanders. They did.

Murdered families followed. Collateral damage. I was the fuse. Johnnie the spark. Maureen my love and saviour.

Icy winds blustered from the Jarvis Strait. This was the winter my Pommy heritage understood. My new gauntlets proved better, at least ten minutes better. Seventy-two dollars allowed me to sit in the saddle a little longer until the same icy pain burnt my fingers. My body remained frozen to the core.

To my west on a distant ridge, wind farms extended as far as I could see. Huge forests of turbines – white giants – sucking green energy from the Roaring Forties. Slowly, slowly, extended arms reached out to grab the wind and reap its power. Kilometres passed and still the turbines lined the hills, turning tirelessly, one blade at a time, weaning society's addiction from an unsustainable present to a better, cleaner future. I needed that strength.

Another stop. Another roadhouse. Another coffee. Another surprise.

The truckies reacted to my entrance like a tickled beehive. My jacket was the source of my infamy. White hair, blue jeans and brown boots removed the jury's doubt. 'You ride a red motorcycle with a stack of shit on the back?' said one, eyes bulging almost as far as his paunch. 'You cross the Nullarbor a couple of days back?' he added.

'I do and I did.'

'How fast were you going? We've got bets,' said another with ears like lamb cutlets edged with cauliflower. 'On the Nullarbor, I mean, top speed?' His eyes narrowed, 'And no malarkey.'

I paused for a second. 'One hundred and eighty-five,' I said, not sure whether to smile or shit.

'I win,' said a third. 'Good on ya. Youse keep an eye on the cops.'

'For sure!'

They all laughed the laugh of larrikins.

'Take it easy,' said the chief interrogator slapping me on the back.

'I will.'

They laughed again. I joined in. Mates.

Forty minutes later, I stepped back out into the cold. Warmer, safer, happier.

An hour on the highway and civilisation returned. I didn't see it coming. Sadly, the outback of Northern Territory, Western Australia and the Nullarbor was far behind me. Three oncoming cars flashed their lights. One, two, three. I slowed and looked ahead for cattle or camels or emus or goats or kangaroos or wombats. Nothing, except a solitary police car hidden off-road – waiting.

Civilisation had its benefits. I stopped at a service station (roadhouses were a thing of the past) and developed a new addiction. I found the dryer in the men's room. I didn't need a leak, but the blast of warm air heated my hands. Not for seconds but for looooooong minutes. The thawing brought a smile to my face. Other men came and went. Raised eyebrows, pursed lips and a couple of exchanged side nods said all that needed to be said. *Crazy guy.*

The service station had even more to offer: a turbaned Indian man stood behind a glass counter clouded with steam. Spread before him was a frozen man's delight. Lamb madras, beef vindaloo, chicken muglai and roast cashew chicken.

'Vindaloo,' I shouted with an urgency of man in the last stages of hypothermia.

The same heads from the men's room turned. *Crazy guy.*

Twenty minutes later, I stepped into the cold. Warm on the outside, volcanic on the inside.

I arrived in the City of Churches at dusk. Today the cold froze my carcass like concrete; stupidly, I kept riding to make a final push to Adelaide's east side. I wanted to make an early start in the morning without the burden of traffic. I needed to make my date with Maureen in Melbourne.

Adelaide greeted me with snarling traffic and impatient commuters. Age had hit me hard. I couldn't 'do' cold, and now I realised I couldn't 'do' traffic either. The first road jams for thirty-five days. Australia's longest road was but a memory. I had chosen a bad time to arrive. Luck led me to the highway on Adelaide's east side and an open road to Melbourne tomorrow. But now I couldn't go any further, not another kilometre. I was flat out. Done. Dusted. Decimated. I pulled into The Bridgewater Inn.

Stiff, cold and exhausted I walked into the pub. 'A room,' I said, 'I need a room.' *Please* and *thank you* had frozen with the ice.

'Sorry,' said the barman. 'We don't offer accommodation.'

'Shit.'

'You okay?'

'Sorry. Rude. I'm exhausted. Been riding all day. Cold. I'm sorry.'

'Try Hahndorf.'

It was an effort to ask what I dreaded to hear: 'How far?'

'Five kilometres.'

An open fire crackled and flamed on the other side of the bar.

'You don't look well,' the barman said. 'Sit by the fire. Warm up first.'

The barman pulled up a chair close to the hearth, stoked the fire, and without asking brought me a hot chocolate. I imagined he would fetch a thermal blanket too. He didn't. While the heat from the hot chocolate and the blazing logs eased the cold, they also fed my exhaustion. I needed to sleep.

'You gonna be okay?'

'Sure,' I lied. 'And thanks.' Five kilometres in the ice of night seemed longer than a butterfly flight to the moon.

Thirty minutes later I tried. I found a cabin in the German enclave of Hahndorf. *Mein Gott.* Today I pushed boundaries I never knew existed. It was $120 a night – I had no strength to look for something cheaper. But it did come with a lavish extra: an electric blanket.

I stopped shaking one hour later. Too tired to sleep, I wrote in my journal instead. I didn't write about my day. I thought about Maureen. Her loyalty, support and love. I thought about Melanie. Her relapse. I thought about my story of the old lady on the train. I thought about prejudice. I thought about alcoholism. I thought about black and white. I thought about grey. I thought about the shape of alcohol. I wrote this:

A Tale of Two Consciences

Alcoholics don't deserve any help from us
So, don't lecture and tell me thus:

'Addiction's not a vice or craven crime
But for God's grace, it might be you another time'
That's a lie, so better to say:
Hell will make them pay
Drunks and skunks
Bums in slums
Thugs on drugs
Beggars and thieves
They are not
Welcome here
We must make them
Understand fair compensation
So don't show hesitation
And try to understand
Hold out our hand
No, we should pray
Lock them away
It's not right to preach
It's sobriety for which they reach
We are strong; They are weak
Don't be naive and believe the lie:
Alcoholics can abstain; stop; one day be dry.

(Now read from bottom to top)

My pen fell to the floor, but not before thoughts of cold Adelaide traffic sucked me down into dreams of straight lines, memories of balmy weather and Australia's longest unwrinkled road.

BIG THINGS AND BUST-UPS

New York has Little Italy: Adelaide has Little Germany – Hahndorf. I rode through this delightful village with flashes of its colonial heritage passing either side: Prussian flags, Kaffeehaus, Otto's Bakery, The Haus, German Arms Hotel, Acrobrau Bierhaus, Wolf Blass Gallery and Museum, Carl Nitschke Memorial Park. The locals, however, did not dress in lederhosen – understandable given the frosty morning. Hahndorf was founded in 1838 as a Lutheran hub for German immigrants escaping persecution from their Prussian King. A contemporary story of yesterday, today and tomorrow.

The Germans created little Hahndorf, but Australians built The Big Olive and The Big Lobster. I rode past both – Tailem Bend and Kingston South East. I'm not sure why the Aussies have a penchant for Big Things: The Big Banana, The Big Ned Kelly, The Big Merino, The Big Lobster, The Big Pineapple, The Big Bogan, The Big Chook, The Big Ugg Boots, The Big Beer Can and The Big Stubbie (remember Day Nine and Larrimar?). There's even a Big Poo, built by local Robertson residents as a protest against a Sydney utility's decision not to reuse wastewater. Perhaps a big country needs big icons.

I nearly had my first accident at Meningie. Luckily for me the town's 50 kph limit kept speeds slow. A driver pulled out of a side road right in front of me. The road was clear and wide. Nothing obstructed his view. I hit the brakes, Yammie lurched and her rear wheel zigzagged into a skid before stopping a nose length from the driver's door. An unshaven man in his mid-thirties looked at me, waved a hand in bleary-blind confusion, then drove off on his oblivious way. The SA government had placed penetrating road warnings across many parts of the state: '**High there? – Time's up for drug drivers.**' Maybe that was the problem. A hiccup in time measured the distance between an ugly accident and the ol' boy's goals.

I followed the Princes Highway. Much of the road passed between low-lying bush submerged in water. Perhaps uncommon rainfall or maybe a regular feature. There was no rain today, just the continuing cold. It wasn't just my low tolerance either; ice fell from Yammie's cover that morning as I undressed her for the day.

The pull of the men's restroom soon became overwhelming. The heaven of a hot-air hand dryer almost trumped the warmth of a *caffé corretto*. The cold bit into me, numbed me, dumbed me. Perhaps to ride like that bordered on an offence too: '**Iced there? – Time's up for frozen riders.**'

In the last hour I battled 'the wall'. So, to keep my blood flowing and senses alert, I invented a sort of ol' fellas twerk – a saddle-bound breakdance and a Gangnam-style bounce with a twist of nutcracker craziness. The music in my helmet helped: 'Roady' by Fat Freddy's Drop. *Yeah*!

I opened the throttle and continued to dance.

Thick pine forest lined the road for twenty kilometres before Mount Gambier's neon lights and streetlamps rose to greet me. I needed a room. My blood needed to shrink the icebergs in my veins.

Potential stopovers littered the street. Several hotel/pubs offered accommodation. Competition kept prices down. Thirty-five dollars bought me a single bed in the Commercial Hotel. Yammie won out too. A dry space in the backyard shed gave her a warm room and would negate any need to de-ice her in the morning. The room was tiny and warm, courtesy of a small oil heater in the corner. I turned it to high and pushed it six inches from my pillow, just far enough not to burn my nose. I would let it percolate the room with heat before attempting to sleep. The pub pulsed with a live band. Friday night freedom. I remembered that feeling. After a shower and a change of clothes, I went downstairs to the bar.

When is rock bottom? Do we ever get there, or are we like the Californians, always thinking the next big quake will be the ultimate disaster? I woke every morning for twenty years thinking I'd hit the bottom. I thought the rock had penetrated my backside and pushed through to my gut. I was wrong. As bad as the horrors got, I never reached the rock. Perhaps the Californian in me said it would be the next shake. Well, that might be tonight. If I've learnt anything though, it's this: rock bottom only arrives when the last nail hammers down your coffin. It's when the last shovel of dirt hits the lid, rattles the box and says, 'now rest in fucking peace'. You've gotta find the bottom before you hit the rock because the cunt of a rock is just an illusion.

I stepped into the bar. After-work drinkers overlapped with the night-has-just-begun crowd. Waiting elbows lined the bar. Mine joined the queue. Five minutes later a young barmaid approached with a big smile as wide as the manager of the pub had no doubt ordered.

'And what can I get for you tonight?' Her smile stretched further.

'A lollipop and a bedtime story,' I said.

'Excuse me!'

'Why, what did you do?'

'What?'

'A soda water,' I said. 'That would be good. Thank you.'

She turned and walked to the soda pump. 'There you go,' she said, placing a large glass popping with soda and topped with a smiley slice of lemon.

'Thank you,' I said. 'And I'm sorry.'

'Why?' Her face softened.

'I'm not as young as I used to be,' I said in clichéd old people speak. I shocked myself with the truth. 'I'm old and I'm alcoholic. This is not easy,' I said as I raised my glass. The present tense amplified everything I thought I'd never say. 'I didn't mean to be rude.'

The barmaid looked at me.

'I was rude,' I said again. 'I'm sorry.'

'Sally,' she said. 'I'm Sally, and you weren't – rude.' She smiled. Easy and warm. 'Enjoy your soda.' She turned to serve her thirsty customers, then looked over her shoulder, 'You're a legend,' she added with a wink.

I finished my soda. Sally had made my night: a confession and a blessing.

Tomorrow, Melbourne. And Maureen.

In another lifetime, in another world, my Friday nights usually started something like this:

After work, I often sat alone in a pub, any pub, but sometimes the 'drink before the commute' finished later than intended, and often, even later than that. So, on Friday nights, when my five am alarm posed no real and present danger for the next morning, the odds of a late one increased. Boogie Woogie Nights. Worrying times. It was easy to lose track of it. Time that is. Easy to lose track of pints. Lager that is. Thoughts and words often folded into meaningless jabber. One beer moved onto the next, but now and then fortuitous encounters with new acquaintances became my reward – mostly other drunks – and unexpected outcomes became extraordinarily common.

One night, I sat strangely satisfied at a 'rediscovered' pub (the previous manager had moved on as had my lifetime ban which probably sat in dusty public-house archives labelled 'undesirables'). The Hitchhiker's Guide to the Galaxy sat in my briefcase, next to my current stressful-project papers. The former was almost finished, the latter not yet started. But Adams had made me think. Made me laugh. I thought about 'Life, the Universe and Everything'. Forty-two. It sounded about right to me.

Sitting on a bar stool next to mine was a man about my age who appeared to have drunk even more than me. It seemed he took injury to one of my innocent proclamations. It may have been something like, 'Looks like rain tomorrow.'

A grunted profanity questioned my forecast and challenged my lineage.

'Heyho brundliebro, methinks thou takest the pisstallydoodles,' I said with Adams-like humour trying to defuse the situation.

Then the fight started.

A simplification. But Monday morning became complicated: my boss, James, had arranged a luncheon meeting with Coutts and Co – bankers for the wealthy. A select group of them to meet a bunch of us. Operational opportunities offered a back for each of us to scratch. 'Us' being an American bank, 'them' being a venerable British one – for clients who had a quid. Or two. First impressions would be important.

I needed to call in my excuses early on Monday morning.

'James, it's Richard.'

'Hey, Rich, big day. Everything okay?' Professionalism pervaded everything.

'No!'

'No?' And the world caved in. 'What's wrong?' James asked already working through a 'Richard-list' of potential answers.

'Look, it might be difficult for me to make the luncheon.'

'Difficult?' James repeated with growing concern.

'Embarrassing actually.'

'Embarrassing?' James said, his question marks more menacing than a torturer's impending kneecapping.

Honesty. Nothing else would do. Say it as it is. Clear. Concise. Credible. 'Well, I was, err, well, mugged.'

'Mugged?'

'Yes, and I've lost two front teeth, my lips look like disembowelled worms and my right eye is like a bloodied beetroot that's still oozing juice. The fact is... Coutts and Co won't be impressed.'

'You've been seen by a doctor? Been to the police?'

'Er, no.' I said to the professional torturer who knew a lie before it was even told.

'Cut the shit!'

'Fight.' I said in a rush to avoid the kneecapping. 'Pub fight.'

'Jesus,' said James.

The line hushed with an ugly silence. One second. Two. Ten seconds.

'Okay, here's what we tell Coutts… It was a rugby match, a clash of heads, the other guy is in hospital. Okay? Got that?'

In England, rugby is played by the privileged elite.

'I understand, but only one part of your excuse is true,' I said.

'What?'

'I don't play rugby.'

'Doesn't matter,' he said bypassing the implication, 'It's a public-school thing. Coutts will love it.'

And they did.

GREAT OCEAN ROAD

This morning I would meet Bill in Peterborough, 230 cold and icy kilometres east. Tonight Maureen, in Melbourne, 520 even colder and icier kilometres east. Coffee, watering needs, hand-warmers and refuelling stops suggested an eight-hour ride.

Today would be big. Tonight bigger.

Mount Gambier froze behind me as Yammie carried me through the Myora Forest. The sun's rays razored deep into the shadowed morning of the trees. Thousands of hectares of pine trees lined my route with military precision. I hit the Victorian border fifteen minutes later and lost another thirty minutes to the state's time difference. After 100 kilometres, the Princes Highway delivered a shock of soles. Hundreds of shoes of all types dangled from a farm fence like lovelocks from a Parisian bridge. Sneakers and slippers, flats and heels, thongs and wellies, sandals and stilettos. A trail of used footwear hung in a message more cryptic than a string of hieroglyphics written by a drunk. Welcome to Tyrendarra. Population: 212. Carol Altmann started the craze. On her travels she saw something similar in New Zealand. 'Why not?' she said. 'Why not' exploded into thousands. My hometown of Coolum Beach broke out in lovelocks at Point Perry a few years ago, but passions were promptly doused by the council.

Maureen and I placed our own lovelock there and sealed our pact with a kiss as a blood-red moon rose over the ocean. *Snip*. Local councils have no heart. *Snip*. The lovelocks disappeared.

The Northern Territory dressed its termite mounds, Western Australia inscribed its boabs, but Victoria lost shoes (and Harold Holt). My curiosity piqued as I considered what my imminent arrival in NSW and the Australian Capital Territory would bring.

Bill, a friend, had a Harley. Facebook posts had alerted him about my madness, and he had volunteered to chaperone me from Peterborough into Melbourne. Bill would accompany me 300 kilometres on one of Australia's most iconic highways: The Great Ocean Road. He would also usher me across metro-Melbourne to Maureen. Bill was both trip-adviser and escort. Secretly, I think Maureen called Bill to make sure I made it. Escort or no, nothing could stop me. Even if I had to crawl. But I still had to make an icy three-hour ride *before* I met Bill.

We met at the junction of the Great Ocean Road and Old Peterborough Road, just before Peterborough. From there we would follow the GOR to Apollo Bay, then north to Melbourne. Late, as usual – me that is – I forgot the thirty-minute time difference between South Australia and Victoria. Bill sat calmly astride his gleaming Harley, stroking his elegantly groomed silver-streaked goatee. After weeks on the road, Yammie looked like a crudded Cinderella: unwashed and unattractive.

Bill gave me his customary firm handshake, followed by a manly hug. His handshake was warm; Bill's Harley had heated handle-bar grips. I looked on with envy. After thirty-six days alone on the road, a shared experience would warm my heart far more than hot gloves on an exhaust pipe.

'You've lost weight,' Bill said.

'I have. A lot. It's good to see you. You've put it on.'

'Indeed,' Bill paused, stroked his beard, remembered his stomach, and continued, 'Indeed, I have. Good to see you too. Let's do it,' he said.

And that was all we needed to say.

Lauded as 'Great,' the GOR deserved its nomenclature.

Bill took me to 'London Bridge' – a viewing platform with stunning vistas of the ocean and towering limestone outcrops that were once joined by a double-spanned natural arch of rock. In 1990, a section of the 'bridge' fell down. A couple had been standing on the far side; the collapse left them surprised and marooned. A helicopter rescue saved the day.

Loch Ard Gorge came next. Named after the famous 1878 shipwreck in which fifty-two souls lost their lives on nearby Mutton Bird Island. The majestic formation of rock reached out into the ocean in a pincer grip that almost shut off the sea from entering its calm lagoon.

Ten kilometres further east, and *the Twelve Apostles* blessed our arrival. Bill grinned at my amazement. Seven limestone stacks – fifty metres high – rose proud and strong against the onslaught of a wild ocean. One collapsed in 2005. The original eight had never been twelve. But the ocean would continue to carve at the cliffs, creating and collapsing new stacks, old stacks, birth and death, rise and fall. Life goes on.

Bill suggested we move on. Time stood still while we gazed in awe at these vistas. But Bill was right. Time to go. My odometer confirmed I had ridden 250 kilometres today. The afternoon pushed on. A long ride lay ahead before I would reach Melbourne, and Maureen. Three hundred kilometres to go.

We fired up. Bill led. His Harley and my Yamaha flew like sisters. The Great Ocean Road trailed across the cliff tops, straight stretches, slow curves, sharp twists. Our bikes rolled and weaved as though at one, with ourselves, with the highway. Bill banked left. I banked left. Bill rocked. I rolled. Slow bend, slow roll, bend, roll, like seagulls sashaying in the wind. Cliffs rose and fell over the ocean, rocky coves, sandy beaches, white surf, distorted angles, hairpins, snake turns, sunbeam and shadow, shifted horizons and shafts of sunlight. Our bikes jived in harmony while two old men swayed to the rhythm of the Great Ocean Road. We landed in Apollo Bay for meat pies and coffee.

'Not too bad,' said Bill.

'The ride or the meat pie?'

'Indeed, all of the above,' Bill said. 'So,' he continued, 'was that good or was that good?'

'Bloody magnificent.'

Bill had escorted me along one of the world's greatest motorcycle rides. In a car it would have been superb. On a bike? Bill and I understood. *I see you.* We sat silent and enjoyed the moment.

'Your ride,' said Bill more seriously. 'Your ride around the block. How's it been?'

Bill knew prior to this adventure Australia had been my adopted home – a home in which my huge backyard had remained unexplored. Bill knew I was an alcoholic. He understood the risks of loneliness and isolation.

How had it been? His question deserved an answer. Could thirty-seven days of reflection around Australia's perimeter be condensed into something concise? Johnnie grinned and the stone in my drive belt flashed a stab of uncertainty. *Don't you forget*, Johnnie said with a sneer. Melanie's relapse now promised hope; a sad crash but a strong resurrection. The Twelve Apostles opposed the onslaught of the ocean. Hope and rebirth kept them going. Storms and smashing waves might grind their strength, but should one fall, and eight become seven, the rage could be harnessed to stand up and rise again. Johnnie believed in storms too. But Johnnie had yet to see my rage.

'Well, Bill,' I said, 'frankly I never thought I'd get this far. But I did. And I can never thank you enough for the ride we did today. The ride has opened my eyes.' I laughed. 'Hallelujah! Australia is truly the lucky country. And for Maureen to allow me to do this trip, I am surely the luckiest guy in Australia.'

'Indeed,' said Bill, waiting for more.

'The Great Ocean Road was the proverbial icing on the cake …' I paused to think, 'but my trip has changed me in a way I can't yet say. Not because I don't want to, but because I'm not sure how to.'

Bill smiled. I didn't need to say more. Bill understood.

'I'll tell you one thing though; I'm chucking in my business when I return. Not that it's doing well anyway, but I need to do something else.'

'Like what?'

'That's what I've got to figure out.'

'Maybe financial planning instead of mortgage broking, maybe car loans instead of houses, maybe …'

I raised a hand to cut him off. 'Bill, the one thing I do know is that whatever it is, it won't be finance.'

'Indeed,' Bill said again.

We settled into another easy silence.

'Bill?'

'Yes?'

'I think I'd like to study.'

'Study?'

'University. Literature. Maybe write a book.'

'Indeed,' Bill said. 'Great idea!'

'It is?'

'You've done things. You've seen things few people would ever see. You've experienced things …' Bill knew about Dominic. The accident. 'You've been through the ringer,' he said. 'You have something important to share.'

'Thank you.' The words came from my heart.

'Go do it,' he said.

Thirty-seven days on the road, and a map began to unfold, but my destination still remained unclear.

'Let's find Maureen,' Bill said. 'You'd better text.'

I did.

See you around 7. Can't wait xxx

We grabbed our gear and strode to our bikes.

Two hundred kilometres to Melbourne. Bill led the way. The traffic collected more traffic and despite it being Saturday, the universe conspired to slow my arrival in Melbourne, a city I didn't know. Maureen waited in a hotel she'd booked close to Lygon Street.

Apparently, the restaurants were to die for. I hoped my pockets were deep enough.

Bill escorted me to the street where Maureen waited. He discreetly stopped at the corner.

'You,' he said, 'are at the end of the road on the right.'

Bill removed his gloves. His warm hand shook my iced fingers.

'Good luck,' he said.

'You too.'

'Indeed,' Bill said as he straddled his Harley and rode off into the Melbourne night.

Maureen stood on the corner. Blonde hair. Big smile. Big love. The Cowell misunderstanding put right. No doubt I would have to explain further, but not tonight.

My body eased from Yammie, old, seized up, exhausted and excited.

We hugged. Kissed. Her love grabbed my heart.

'I've missed you,' she said. 'I've worried myself to sleep every night. But now you're here.'

'I am. And I'm good.'

'You've lost so much weight. Your face is gaunt.'

'I'm fine.'

'I've booked a table at DOC. Italian pizza just down the street. At eight. We have an hour. Are you too tired?'

I smiled as my energy rose and my exhaustion evaporated.

'Sixty minutes?' I said, smiling the smile of a boy after his first kiss.

'Let's go,' Maureen said with a wicked grin.

Saucy and sweet, buttered and baked, deep-dish delicious, spicy scrumtitilumious, the pizza punched a pack to the senses. Alive and here. Maureen and Melbourne. Life was good.

SUNDAY MORNING EASY

unday morning: easy, strawberry fields, music playing, my love was waiting, homeward bound. My eyes opened slow and lazy. Soft and sultry sunlight crept through the window. It was nearly noon. I had slept for twelve hours. A radio stirred with gentle ballads. Maureen lay next to me.

'Hey there,' she said.

'Hey, yourself.'

'I put the radio on thirty minutes ago. It's nearly midday.'

I smiled and pulled Maureen close.

'I've missed you. Can you believe it? I'm nearly there,' I said.

'Just make sure you make it back to Coolum.'

The mileage paled into insignificance compared with the unspoken risks.

'I will. All good,' I said.

All bad, whispered Johnnie.

'Let's do the Melbourne Star.'

'The what?' I said.

'The Melbourne Star – the Ferris wheel.'

'Like the London Eye.'

'Yes, an authentic Australian copy.'

'Sure,' I said.

And that's what we did. Second.

Food, coffee and love. The early afternoon meandered into a late breakfast at Melbourne's Docklands. Eggs Benedict our mutual choice: salmon for Maureen, ham for me. And copious cups of exquisite, ground black coffee.

An hour later, we stepped onto the Ferris wheel. The Melbourne Star swooned slowly over the city; its snail-paced orbit unveiled a landscape of glass. Surreal imagery, as though we had edged through honey at the speed of light, from camels to cars, from stone-age deserts to spaceships. An odyssey. I imagined waltzing with Maureen across time, the Blue Danube, forward, ever closer...

'Are you still with me?' Maureen said.

I snapped awake. 'Sorry, I dozed, just a second...' I said in meek defence. 'Wow! It's beautiful.'

'Are you okay?'

'I am completely operational, and all my circuits are functioning perfectly.'

'What?'

'Artificial intelligence,' I said. 'HAL 9000.'

'You're crazy,' Maureen said as she reached for my hand.

We strolled the city and by late afternoon Melbourne's chic eateries had touched alternative addictions: frozen yoghurt at Yo-Chi's and coffee and cookie cheesecake at Brunetti's. Yo-Chi's struck my sweet tooth with dangerous mix-and-match flavours: dark chocolate and coconut, salted butterscotch (with a touch of sea salt), mandarin and poppy seed, coffee (made with organic coffee beans) ... the list disappeared into my belly along with toppings dusted with honey-roasted cashews, crushed almonds, organic chocolate soil, banana in caramel. Maureen thought I was gaunt. Thin and wasted needed to be fixed. I did my best.

A repeat visit to DOC later that night helped some more. We almost missed our table. The maître d' told us we would have to wait forty minutes. I took Maureen for a drink in the pub across the road to fill the void. When we returned, a long queue snaked out the restaurant. We were late. I asked the waiter how long. His hand wagged up and down: '*Reeeechar*,' he said, I call you a *meeeeleeon* times!'

I apologised. '*Sono cosi dispiacuto.*'

He found us a table.

A platter of mixed antipasti arrived against the advice of my stomach which insisted I skip dinner altogether. The dish arrived with Italian flamboyance.

'*Reeeechar*, enjoy. But you donna be late again, eh? *Buon appetito*!'

The dish looked too big for the table: fried mozzarella and provoloni, melon and parmesan, artichokes, bresaola, Scamorza, deep fried olives in breadcrumbs and, of course, a basket of focaccia.

One day in Melbourne, and my food intake had exceeded my total calorie count for thirty-six days on the road. Perhaps *una grande esagerazione*. Perhaps.

It was a day to remember. Full, yet short. Canberra tomorrow. A long ride. The cold waited. And my body shivered at the thought.

RAROTONGA WEDDING

We hugged our goodbyes. Maureen raised a smile, but the unspoken tension sat like a cloud. So near but still so far. The underground carpark felt like an unoccupied bunker. A relic of the Cold War.

'Be good. Be careful,' Maureen said. 'See you in Sydney.'

'Sydney!' I repeated as though it were a cocktail toast meant to rouse the troops and muzzle their fear. My words ricocheted off the walls. I turned Yammie's key and the roar rocked us both. 'I will…' my mouthed mimed as I pulled on my helmet, 'be good.'

My wing mirrors framed Maureen. Drab yellow light lit her hand as she held it high in a wave. I raised a glove and rode up the ramp towards Monday morning and the cold.

Sydney, I thought. One thousand kilometres. Canberra stood somewhere in between.

Monday wheezed with blue fumes drifting through the cold, frustrated Melbournian traffic. Cars, trams, trucks, vans, utes, taxis and busses pumped plumes of exhaust knotting me into commuter claustrophobia. City workers slow-danced a stop-start shuffle: five-feet forward, breathe, exhale, slap wheel, glance at watch, sluggish sigh, five-feet forward. Five-days groundhog for them. Five days closer to closure for me. *Closure?* Yammie did a slow slalom on tick-over as we crawled through metal and fumes. Lightning struck: a handsome twenty-year-old glanced up from the steering wheel of a battered ute. The young man smiled a smile of serenity, of encouragement. The rumble and grind of a thousand jammed cars were silenced. Time stitched for a second. A flash of recognition. A car horn blared. An unseen traffic light turned green. He turned left. I pushed ahead. The illusion vanished.

Thirty minutes into Melbourne's car conga to nowhere, there were still no signs of escape. My mobile sat in its holder on the handlebars. It flashed.

Where R U?

———

Coolum Beach, Australia January 2004

It was the best of times; it was the worst of times.

Tony Blair led Britain, Bush Jr the United States, Howard, Australia; Saddam Hussein rotted in prison; Vladmir Putin ruled Russia; Hu Jintao chaired China's Communist Party; Greece hosted the Olympics, Federer won three Grand Slams; Ronaldinho lifted FIFA's Player of the Year; *Million Dollar Baby* won best picture; Usher topped the charts. Marlon Brando died. And I got married. In the Cooke Islands.

Two months earlier, over dinner at an outside table by the beach at Coolum, a man needed to pop a big question. But instead it sat corked in a struggle between hope and anxiety. Documents wedged tight in his jacket pocket rustled to be released. The man's heart pumped the sheaths of paper so hard, he was sure they sounded like books fanned by a million frantic thumbs. Small talk poured from his mouth; significant words stayed stuck in his throat. Big talk needed to take command. This Coolum Beach moment had been plotted and planned for months. A perfect summer's evening lent a hand. Jasmine floated on a gentle sea breeze while cicadas hummed a lullaby.

A refusal would dump the man into a dark world of *coulda* and *shoulda* – a regret-riddled boxer like Brando's fighter.

The man pushed aside the table and knelt on one knee.

'Marry me?' he said.

'Yes,' Maureen said, without a pause, a hiccup, or a stutter. Just a smile.

The man punched the air like a champion finally lifting the title. The underdog who upset the pundits. A Rocky Balboa. A Raging Bull. An Apollo Creed… the other diners looked both amused and startled. The man sat down, coyly smiled and removed the documents from his jacket.

Tickets to Rarotonga. A bare-foot beach marriage in the South Pacific: one celebrant, one ukulele player, one honeymoon suite, two frangipani leis. And no guests.

Maureen laughed. 'When?' she said.

'Six weeks…' the man said. He paused. 'On my fiftieth birthday.'

————

Where R U now?

Melanie would have to wait.

Congestion eased and soon dairy-cattle-dotted fields confirmed my escape from Melbourne. The temperature lowered as my speed picked up and the relative shelter of the city warmth evaporated. Speed cameras regarded my progress with interest; I regarded theirs with alarm. My eyes flicked from speedo to camera, camera to speedo. My licence already hung in the balance. Speed control meant the difference between keeping my licence and losing it. It might also mean the difference between life and death. I had learnt my lesson. But these traps and controls were time-over-distance speed cameras. So, velocity between two undefined points calculated your average speed. Slowing down and saying cheese for a visible camera didn't cut it. Conformity to legal limits *over time* was all that mattered. Changing your reckless ways halfway through did not negate what you had done before. A horrifying fact wagged a finger like a sentencing judge. *Life over time*:

did today's good acts or tomorrow's kindness redeem yesterday's murder? I slowed down.

Maureen had used her initiative to extend my resilience against the cold. 'Hot hands,' she said. I liked the idea and wanted to find out more. Hot Hands were single-use heat packs sold by pharmacies. The 'pack' is like an oversized tea bag with chemicals that when exposed to air react to produce instant warmth for hands and feet. Maureen smiled. 'Try them,' she said.

At six o'clock that morning, I checked Canberra's temperature: minus two degrees. Anything deserved a try; my fingers demanded it. Brass monkeys agreed. I gave Hot Hands a go.

I pushed a single sachet down into each glove so that a magic pouch lay over the back of my hands, securely wedged with gloves. Now here's a tip I never follow: always read the instructions. After two hours of riding, the soreness in my hands trumped the cold. At the next coffee break, I pulled off my gloves to reveal blistered knuckles. That night I read the instructions. *People with sensitive skin, especially babies, diabetics and particularly the elderly, may have a reduced sensation to heat.* Anyway, the conclusion was obvious. I'm not a diabetic, so as much as I hate to say this, I must have fallen into the elderly category. Now my hands glowed with red-blistered skin. My reduced sensation to heat hadn't told me my hands were on fire. Back to the drawing board.

I stopped at a service station for fuel and other addictions and checked my mobile.

Let me know.

Melanie had sent the other two texts six minutes after the first. Last time we texted, her Beetle was on its way to Coober Pedy.

Headed for Canberra. You?

Wow! Exclaimed the text before being bumped by another: *Then?*

Sydney.

I'm already there! Dinner tomorrow night?

I paused. Anxious.

I'm meeting Maureen.

Great. We can all catch up.

During my stopover in Melbourne, Melanie must have overtaken me. I had ridden fast. Long distances too. Admittedly, I hadn't started at dawn or ridden late into the night, but Melanie's bug had must have done some motoring to rack up such distances.

Time to think. Time to … Not a good idea. No.

I needed to ride on. Canberra was 400 kilometres away. Maybe a city too far.

Let's see how I track, texted my blistered fingers.

Forget it.

Shit.

Late afternoon. Canberra was still 200 kilometres farther east. Yesterday's rest had not extended my endurance. Maureen told me many times to watch my weight. For the first time in my life, my body needed more food. I felt sure I'd dropped beneath sixty-five kilos. The loss of body mass did little to fight the cold and added much to my fatigue. I was too tired to continue. Canberra would have to wait.

GUNDAGAI said the turn-off. One kilometre on the other side of the Murrumbidgee River. I turned right and checked in to the first motel I found: Bushman's Retreat. Old and tired like me.

Maureen had made me promise I would call as soon as I arrived in Canberra.

'I've arrived.'

'Canberra?'

'No,' I said. 'A motel.'

'Where?'

'Not Canberra.'

'Where then.'

The motel check-in sheet offered the prompt I needed. 'Gundagai,' I said pronouncing it *Goondergay.*

'Gun-da-guy,' Maureen repeated.

'Yes. You've heard of it?'

'Of course. Everyone knows Gundagai.'

'I don't.'

'That's because you're a bloody Pom,' she said laughing. 'It's where the dog sits on the tucker box,' she added.

'What?'

'It's a song,' she said. 'By Jack O'Hagan.'

'Who?'

'You know,' she said as though to a child. '"Along the Road to Gundagai." There's a track winding back, To an old-fashioned shack, Along the road to Gundagai.'

'Sorry,' I said heavy with sarcasm, 'but it didn't hit the London discos of my youth.'

'Funny,' Maureen said. 'What about "Whiplash"'. She sung the opening bars: 'Mulga woods and deserts, the stage thunders by, From Sydney to Campden and onto Gundagai, Whiplash, Whiplash …'

'Okay, okay. Stop. I know it. I do.' Now it was my turn to dig deep, '…Graves,' I said, 'Peter Graves of Mission Impossible.'

'I'm impressed,' Maureen said. And the unspoken stress evaporated for the moment. We laughed.

'Frank Ifield,' I said. 'He sang the theme song.'

'Sharp,' Maureen said. 'Very sharp.'

The old boy was back in favour.

Maureen's flight had just arrived in Sydney. She would wait there for me tomorrow.

My appetite deserted me. Too tired to find somewhere to eat I made do: a mug of sweet tea, the motel's courtesy biscuits, an apple and the remainder of my cheese and crackers. After a hot shower the old man was done and truly dusted. I fell asleep with the weight and speed of a road train.

BOGGED BULLOCKS

Hunger hit hard when the soft dawn light eased through my window. Zero degrees. My plan was simple: breakfast in Gundagai, lunch in Canberra and dinner in Sydney with Maureen.

Gundagai was a frontier town with a folklore to match its heritage. This much Maureen had told me, but I needed to see it for myself.

Sheep and cattle surrounded Gundagai on lush green fields that twinkled with dewdrops enjoying the morning sun. My road to find the bakery paralleled the Prince Alfred Bridge and the timber railway viaduct that stretched across the Murrumbidgee flood plain. The bridge spanned the plain with a latticework of immense timber trusses, strong and seemingly invincible. Time and nature had weakened its structures and it was now fragile and dangerous, although age had not diminished its magnificence. A large timber-framed railway station built in 1886 stood at the end of line, also retired from active duty in 1984. Now it lent its services as a museum – the custodian of the town's memories.

The bakery bustled in the otherwise quiet but historic Sheridan Street. The bakehouse boasted of being the oldest working bakery in Australia. Breakfast smelt good and tasted better. I sat outside, hot coffee in one hand, a gourmet sausage roll in the other. I slung a salute to William Bibo, the German immigrant, who built and opened the bakery in 1864.

Fifty metres on the other side of the road, the ochre-coloured, art deco Gundagai Theatre built in 1929 still looked elegant. The theatre was now labelled as the *Arts and Crafts Emporium* and sold antiques and vintage clothing. The Lotts Family Hotel was next door. Built in 1858, it originally operated as the Fry Hotel and housed Cobb and Co – the classic stagecoach company immortalised in the seventies TV series *Whiplash*. Gundagai was thought to be close to a favoured meeting spot at Five Mile Creek: a place to camp and to tell stories and poems. Bullockies, bards, travellers, shearers and drovers passed through. But the Gundagai flood of 1852 created the real heroes of the town: two Aboriginal men – Jacky and Yarri from the Wiradjuri people. Using their frail bark canoes, they rescued one third of Gundagai's population. The two men risked their lives and saved sixty-nine souls. Eighty died. This disaster and loss of life is one of Australia's most significant, yet least remembered.

Banjo Patterson's poem *The Road to Gundagai* laments the loss of a *maiden of fair face* to another man *along the Sydney track*, so *with a sigh* he turned and took *the lonely road to Gundagai*. Bowyang Yorke penned another that opens with – *There goes Bill the Bullocky, He's bound for Gundai* – but dire straits with his bullocks ends with a loyal dog waiting for a master that would never return: *The dog sat on the tucker box, Nine Miles from Gundagai*. Seventy years later, Jack Moses, bush poet, journalist and whisky salesman took up the reins with his poem 'Nine Miles from Gundagai'. A sheep drover narrates: *I've been jilted, jarred and crossed in love, And sand-bagged in the dark, Till if a mountain fell on me, I'd treat it as a lark, It's when you've got your bullocks bogged, That's the time you flog and cry, And the dog sits on the tucker box, Nine Miles from Gundagai.*

Moses's poem inspired the creation of a sculpted bronze dog that sits on a stone tucker box at Snake Gully, nine kilometres from Gundagai. Australian Prime Minister Joe Lyons unveiled the statue as part of 'Back to Gundagai Week' and the 103rd anniversary of Charles Sturt's 1829 crossing of the Murrumbidgee River. Jack O'Hagan,

Australia's Irving Berlin, immortalised the poetry with his song trilogy: 'Along the Road to Gundagai' (1922) and 'Where the Dog Sits on the Tucker Box' (1938) and 'When a Boy from Alabama Meets a Girl from Gundagai' (1942) – a nod to the thousands of American soldiers who came to Australia during the Second World War and wooed the women.

From Gundagai, I took away a deeper sense of Australia, its people, and its heritage. O'Hagan's lyrics spoke to me, too. Aren't we all looking for our home, our haven, our safe place? Our place without grief, without pain, where the gum trees sway, where once more we can play? And no matter how heavy the load, it ain't ever gonna be as bad as when your *bullocks are bogged* and *The dog sits on the tucker box, Nine miles from Gundagai.*

Maureen, my *maiden fair of face* waited in Sydney, 500 kilometres north-west. Canberra was 150 kilometres from Gundagai. It would be a cold day. Dry. And at one time – 'prohibition' dry.

Johnnie Walker stirred. *Dry? Prohibition? Teetotallers?* Johnnie didn't like the words; he didn't like the implications. King O'Malley struck Johnnie with fear. O'Malley, an American immigrant, declared alcohol 'stagger juice.' In 1911, as Australia's Home Affairs Minister, O'Malley became instrumental in making alcohol illegal in the Australian Capital Territory. Prohibition reigned for seventeen years. Canberra was an adolescent of sorts. The 1901 Australian Constitution demanded a truce between Sydney and Melbourne while the federation decided where the capital and the seat of government would lie. Neither would be allowed to be Australia's capital. The two squabbling cities retired to the ropes when the Constitution demanded that Australia's capital be seated somewhere, anywhere as long as the chosen site be 'distant not less than one hundred miles from Sydney'. No-man's-land.

In 1911, New South Wales ceded land for the creation of the Australian Capital Territory. Two years later workers drove the first construction peg into the ground – 150 miles from Sydney, but almost 300 miles from Melbourne. As a consolation the Australian seat of government stayed in Melbourne until the completion of its new home.

And in 1927, twenty-six years after the Constitution, and fourteen years after the first peg smashed into the ACT's earth, Parliament moved to Canberra's new (now Old) Parliament House. Slowly other government offices followed. But after seventeen years of prohibition, with Parliament now ensconced in Canberra, thirsty politicians legalised 'stagger juice' with the speed of greased lightning. The United States would have to wait another five, but then the Americans started their experiment ten years after the Australians. Politicians had drowned O'Malley's dream of an alcohol-free Australia. Johnnie breathed easy. My visit would be short on time, long on emotion. All I wanted, and all I had time for, was to ride down Anzac Parade to cruise around Parliament House (the new one) and to eat a slice of Gundagai pie on the steps of the Australian War Memorial. Wrapped in a brown paper bag and insulated in my pannier, the pie had fared far better than my hands. Warm gravy dribbled over cold fingers as Bibo's steak pie disappeared into my mouth.

Canberra was colder than Gundagai, but the view from the steps of the Australian War Memorial moved me more than most grand old city vistas could. London, Athens, Paris or Rome might throw historical and architectural wonders at every corner, but the simple grandeur of this magnificent panorama drew tears the cold breeze could not excuse. Blue gums stood to attention in a perennial salute in remembrance of all that served, lining the wide avenue that led to Parliament House three kilometres away on Capitol Hill. A huge spire crowned the seat of government, topped at its apex with an eighty-metre flagpole where a squash-court-sized Australian flag billowed like a yacht's sail.

Time to go. Yammie waited in the Australian War Memorial's car park.

I rode down Anzac Parade at a slow pace, in respect to the memorials to various conflicts lining our route. We crossed Lake Burleigh Griffin and turned into Kings Avenue towards Parliament House. Security cameras swivelled to monitor my movements. The present Prime Minister had been reinstated some thirty days ago after a risky double-dissolution and a general election that cost him fourteen seats. He hung onto his majority by one seat. I sat safer in mine. I did three circuits of Parliament House before heading towards Sydney where Maureen was waiting.

The afternoon faded and the temperature followed. Sydney was a mission but not impossible. One hundred and fifty kilometres. Maureen waited. One hundred. Maureen waited. Seventy-five. A hot coffee and Mars Bar. Fifty kilometres. Maureen waited. My energy started to sink as the mercury slid. Maureen waited.

A miracle – on the boundaries of Sydney the temperature surged ten degrees. Warmth, like a glove stuffed with Hot Hands, filled my gloves, my boots, my body. And no blisters. I stayed warm for the rest of the journey. This rider had come in from the cold. But now Yammie had to battle the Sydney traffic. In belching exhaust and fraying tempers, we contested every metre, every blaring horn and every middle finger. *Aaaah*, I wasn't that bad … just in a hurry. Maureen had booked a room at the Mercure and waited outside. I had called her twenty minutes earlier to tell her I was close.

Wow! She looked beautiful. We hugged like teenagers as rush-hour madness motored on its oblivious way. We'd only been apart for forty-eight hours. But separate we must. Maureen took the hotel's elevators down to the underground carpark while I rode Yammie to her quarters in the underground carpark several floors below the hubbub of the street. Maureen waited at Yammie's allotted parking bay. We hugged again.

'We're on the tenth floor,' Maureen said. 'And I've got a surprise.'

The room, a standard double, looked like a rock star's suite. 'Wow,' I said, looking at my bug-stained jacket, grime-encrusted jeans, and scuffed boots. Maureen sent me to the shower with fast-flicking hand movements that gave no chance of further parley until the ol' boy had scrubbed every last remnant of road dirt from his ageing body.

'Well, well.' Maureen smiled, 'It's my husband.'

'Let's go,' she added with an urgency I adored.

'Wow,' I said again, smiling like a delinquent grey nomad hiding behind the cover of silver hair.

'Spice Alley.'

'What?'

'Get dressed,' Maureen said.

My face dropped. One minute later we stepped out in the corridor holding hands, down to the neon-lit street. 'Where are we going?'

'Wait and see.'

We walked along George Street, crossed Regent Street and onto Broadway where a left turn took us into Kensington Street. A few hundred metres down the dark street, a narrow lane told me we had arrived. Spice Alley: a cobbled lane of Asian culinary delight.

'Wow,' I said again.

Maureen agreed. 'Fantastic.'

We held hands and walked in. Steam spiralled from open counters shoulder to shoulder along the lane. Multiple woks cheffed by jugglers sizzled and flared; spiced aromas wafted along the narrow street with tantalising notes of sesame, chilli, aniseed, ginger and garlic. Shouting cooks, click-clacking chopsticks, chatting diners and clinking glasses filled the alley. People sat in nooks and crannies, outside, inside, eating, choosing, sharing, savouring, talking, laughing. Gin Alley elbowed the lane and offered eighty brands of juniper-laced alcohol that only the good and strong could enjoy. We stood among a cocktail of humanity and considered each dish with far greater thought than I considered where to sleep. Maureen took the plunge: Pipi Sambal. I took my dive soon after: Shanghai Dumplings. Coke for Maureen. Soda water for me. We smiled, we ate, we held hands. I told Maureen stories of a London boy lost in Gundagai. Of bogged bullocks, of a dog that sat on the tucker box, of tough men who took it all, of loves lost, of courage, of Jacki and Yarri, of Bibo's bakery, of loyalty, of wars, of pride, of prohibition, of Parliament. Everything. Except Johnnie Walker. And an alcoholic friend. One thousand kilometres to go.

'Dessert?' I asked.

Maureen smiled. 'Our room. Ten minutes.'

THE TOURIST

Noon arrived like dawn. Maureen and a long sleep led me to a level of relaxation that nothing else could. I enjoyed the snug warmth of late morning. Dust mites floated lazily in the sun stirred by our breath. Long and slow. Yesterday and tomorrow hid under a soft blanket of inconsequence. Breakfast, lunch more like, came with a knock at the door and a waiter holding a tray with a plunger of coffee and two silver-domed plates struggling to contain the aroma of bacon and eggs and sausages and mushrooms, tomatoes and hash browns.

'Luxury!' I said. 'You must be really worried about my weight. When did you order this?'

'Yesterday. Before you arrived.'

'You thought of everything.'

'I did. Eat well because today you're walking,' Maureen said.

'Walking?'

'All day! Or at least what's left of it.'

And we did: Circular Quay, Darling Harbour, the Opera House, Harbour Bridge, Botanical Gardens, Parliament House and the Mitchell Library (New South Wales State Library – Australia's oldest).

We ended the day on The Rocks: a neighbourhood of historic laneways hidden under the shadow of the Harbour Bridge. Tourists meandered through its old pubs, ate its street food, savoured its chic eateries and boogied with its buskers. We finished with a beer for Maureen, soda for me, and 'parma' pizza to share.

But of everything we did, and saw, of everything Sydney had to offer, there was one little big thing I had to do: see Trim – Matthew Flinders' cat. Trim, sculpted in bronze, sat on a windowsill in the state library behind the statue of his master. Named after the butler in Sterne's *Tristram Shandy*, Trim was the first cat to circumnavigate Australia. He did this between 1801 and 1803 aboard commander Matthew Flinders' ship, *HMS Investigator*. Man and cat had a strong bond. Flinders said Trim was 'the most affectionate of friends, faithful of servants, and best of creatures. He made the tour of the globe, and a voyage to Australia, which he circumnavigated.' I had ridden past a bronze tribute to the pair in Port Lincoln one week earlier. Another presides in London's Euston Station. Flinders mapped Australia's coastline and is largely responsible for its name. He died peacefully in England. Trim was eaten by a hungry slave in Mauritius. A moment of misfortune even an Australian might deem a day to declare the bullocks as truly bogged.

Coolum Beach was 1,000 kilometres north-east. So close, yet still so far. A stone stuck in my drive belt threatened to split; Melanie's relapse stuck in my throat, and Johnnie Walker stuck in my saddlebag.

Maureen removed all thoughts of bogged bullocks.

'I've decided,' she said. 'Let's end your journey with two days in Byron Bay. Two days of rest before your last ride.'

'Last ride?'

'Could you make Byron to Coolum in a day?'

'Sure.'

'It's settled then.'

'Fantastic,' I said, thrilled two days rest would precede my last ride. 'I'll shoot for Port Macquarie tomorrow, Byron Bay the next. Weather permitting I'll be there in two days.'

Maureen smiled. 'You've done it,' she said.

'Ever hear of the fat lady?'

One more night alone to kill the beast and free the Murderer.

EXECUTION

A warm morning and another farewell from another underground carpark. Maureen flew to the Sunshine Coast where she'd spend the night before driving south to Byron Bay. Two days and one night before we would meet again. *You've done it*, Maureen said yesterday. I hadn't. One thousand kilometres still remained. Three days of riding.

Yammie weaved her way northbound, across the Sydney Harbour Bridge, through an hour of rushing traffic until we crossed into North Sydney and cruised onto the Pacific Highway. The sun shone in a cloudless sky. It was the warmest day since my escape from Fremantle Prison seventeen days and 5,000 kilometres ago. But I had begun to sneeze and cough; a head cold had crept up on me somewhere during the night. My muscles ached and my sinuses throbbed. My helmet squeezed my head. Suffocation at 110 kph forced me to stop. With a coffee in my hand, guilt pushed me to send a text.

How are you?

CONFUSED, Melanie shouted back.

A lower-case text followed six seconds later: *Call me.*

The service station bustled with chatter, cutlery and commerce. Truckies, tradies, travellers going about their business, all in their own world, but not a soul crossed into mine. My coffee grew colder as I considered what I should do. What I should say.

Then my phone rang.

Forty-two days on the road, 15,000 dry miles, and the fat lady still hovered in the wings. Grief and regret squeezed my memories. *We're back.* But despite the tension, I felt today would be different. Today, the sunlight would drive past shadows where they belonged: *Yesterday.*

Let It Be, I heard Dom say. *Here Comes the Sun.*

And today, the blessing of what had been given started to eclipse what had been taken away. Dominic rode with me. He did. I saw him. And Maureen had been my saviour. Not for forty-two days, but for the 'lifetime' we had been together. Time apart exponentially raised the risks of relapse. This time though, my tormentor would be my alibi. Johnnie would be the proof. My witness. My jury. And Dominic would be my judge.

'Melanie,' I said, 'Where are you? How are you?'

'Cracking!'

'Cracking?'

'I'm not coping.'

'Shit.' I said. 'Where are you?'

'Driving … just driving … just moving. If I stop …'

'Are you drinking?'

'No … Not yet!'

'Not yet?'

'I'm afraid. Everything's falling apart.'

'Jesus! Are you still in Sydney?'

'You didn't call. You didn't …'

'Melanie. I'm sorry. I really am. Look, this is difficult. On the phone, I mean. Are you still in Sydney?'

'No,' she said.

I waited. 'Then, where are you?' I asked again.

'I left Sydney this morning. I'm near Newcastle.'

'Newcastle? That's home, isn't it? Your sons live there.'

'It's where I *had* a home. I have no sons.'

'What? But you said …'

'I lied.'

'You lied?'

'I didn't mean to. I just wanted people to believe I have family. That I had children. That I was a mother.'

I couldn't answer. A black sadness shook me to my boots. Johnnie stirred.

'I was pregnant and took a beating,' she said. 'No kids for me.'

'I'm so sorry, Melanie. I'm sad for you. I … look, I'm heading for Port Macquarie. Byron Bay tomorrow. Maybe I could meet you in Newcastle. I'll be there in under an hour.'

'I'm not stopping there,' she said. 'I won't.'

'But …'

Melanie cut me off. 'I have an old AA friend, Eva. She lives near Port Macquarie. I'm staying the night.'

'Just a night?' I said.

'One night. I didn't lie about continuing my trip. Mum left me money. Not much. Enough to see me through six months. Until I find work, the place I'm looking for, until …'

'But you need help!'

'Meet me tonight,' she said.

'Melanie, tonight is tough. I've …'

'You're making excuses. It would help me … A LOT.'

'I'll call you when I get there.'

Tonight is tough. I sounded weak. But, *If you can keep your head when all about you are losing theirs / If you can trust yourself when all men doubt you / Yours is the earth and everything that's in it / And – which is more – you'll be a man my son*!

I remember, Dad. I remember. But remembering had never been enough.

Port Macquarie lay 300 kilometres north-east. I took the Tuggerah turnoff. I needed things for tonight. Important things … Forty minutes later, Yammie glided back onto the Pacific Highway. We were back on track. I had what I needed.

My helmet held my head in a vice. Flu waited around the corner. The day stayed dry. Wet weather threatened. Then retreated. Kilometres stretched ahead signposted with hours. Four hours. Three hours. Two. A fever wound a weepy crawl through my already exhausted body. My helmet snapped with sneezes and shuddered with coughs.

'FOCUS,' I shouted. My blue-tooth headset answered: 'service not available'. My concentration faded and a collision almost followed. A Toyota's brake light flagged its intent. I didn't stop. I couldn't stop. A zag, a zig, another zag and with a miracle, I missed the four-wheel drive. *Shit.* Close call. One hundred kilometres to Port Macquarie. The fat lady waited in the wings.

Light faded as the balmy afternoon descended into a cold evening. There were no obvious choices to stay in Port Macquarie. Too tired to look for options, I took a room in a small resort just a few kilometres outside the town centre. I had a phone call to make, but it would have to wait. Hot shower first. Twenty minutes later, refreshed and warmer but anxious, I packed the things I needed with the stuff I bought in Tuggerah. I pushed, shoved, squeezed and prodded everything into my rucksack, its zippers struggling to contain the load.

Yammie was still warm from the day's ride. The sun would set in fifteen minutes and although I'd have light for maybe another thirty, the torch in my jacket would be essential. I rode along the beach road. North and south. I chose Flynns Beach: a short beach, no more than 500 metres long, it sat between two rocky headlands – Nobby Head to the south and Flynns Point to the north. The headland to the south looked the most promising.

I hefted my load along the beach towards Nobby Head, frequently shrugging my swollen backpack to stop the contents stabbing my back. At the base of the headland, a narrow path led upwards through dense bush to the summit. Near the top the shadows deepened, and my torch became a necessity. Several trails branched off the main track. I chose one and hung my chequered handkerchief on a branch. Thirty metres down the almost hidden trail, the dirt path widened like a swollen artery, small, but big enough for my purpose. I dropped my pack, took out my bush knife and started to dig.

Thirty minutes later the blackness of a moonless night descended on my work. It was done. I retraced my footsteps down to the beach and to the carpark where Yammie waited. I called Melanie.

A female voice answered. 'Richard,' said a woman I guessed was Eva.

'How …'

'Melanie's asleep. She said you'd call.'

'But…'

'She's okay.'

'Can…'

'She wanted me to wake her. Hold a sec …'

Two minutes later the mobile passed from Eva to Melanie.

'Where are you?'

'Nobby Head. Can you get here?'

Melanie consulted with Eva.

'Give me fifteen minutes.'

'I'm in the car park,' I said.

Twenty minutes later Melanie's Beetle pulled up against Yammie. A hug said everything. Comrades. In arms against a common foe, against a future we feared, against a past that blinded the present.

Silence and surf. I switched on my torch, took Melanie's hand, and led the way.

'What…?'

I held a finger to my lips.

She said nothing more.

The surf exploded with the *WHUMMMP* of heavy artillery. The ocean rushed up the beach until its strength dribbled to nothing. It sighed, heaved, drew strength, then unloaded another barrage. *WHUMMMP*. The assault advanced. The beach receded. We reached the trail and hiked upwards to Nobby Head. My torch lit the path. Ten minutes later my chequered handkerchief told me we had found the hidden trail that led to my empty rucksack.

Melanie said nothing; her face said it all. A small pit brimmed with firewood – two feet deep, two in diameter. Seashells circled the perimeter. A bottle of whisky sat on a book while Johnnie Walker looked on from his red label like a circus ringmaster waiting to crack his whip. Two chipped enamel mugs and a white flask sat on the opposing side. A lighted candle, shielded by plastic, flickered in between. Soft candlelight wavered across the tiny clearing, curtained by the blackness of the bush, chorussed by the distant rumble of the surf.

'What is this?' Melanie said without fear.

'Please sit,' I said as I pulled the bush knife from my jacket. 'And listen.'

'I'm a Murderer.'

Melanie's eyes widened.

'Today,' I said, 'As I do every day, I think of Dominic. My son. He died in a car crash. With Heather, my ex-wife. A head-on. A truck. I'm to blame.'

I tapped my knife on the bottle and ran the blade beneath Johnnie's throat. 'Johnnie,' I said tapping the bottle, 'Mr Walker, has been stashed in my pannier for forty-two days.'

'Richard…'

'Please.' I held up my hand. 'I didn't know whether I'd drink him or kill him. Dominic died thirteen years ago. As of today, I've covered fifteen thousand kilometres. And I've seen him, Melanie. I see Dominic driving trucks. I see him in crowds, in my dreams. I see him with a smile. *I see him!* I know he wants me to do this. He helped me make it. I'm grateful. To him. To Maureen. Without them, that bastard,' I said, pointing the knife at Johnnie, 'would have laughed all the way to my grave. Dominic's memory disgraced; Maureen's trust abused.'

'Richard, were you in that car?'

'No.'

'Then …'

'But I should have been. I WASN'T THERE. Often, I prayed I was. But you know what? That's my dishonour. Because on the day he died, miracles happened too. Gabby, my daughter, survived without a scratch. And Jamie, my eldest, stayed at home. Two miracles and a car cursed to crash. I should have seen the blessing – it had no disguise. Instead booze beat me into self-pity. Grief could be expected, but self-pity? Abhorrent. And I made it worse. I created pity for myself with the passion Frankenstein created his monster. We were both set to self-destruct.'

Melanie started to cry.

'I've brought you here today, tonight, because I wanted to share this moment. That bastard is gonna die.' I waved my knife at the whisky like a preacher exorcising the devil. 'Dominic gave me the chance. Maureen gave me the love. Maureen gave me more than I deserve.'

I pulled matches from my jacket and lit the firelighters and kindling. Melanie stopped crying. The wood sputtered but the fire took.

'Melanie, you stayed dry for ten years. I've hit over two thousand days. But that's to Maureen's credit, not mine. You're stronger than me. I'm sorry for your loss. I'm sorry about your mother. But you don't need to invent a life … to invent sons … you don't need to be an actress in someone else's script. You are a wonderful human being. *You are YOU!*'

Johnnie Walker's grin started to fade. I picked up the bottle. 'Help me,' I said.

'How?'

'Hold the bottle over the fire. Two hands. One at each end.'

'Like this?'

'Yes.'

I raised the bush knife into the air. 'Ready?'

She nodded.

My knife fell with a weight and fury that surprised us both. Johnnie crumpled as the bottle broke and the flames roared. Mr Walker died a violent death, devoured by fire, whisky and glass. May he rot in hell.

The fire belched as though a huge hunger had been sated. We studied the flames, silent like lambs. The devil dead, the fire began to calm.

'Richard?' Melanie touched my arm. 'Richard?' she said again, 'are you okay?'

'I think we just watched the fat lady sing.'

'Johnnie's final song,' Melanie said.

In our own way, with our own translation, the significance of the alcoholic sacrifice had pierced our hearts like a spear of stone-age bone.

'Now I propose a toast,' I said.

'A toast?'

I picked up the two chipped enamel mugs. 'Take these,' I said, as I unscrewed the lid of the flask and poured hot chocolate. Melanie smiled. A sense of palpable relief drifted across the trail as real as the heat, the smoke, the smell of cocoa, as real as today. I AM.

'To Dominic, to dry horizons, to the present tense.'

'To Dominic, to dry horizons, to the present tense. And to new lives,' said Melanie raising her mug.

We chugged thick chocolate. Hot and sweet. 'Cheers,' said two voices.

One thing remained: The Book. It had ridden a long way too. It had sat next to Johnnie, shoulder to shoulder in my pannier. A beautiful reminder of the ugliness of alcoholism. Its voice raw and true. I had read it often, like a bible.

'This is for you,' I said. And handed her the book.

'*Drinking: A Love Story.*' She looked puzzled. '*By Caroline Knapp?*'

'Yes. It helped me. Drink the words. Remind yourself every day of what alcoholism was like. Caroline died young. Younger than us, but she left a poignant memory.'

Melanie opened the book.

'You've written in it,' she said, and began to read, '*To Melanie, you'll understand this book like I did. Your strength will see you win. Stay strong, stay sane, stay sober. Help yourself like you've helped me. Help others. Family is not always bred of blood. Ten years of courage. Now make it an eternity. Rich X,*'

She stopped; she teared. 'There's a P.S …'

'Read it,' I said, 'because that's the essence of what we alcoholics have to do.'

Melanie began to read: '*P.S. Caroline Knapp said this about her affair with alcohol: "I fell in love and then, because the love was ruining everything I cared about, I had to fall out."*'

'Thank you,' she said. 'Thank you.'

'Let's go. Eva will worry.'

We placed the shells over the dying fire and kicked dirt onto the pit. Tomorrow no-one would know we had been here. Our sacrifice would remain a mystery. Tonight, the Murderer went free.

OYSTERS

I awoke from the sleep of babies. Rested and restored. No sign of a cold or flu. This was to be my penultimate ride. I would meet Maureen in Byron Bay. She would arrive lunchtime. I should get there by late afternoon. We would have two days together. A blissful bonus, a second honeymoon, a celebration. A personal victory for me; a huge relief for Maureen. I would start a new philosophy. The stone in my drive belt was just that: a stone in my drive belt. Johnnie was dead. Melanie had a good chance of victory. And, for once, I believed I did too. The fat lady could sing whenever and wherever she wanted. I didn't care. Maureen was my wife, my love, my sanity, my mate. Today, in this moment, a glass of whisky didn't sit in my hand. One step today, 2,000 tomorrow, 4,000 the next, an eternity. Today Maureen waited in Byron Bay. Today and the present tense were all that mattered.

It was a 'no gloves' day – warm, calm and satisfying. The serenity of it settled on me like a prayer. Kilometres trailed behind us as Yammie purred like a marathon runner on the last stretch.

Four hundred kilometres passed with ease: Coffs Harbour, banana plantations, sugar fields, the Richmond River – pastel water colours –

all a pleasing blur as Bryon Bay emerged from the late afternoon with the promise of paradise.

Maureen waited at the corner of Clarkes Beach. She looked like she did the day we married on a Pacific island. A princess.

We had a cabin for three nights before my final ride to Coolum. First a shower, then an arm-in-arm stroll along the beach.

Friday night: hippies played drums, happy crowds danced, hooch was drunk. A crimson sunset cued the night as tendrils of weed whispered around Byron's perfect people.

'We couldn't have designed a better finale,' Maureen said.

'But it's the beginning.'

We both laughed. The significance of my trip needed no further discussion. Maureen understood.

'It's happy hour at the Balcony Bar,' Maureen said. 'Coffin Bay oysters are a dollar an oyster.'

'Then let's get happy. Count me in for dozen.'

'You know what they say about oysters,' she said.

'Make it two dozen.'

Youth with grey hair and wrinkles. Twenty-one-year-old hearts with sixty-something birth certificates. Spirits that would never age. A love that would never die.

MEDIA MANIA

Final day. Final ride. Final goal. Coolum Beach was a serene 285 kilometres north. Maureen slept. I wallowed in the warmth of the bed, hands held relaxed behind my head. Forty-six days and a circumnavigation of Australia. Sixteen thousand kilometres and 6,000 charity sponsored dollars. Beyond Blue would be pleased. Today would be short but I didn't want it to end. Byron tugged me with its charm. If the morning before, two Bryon-days before, could be locked into a looping Groundhog Day of lazy love and sunsets – count me in.

Last night ABC radio contacted me. A reporter would call in the morning. They wanted a live interview.

The phone rang, Maureen woke, and a female voice said, 'Richard, this is Terri Begley of 612 ABC Brisbane.' For two minutes I babbled nonsense about an old man riding a motorcycle in pursuit of Australia and a dream. The truth didn't seem important; the reality inconsequential. Except to me and Maureen. The interview went well and Beyond Blue got a good plug. *Thank you, Terri.*

Channel Seven ran the story of my departure forty-six days ago, and ABC radio covered my return. A win for *Beyond Blue*. And a very private victory for me.

Coffee and toast on the deck. I took my time and finished loading Yammie for our last ride. Mid-morning, I was ready. I gave Maureen a hug, and with a triumphant, ungloved hand, waved farewell. Man, and bike roared rudely out of peaceful Byron Bay. Yammie headed for the highway.

A surprise phone call interrupted a fuel stop just south of Brisbane. ABC Sunshine Coast Radio 90.3 wanted an interview for their DRIVE program with Sheridan Stewart. They asked if I could attend the radio's studio in Maroochydore that afternoon. How could I refuse? The ABC studio was just a fifteen-minute ride from Coolum Beach and the end of my 16,000-kilometre journey.

Sheridan bubbled like champagne – an Olympic yellow-ribbon finish line to a forty-six-day marathon. Celebrity status, if only for a minute, and a further plug for charity. I don't remember what I said, but I'm sure the interview ended something like this:

'So, what's next, Richard?' Sheridan said. 'Maybe a book?'

Maureen, family, friends and my dog greeted me with banners and bunting, champagne and cake, handshakes and hugs, tears and wagging tails. Soda water for me. Champagne for Maureen. We were both winners.

It was over.

Bill Bryson said in his book *Down Under:* 'What a preposterously outsized country this was. But that is of course the thing about Australia – that there is such a lot to find in it, but such a lot of it to find it in. You could never see the half of it.'

Bryson was right of course, but I found much more. I found myself.

THE BEGINNING

T he sun hovered on a new horizon. Maureen slept. Sunbeams edged the day into a new morning. A cool breeze floated through the window. I savoured the tranquillity like a jewel. Slowly. I breathed in … breathed out. In. Out. My abdomen rose, a yacht's sail in a gentle, satisfying billow. Each breath calm, fulfilling, rich. The beauty of the present tense. I smiled. 16,034 kilometres. And a lifetime remembered.

A long-forgotten story fluttered from an old alcoholic parable. At first it had no shape, no sharpness, until I massaged the words, until the tale unfolded like a butterfly:

I see an old African man. Uma. He sells his fertile farm to search for diamonds. Uma has listened to the stories of travellers from antique lands. They tell of precious stones littered in abundance across the continent. Diamonds and dreams, Everywhere but nowhere. He used the money his fields had harvested and left his 'nowhere' farm to travel 'everywhere' in search of fortune. Uma chased whispers of wealth in the mountains and valleys, riverbeds and caves. The old man dug and dredged distant terrains from corner to corner, his energy and money fading painfully like his health. He knew those sparkling rocks with seductive glitter would gleam for him. Tomorrow, next week, next month. But each year passed in frustration and pain. But Uma's defeat could not break his dream. Gone was his self-respect, loved ones, friends, home, health – and spirit – until one morning the old man could no longer endure his life another day. Uma stood sad and sick at the edge of a gorge. A raging river snaked below in a dark scar the sun did not reach. Uma toppled downwards like a gnarled log slowly turning until his broken body splintered onto the rocks. And into oblivion. But as the old man's soul rose, he saw his farm. Uma glimpsed the man who had bought his land. The new owner's plough had uncovered an unusual object, partly obscured by mud. A goose egg of rock, like translucent glass. Uma saw the farmer touch its oily film and look into the rock's metallic lustre. He saw the farmer pocket the peculiar rock without another thought and then continue to toil his fields. Weeks later a passing traveller stopped by the farmer's paddock asking for refreshment. The farmer gladly shared his food and showed his acquaintance the strange rock.

'It's a diamond,' the traveller said, 'you're a rich man.'

The following day the farmer found more of these curious stones. Diamonds covered his farm – veiled with dirt; obscured by greed.

Uma had created nightmares while living in the presence of his dreams. He sold a truth to die for a lie. Uma never saw all the light that was everywhere to see.

Maureen stirred. Sleepy awake.

'Hey babe, can you believe it?' I said.

'No,' she said, mistaking my meaning, 'But you did it. You actually did it.'

'No, I mean, I'm Uma.'

'Uma?'

'The African farmer.'

'A farmer?' said Maureen.

'Uma. Diamonds. But I have another chance.'

'What?'

'I never saw all the light that was everywhere to see.'

'You're crazy,' said Maureen.

Then in a little seaside town, on a sun-blessed winter morning, life began again.

One day at a time.

ACKNOWLEDGMENTS

I'm still sober. Yesterday and today – one day at a time. A huge hug and thanks to Maureen who not only blessed my crazy ride but saved my life several times – literally and metaphorically. The cliched author acknowledgement of 'I couldn't have done it without her' is a monumental understatement – I wouldn't be *here* without her. Maureen believed in me, my purpose and my book. She, more than anyone else, knew the emotional dangers of my ride, my journey and my craziness. She never flinched. She knew it had to be done.

My children's bravery carried me through tragic times, but their trauma was far greater, much of which I inflicted. Gabby and Jamie were inspirations. It should have been the other way around. My heartfelt apology is the most important acknowledgement I can make. My alcoholism hurt many, none more than Maureen, Gabby and Jamie. I'm deeply sorry, as I am to Dominic and Heather, and to a significant list of others too many to include.

Writing a memoir has been a long and indulgent journey. I never thought I'd get this far, and while on the subject, I never thought I'd complete the ride – let alone in 46 days. Good luck, good weather, and a good motorcycle overcame bad planning and poor risk management, although my mission hid an altogether different purpose.

'Anti-clockwise' didn't cut it as a 'detailed' plan on how to ride a motorcycle, bought ten days earlier, for a 16,000-kilometre circumnavigation of Australia. An enormous debt of gratitude goes to my bike, Yammie. She kept me upright, she stayed strong, and she went like hell. I can't thank her without thanking Steve McLaren, her previous owner, who cared for her with a passion. He handed over a beauty, but bike and rider still needed equipment. Mal of Biker Life in Maroochydore came to my rescue and guided me to sensible decisions. 'You'll need boots,' Mal said first. 'What's wrong with these? I said showing him my office loafers. To discuss my needs further, Mal needed to understand my goals. 'You're gonna do what?' he said, face sinking with anxiety and trepidation. 'Why don't you just take her away for a weekend first?' He was right of course, but 'right' didn't describe the way I did things. 'All or nothing,' I said. Out of fear and concern, Mal contacted a group of riders – The Cooktown Crusaders – who were leaving around the same time as me. 'Why don't you ride with them for a while,' he said. 'Learn the ropes. They're riding to Cape Tribulation. I'll get Heckle to give you a call.' Mr Heckle rode to raise money for autism and led the Crusaders. I didn't ride with them but camped with the riders on my third night and am grateful for their company and insight. Thanks, Heckle. Thanks, Mal.

My ride was important for the selfish reasons covered in the book, but I still wanted to generate something positive for others. I decided to raise money for charity – another last-minute decision, but it was a simple choice: Beyond Blue. This charity helps Australians who suffer with anxiety, depression or thoughts of suicide. Many kind people donated generously – together we raised $6,000. Jetts gym contributed a whopping $1,100. Newspapers and TV stations helped. The *Sunshine Coast Daily* gave me a big spread. Thank you, Shirley Sinclair. And thank you Myra, my mother-in-law, who donated $500, but died in our arms two years later, on Father's Day, three hours after treating me to an Indian take-away.

But if the book is the icing, who was responsible for the cake? First, I'd like to thank the University of the Sunshine Coast for providing an amazing lecturers and tutors that guided me through my

Bachelor of Journalism degree. A special thanks to Dr Jane Stephens and Dr Peter English. Both were inspirational. They were always there, eager to listen and help. As an old boy among young, smart and energetic students it was often difficult to keep up. The semester I attended the local courts almost every week for two months particularly stood out. The courts moved me in ways I could never have imagined. I listened to hearings of extreme crimes that often brought me close to tears. Other times I heard kooky cases that made me laugh so loud I thought I would be escorted from the court, but the closeness of the crimes shocked me – the next-door neighbour, the people across the street, the couple across town, the kid from the high school, the old man up the hill, the drunk from the pub. It made me think of fate and circumstance. It made me reflect: 'There but for the grace of God go I.'

The ride had many purposes, but a major by-product of long hours and many days in the saddle created an overwhelming desire to write. About what? It didn't really matter, although I felt my story might be a fitting place to start. It would be painful. It would be demanding. It would require more skill than I had. I would need help.

I joined the Sunshine Coast Writers' Group – a friendly and talented group of writers who read their work aloud every Monday afternoon. A short critique from each member followed. At first it was daunting, but slowly my confidence increased, and as the weeks passed, I learnt and experimented, little by little, with both my writing style and my secret. 'Hi, I'm Richard and I'm an alcoholic.' It's one thing to say this at an AA meeting; it's entirely another to write it down and wait for the writing club to examine every word. The group accepted my admission with grace and respect. In all honesty, I think it was this body of men and women, of novelists and poets, of memoirists and short-story writers who gave me the nod to consider going further. Irena Sprey ran the group and with her encouragement I entered the club's annual short story competition for both fiction and non-fiction. I won both. I thank the group sincerely and I believed I was on a roll. Little did I know the dice had barely moved. I give further thanks to Irena who, along with Saffron Drew, helped me secure a $2,000 Regional Arts Development Fund (RADF) grant to further develop my memoir. Thank you, Irena and Saffron.

The grant provided financial support to secure the coaching and editing services of Carolyn Martinez. Carolyn helped to shape my work and drive it to the next level. I thought my work was good, but – and here is the failing of many wannabe writers – it wasn't. Not even close. Thank you, Carolyn, for guiding me in the right direction.

Linda Morse, a member of the Sunshine Coast Writers' Group, suggested enrolling Masters in Creative Writing might be good idea, as she was going to do. I dismissed the idea at first, as too expensive and time consuming, though contacted Dr Paul Williams, a Senior Lecturer in creative writing at the University of the Sunshine Coast, anyway. Paul was encouraging and inspirational, but it took six weeks for me to make my decision and apply. By then my start date had to be deferred until the following year. First, I needed to be accepted into the program. My Bachelor's degree was a pathway, but I also needed to submit a portfolio of writing projects. My Sunshine Coast Writers' Group contributions helped my application, as did material created during my journalism degree, and I was accepted. Thank you, Paul and Linda.

Then the real journey began. A group of passionate students, young and old, began their Masters with Dr Paul Williams and Dr Shelley Davidow. We sucked up their every word like whiskeys before last orders. The course was inspirational and demanding. There was camaraderie and conflict. From this eclectic mix of people, I forged long-lasting friendships. We had to critique each other's work and referred to these critiques as shit sandwiches. A little praise wrapped around a thick wedge of … It was tough to swallow – tougher still to hand one out. Most of us made it.

The words multiplied, chapters took shape and our darlings grew. Paul and Shelley led the way. I'm sure I speak for the entire USC Masters class of 2018 when I say these lecturers changed our lives. Thank you, Paul and Shelley. Thank you, fellow students. After graduation, however, we realised the hard work had only just begun.

My draft manuscript continued to develop, rewrite after rewrite, in the garbage, out of the garbage, old ideas dumped, new ones inserted. But I hit gold when I found an excellent editor to help me – Dr Melanie Myers. Sometimes writers continue to believe their darlings are sandwiched with the best cut of beef you'll ever find and smell delicious. You need someone like Mel to tell you they aren't. Over and over again! Until you believe peace must be near and you raise the flag. I'm done. Then Nikki Stephens stepped in with a proofread to make it even better. Thank you, Mel and Nikki.

I have much to be thankful for. A higher power kept me on this earth longer than I ever deserved and gave me a beautiful wife and three exceptional kids. One lives in heaven. He's twenty and will be forever.

'Remember, hope is a good thing, maybe the best of things, and no good thing ever dies.' (Stephen King)

IF by Rudyard Kipling (1865-1936)

If you can keep your head when all about you
Are losing theirs and blaming it on you;
If you can trust yourself when all men doubt you,
But make allowance for their doubting too:
If you can wait and not be tired by waiting,
Or, being lied about, don't deal in lies,
Or being hated don't give way to hating,
And yet don't look too good, nor talk too wise;

If you can dream - and not make dreams your master;
If you can think - and not make thoughts your aim,
If you can meet with Triumph and Disaster
And treat those two impostors just the same:.
If you can bear to hear the truth you've spoken
Twisted by knaves to make a trap for fools,
Or watch the things you gave your life to, broken,
And stoop and build'em up with worn-out tools;

If you can make one heap of all your winnings
And risk it on one turn of pitch-and-toss,
And lose, and start again at your beginnings,
And never breathe a word about your loss:
If you can force your heart and nerve and sinew
To serve your turn long after they are gone,
And so hold on when there is nothing in you
Except the Will which says to them: "Hold on!"

If you can talk with crowds and keep your virtue,
Or walk with Kings - nor lose the common touch,
If neither foes nor loving friends can hurt you,
If all men count with you, but none too much:
If you can fill the unforgiving minute
With sixty seconds' worth of distance run,
Yours is the Earth and everything that's in it,
And - which is more - you'll be a Man, my son!

Lightning Source UK Ltd.
Milton Keynes UK
UKHW010636100920
369682UK00003B/618